Claudia Schwabe (Ed.)

The Fairy Tale and Its Uses in Contemporary New Media and Popular Culture

MDPI

This book is a reprint of the Special Issue that appeared in the online, open access journal, *Humanities* (ISSN 2076-0787) in 2016, available at:

http://www.mdpi.com/journal/humanities/special_issues/fairy_tales

Guest Editor
Claudia Schwabe
Assistant Professor, Department of Languages,
Utah State University,
USA

Editorial Office
MDPI AG
St. Alban-Anlage 66
Basel, Switzerland

Publisher
Shu-Kun Lin

Assistant Editor
Jie Gu

1. Edition 2016

MDPI • Basel • Beijing • Wuhan • Barcelona • Belgrade

ISBN 978-3-03842-300-3 (Hbk)
ISBN 978-3-03842-301-0 (electronic)

Table of Contents

List of Contributors

Erin Kathleen Bahl is a doctoral candidate in the English department at the Ohio State University studying digital media, composition, and folklore. Her research investigates the possibilities that new media and digital technologies offer for creating knowledge and telling stories. She is currently working on a dissertation exploring the relationship between technology, invention, and design in composing new media scholarship. Her work has been published in *Computers and Composition, Composition Studies, Humanities Journal, Harlot of the Arts*, and *Showcasing the Best of CIWIC/DMAC*, with forthcoming work in *Signs and Media, Computers and Composition Online*, and *Computers and Composition Digital Press*.

Savannah Blitch is currently completing her final year of study towards a Bachelor's Degree in English Literature. She has had poetry published in the local magazines *Lux* and *Four Chambers* and recently presented a paper at the 2016 Annual American Folklore Society conference in Long Beach.

Sara Cleto is a doctoral candidate at the Ohio State University, where she studies folklore, literature, and the places where they intersect. Her areas of specialization include fairy-tale studies, folk narrative, nineteenth-century literature, and disability theory, and she is currently working on a dissertation that explores representations of disability in nineteenth-century fairy-tales and fantastic literature. Her scholarly and creative work can be found in *Humanities Journal, Louise Pound: A Folklore and Literature Miscellany, Supernatural Studies, Faerie Magazine, Goblin Fruit*, and others.

Jason Marc Harris is an Instructional Assistant Professor at Texas A&M University in College Station, TX and teaches creative writing, folklore, and literature. He has a Ph.D. in English Literature from the University of Washington and an MFA in fiction from Bowling Green State University, where he served as Fiction Editor of Mid-American Review. His books include *Folklore and the Fantastic in Nineteenth-Century British Fiction* and (with Birke Duncan) *The Troll Tale and Other Scary Stories*, and *Laugh Without Guilt: A Clean Joke Book*; and fiction in *Every Day Fiction, Masque and Spectacle, Cheap Pop*, Arroyo Literary Review, *Psychopomp Magazine*, and *Midwestern Gothic*. http://www.jasonmarcharris.com/

Anne Kustritz is an Assistant Professor in Media and Culture Studies at Utrecht University. Her scholarship focuses on fan communities, transformative works, and digital economies. Her teaching specializes in sexuality, gender, media ethnography, and convergence. Her articles appear in *Camera Obscura, Feminist Media Studies*, and *The Journal of American Culture*. She serves on the editorial board of the journal *Transformative Works and Cultures*, an open-source, peer-reviewed on-line academic journal affiliated with the non-profit Organization for Transformative Works which seeks to offer fans legal, social, and technological resources to organize, preserve their history, and promote the legality of transformative works.

Julianna Lindsay is from Las Vegas, Nevada. Her academic background is in English literature, history, anthropology, archaeology, and heritage studies, receiving her doctorate in heritage studies in 2015. She enjoys researching nostalgia, culture, and the ways in which these pop into modern activities with a pointed interest in American culture and 1980s childhood nostalgia. Lindsay currently works for the Texas Historical Commission as a site educator and interpreter. She currently resides with one husband, plants of average size, and one black cat of unusual size, Belfry.

Jarom McDonald is an independent scholar who specializes in algorithmic media analysis. Recent projects have given him the opportunity to look at data-driven narratives and social television engagement. In his spare time, he works as the chief technology officer of a streaming media company.

Jane Orton has degrees from Durham, Oxford and Edinburgh Universities (with a supervisory period at the University of Bologna) in Politics, Himalayan Studies, Classics and Philosophy. Her work takes her to the Indian Himalayas, where she researches local folklore and records traditional Himalayan music. Dr. Orton also has an interest in the folklore surrounding how to gain entry into the world's most exclusive night clubs.

Jill Terry Rudy, Associate Professor of English, Brigham Young University, researches the history of American folklore scholarship, fairy tale and folk narratives, intermediality, family folklore, and foodways. She teaches folklore courses as well as a Late Summer Honors, senior seminar, and graduate seminar on fairy tales and media. She has published in *College English, Journal of American Folklore*, and other folklore journals. She edited *The Marrow of Human Experience: Essays on Folklore* by William A. Wilson and co-edited *Channeling Wonder: Fairy Tales on Television* with Pauline Greenhill. She directs a digital humanities project with a searchable, interactive website at fttv.byu.edu.

Kylie Schroeder is currently pursuing her Master's Degree in Utah State University's Folklore Program. She completed her undergraduate degree at the University of Wisconsin-Madison in 2014 with a major in anthropology and certificates in religious studies, folklore, and Celtic studies. Some of her research interests include supernatural tourism, culinary tourism, and living history as alternative education.

Claudia Schwabe, Assistant Professor of German, teaches German literature, language, and culture classes with an emphasis on fairy tales at Utah State University. She co-edited *New Approaches to Teaching Folk and Fairy Tales* (2016) and is currently working on her monograph *Craving Supernatural Creatures: German Fairy-Tale Figures in American Pop Culture*, which is under contract with Wayne State University Press's Series in Fairy-Tale Studies. Her articles, book chapters, poetry, and reviews have appeared in *Marvels & Tales: Journal of Fairy-Tale Studies*, *Contemporary Legend*, *Channeling Wonder* (2014), *Journal of Folklore Research*, *The German Quarterly*, *Cultural Analysis*, *Poetica Magazine*, and elsewhere.

Brittany Warman is a PhD candidate in English and Folklore at The Ohio State University. Her main interests include folkloric retellings, fairy tales, 19th-century literature (particularly the Gothic and Fantastic), supernatural folklore (especially conceptions of magic and fairy-lore/witch-lore), feminist and queer theory, speculative literature, experimental literature, and digital media. She is currently working on her dissertation about fairy-lore, fairy tales, and Gothic literature.

Kristiana Willsey has a PhD in Folklore from Indiana University, and has taught classes on fairy tales and folk narrative at Otis College of Art and Design, UCLA, and Indiana University-Purdue University Indianapolis. She is currently a visiting scholar at the American Academy of Arts and Sciences.

Preston Wittwer is a Master's student studying English, rhetoric, and media at Brigham Young University (BYU). Between teaching freshman writing courses and studying folklore, he is currently writing his thesis on the rhetoric of the presidency and how the president has increasingly become a pop culture fixture, specifically through appearances on late night comedy talk shows. Preston is from Murray, Utah, and, following his time at BYU, plans to pursue a doctoral degree in media studies and commit full time to academia.

The Fairy Tale and Its Uses in Contemporary New Media and Popular Culture Introduction

Claudia Schwabe

Abstract: Ever since the beginning of the 21st century, the fairy tale has not only become a staple of the small and silver screen around the globe, it has also migrated into new media, overwhelming audiences with imaginative and spectacular retellings along the way. Indeed, modern fairy-tale adaptations pervading contemporary popular culture drastically subvert, shatter, and alter the public's understanding of the classic fairy tale. Because of the phenomenally increasing proliferation of fairy-tale transformations in today's "old" and "new" media, we must reflect upon the significance of the fairy tale for society and its social uses in a nuanced fashion. How, why, and for whom have fairy-tale narratives, characters, and motifs metamorphosed in recent decades? What significant intermedial and intertextual relationships exist nowadays in connection with the fairy tale? This special issue features 11 illuminating articles of 13 scholars in the fields of folklore and fairy-tale studies tackling these and other relevant questions.

Reprinted from *Humanities*. Cite as: Schwabe, C. The Fairy Tale and Its Uses in Contemporary New Media and Popular Culture Introduction. *Humanities* **2016**, 5, 81.

Following the increasing influence of visual culture on fairy-tale productions since the 20th century, the digital revolution has contributed significantly to the dissemination of the fairy tale and has solidified its presence in late-20th-century and 21st-century popular culture. Similarly to cinema and television, which are considered "old" media, so have "new" media (the Internet and websites, such as online platforms and blogs, social media, online newspapers, wikis, and video games) made frequent use of fairy-tale materials and thus kept the genre in the public consciousness. Although fairy tales are constantly migrating into new cultures and different media, reinventing themselves along the way, recent years in particular have seen a wave of highly innovative but also highly disputable fairy-tale retellings in popular culture. On television, popular fairy-tale series that are based explicitly on fairy-tale figures and motifs are, for example, American Broadcasting Company's (ABC) *Once Upon a Time* (2011–present) and National Broadcasting Company's (NBC) *Grimm* (2011–present) [1]. These shows drastically subvert viewers' expectations of traditional fairy-tale structures and characters. To promote interest in the series, both "*Once Upon a Time* and *Grimm* make use of print- and web-based paratexts that give the reader the potential to engage with the programs beyond the televised text itself" ([2], p. 1010). The same subversive tone unsettling familiar fairy-tale conventions is noticeable in many recent fairy-tale film adaptations, including *The Huntsman: Winter's War* (2016) [3] and its prequel *Snow White and the Huntsman* (2012) [4], *Hansel & Gretel: Witch Hunters* (2013) [5], the *Shrek* films (2001–2010) [6–9], or the Disney productions *Into the Woods* (2014) [10], *Maleficent* (2014) [11], and *Frozen* (2013) [12]. Contributing to this new and transformed pervasiveness of the fairy tale in today's culture is its hypercommodification and mass-mediated hype, especially in the United States. One major, though by no means exclusive, focus of this Special Issue is tackling the questions: How do we read popular culture's employment of the fairy tale? How, why, and for whom have fairy-tale narratives, characters, and motifs metamorphosed in the 21st century? What significant intermedial and intertextual relationships exist nowadays in connection with the fairy tale?

The continuing proliferation and diversification of fairy tales in our society permeates a wide range of media: from film and television to commercial platforms, advertising, and marketplaces capitalizing on consumer products (including clothing, toys, household items, and more), and from popular literature and graphic novels to new media. Thanks to the electronic accessibility of fairy-tale texts and fairy tale–inspired materials via websites and online publications, they now have become a multimedia phenomenon. Technological tools, such as computers, tablets, and smartphones allow us to watch, read, listen to, play, and generally engage with fairy-tale material from any place in the world. The same tools give us the ability to navigate the "fairy-tale web," as Cristina Bacchilega [13] coined the term in her book *Fairy Tales Transformed* (2013), and to control the way fairy-tale texts are presented to us and to others. Donald Haase noted in the Greenwood Encyclopedia *Folktales and Fairy Tales* (2016): "As a genre characterized by endless variation and adaptability, the fairy tale lends itself especially well to reinvention under these circumstances. As technology continues to advance and the visual experience becomes increasingly creative and interactive, it will be interesting to see how the production and reception of the fairy tale changes to take advantage of these new possibilities" ([2], p. 1010).

This development of what can be described as "fairy-tale hype" in the media has not only informed scholarly perspectives but has also taken hold in popular consciousness. An essential question that must be asked in this context is: How is contemporary media changing the face of the fairy tale and to what effect? At the same time, thanks to the fast-growing field of modern technologies, we are now in a better position than ever before to explore and discuss the intersections of fairy-tale studies with media and technology. The advancement of online fairy-tale databases that are publicly accessible, such as the International Fairy-Tale Filmography (http://iftf. uwinnipeg.ca) and the Fairy-Tale Teleography and Visualizations digital humanities project (http://fttv.byu.edu), two archival online tools for intermedial fairy-tale research, offer significantly evolving opportunities to examine the relationships between tales and popular culture within the framework of new media. Heidi Anne Heiner's invaluable website SurLaLune Fairy Tales (http://www.surlalunefairytales.com) features hyperlinked textual annotations to numerous international fairy tales, histories of tales, bibliographies, illustrations, modern interpretations of tales, a blog, and book galleries. Tracey A. Callison's research website Folk and Fairy (http://www.folkandfairy.org) offers a vast selection of print sources from literary traditions ranging from feminism to psychology to Marxism. Noteworthy blogs online are Maria Tatar's *Breezes From Wonderland* (http://blogs.harvard.edu/tatar/), Kristin's *Tales of Faerie* (http://talesoffaerie.blogspot.com), Tahlia Merrill Kirk's *Diamonds & Toads* (http://www.diamondsandtoads.com), and Amy Kraft and Sophie Bushwick's *Tabled Fables* (http://tabledfables.tumblr.com/podcasts), which also features eight illuminating fairy-tale podcasts.

This special issue offers 11 insightful articles of 13 scholars in the fields of folklore and fairy-tale studies. In their thought-provoking contributions to this Special Issue, the authors analyze and discuss topics, including the generic complexity of recent fairy-tale adaptations with regard to genre mixing and mashing; fairy-tale hybridity; intertextuality and intermediality; international reinterpretations and reboots of classical fairy tales in old and new media; intersections of fairy-tale studies and digital humanities scholarship; responses to "Disneyfied" fairy tales on social media platforms; digital forms of storytelling; international dissemination of fairy tales using new media; transmedia approaches to fairy tales; artifactualization; ideological aesthetics of fairy tales in television series; fan fiction culture; fairy-tale alternate universe stories; happily-ever-after endings; definitions of the fairy-tale genre; the queering of fairy tales; feminism and fairy tales; the concept of the *folkloresque*; magic realism; science and fairy tales; fairy tales as filmic art; fairy tale–inspired comic book series and anime; and televisual fairy-tale iconography in advertising.

"Between Earth and Sky: Transcendence, Reality, and the Fairy Tale in *Pan's Labyrinth*" is the title of a chapter by Savannah Blitch, a student of English Literature at Arizona State University. Blitch focuses on Guillermo del Toro's *Pan's Labyrinth* (2006) [14], a film that plays upon our deep-rooted and mercurial relationship with fairy tales and folklore. By turns beautiful and grotesque, *Pan's Labyrinth* is a complex portrait of the clash between the protagonist's (Ofelia) fairy-tale world and that of the brutal adults around her. Blitch provides an illuminating analysis of the juxtaposition of the film's imagery of closed/open circles, their respective realms, and how Ofelia moves between the two spaces. Blitch argues that these aspects create an unusual relationship between the fairy-tale universe and the physical one, characterized by simultaneous displacement and interdependency. Ofelia acts as a mediatrix of these spheres, conforming to neither the imposed rules of her historical reality nor the expected structural rules of fairy tales, and this refusal ultimately allows her transcendence from the circumscribed realm of the liminal into Victor Turner's "liminoid" space, escaping the trap of binarism.

In her chapter "'All That Was Lost Is Revealed': Motifs and Moral Ambiguity in *Over the Garden Wall*", folklore scholar Kristiana Willsey claims that unlike the majority of fairy-tale films and television shows of the last decade, Patrick McHale's animated miniseries *Over the Garden Wall* (2014) [15] does not self-consciously disrupt or critique fairy-tale norms. Instead, the miniseries strips away a century of popular culture associations and uses motifs in the way oral narrators use them, to create resonant images—what Max Lüthi called "the shock effect of beauty" ([16], p. 3). In her intriguing analysis, Willsey describes *Over the Garden Wall* as pointedly nostalgic in both its source material and storytelling approach, and identifies the miniseries as an argument for singular fairy tales in an increasingly transmedia-driven narrative landscape.

Jill Rudy, Associate Professor of English at Brigham Young University, and Jerom McDonald, an independent scholar who specializes in algorithmic media analysis, co-wrote the chapter "Baba Yaga, Monsters of the Week, and Pop Culture's Formation of Wonder and Families through Monstrosity". The authors highlight the fact that in television shows outside of Slavic nations, Baba Yaga often appears in Monster of the Week (MOTW) episodes. Their chapter considers transforming forms in this trope. Whereas some MOTW are contemporary inventions, many are creatures from folk narratives. Employing the *folkloresque* concept, Rudy and McDonald explore how contemporary audiovisual tropes gain integrity and traction by indexing traditional knowledge and belief systems. Using digital humanities methods, the authors built a "monster typology" and used topic modeling to investigate central concerns, finding connections between crime, violence, family, and loss. Rudy and McDonald recognize Baba Yaga's role as a villain and acknowledge that the narrative arcs build close relationships between characters and among viewers.

Sara Cleto and Erin Kathleen Bahl, two doctoral candidates at the Ohio State University, focus on the anime series *Puella Magi Madoka Magica* (2011) [17], in which middle school girls fight witches in exchange for a wish. Many of the series' action sequences unfold in "labyrinths", magical spaces controlled by witches. Cleto and Bahl investigate these labyrinths as creative acts of embodied composing that negotiate grief and despair. By composing a labyrinth, witches can simultaneously reshape their environment and create a powerful statement about identity in narrative spaces that they control. In particular, Cleto and Bahl argue that both the frameworks of "fairy tale" and "new media" give us useful analytical resources for beginning to make sense of the complex phenomenon of *Madoka*'s labyrinths.

Brittany Warman, a doctoral candidate in English and Folklore at the Ohio State University, examines in her chapter the popular television show *Once Upon a Time* (2011–present) [18] and takes a closer look at the character Ruby/Red, the series' version of Little Red Riding Hood, who *is* the wolf. As a werewolf, Ruby/Red must wear an enchanted red cloak in order to keep from turning into a monster. Warman argues that though Red's story certainly calls on the classic fairy tale, it also makes deliberate use of the less familiar tale "Snow White and Rose Red" (ATU 426). Taking queer readings of this text as starting points, Warman demonstrates that this allusion opens up space for a compelling reading of Red's werewolf nature as a coded depiction of her later confirmed bisexuality.

In his chapter "Don Draper Thinks Your Ad Is Cliché: Fairy Tale Iconography in TV Commercials", Preston Wittwer, a master's student at Brigham Young University, zooms in on the history of fairy-tale iconography in advertising and the relationship between advertising and fairy tales. Wittwer investigates how, and for whom, fairy-tale figures have been adapted decade by decade in order to examine popular culture's commercialized and hypnotic relationship with fairy tales in the most direct format available: television commercials. In his text, Wittwer draws on Don Draper, the fictional character and the protagonist of the television series *Mad Men* (2007–2015) [19], who rejects a shoe commercial pitch featuring Cinderella, calling it "cliché". Wittwer illuminates that the temptation for advertisers to use fairy-tale iconography continues today and highlights that some ads feature fairy tales, which are innovative for their time.

Anne Kustritz, an assistant professor in Media and Culture Studies at Utrecht University, contributes the chapter "'They All Lived Happily Ever After. Obviously': Realism and Utopia in *Game of Thrones*-Based Alternate Universe Fairy Tale Fan Fiction". Kustritz's chapter focuses on how fan fiction alternate universe stories (AUs) that combine the popular television series *Game of Thrones* (2011–present) [20] with fairy-tale elements construct a dialogue between realism and wonder. Kustritz argues that realism in "quality TV" often rejects feminine genres, while the happily-ever-after ending also receives significant feminist criticism. However, because fan fiction cultures place stories in dialogue with numerous other versions, the fairy-tale happy ending can serve unexpected purposes. By examining *Game of Thrones* fairy-tale AU fan fiction, Kustritz's chapter demonstrates the genre's ability to construct surprising critiques through strategic deployment of impossible wishes made manifest through the magic of fan creativity.

A master's student in Folklore at Utah State University, Kylie Schroeder's case study sheds light on how YouTube artist Paint, a.k.a. Jon Cozart, challenges Disney's "happily ever afters" through comedic satire and creates parodied storylines, bringing four animated Disney princesses into the real world. Schroeder's case study looks at the global recognition of Disney and how it allows the creation of social commentary, while an increasingly digital world impacts the capabilities of the creator and the viewers. Cozart's fairy-tale parody takes on content and a form that reflects the increasingly globalized and digitized world.

Julianna Lindsay, who holds a doctorate in Heritage Studies from Arkansas State University, adds the chapter "The Magic and Science of *Grimm*: A Television Fairy Tale for Modern Americans." Lindsay argues that NBC's television series *Grimm* (2011–present) uses fairy tales and an altered history to explore modern issues in American society, such as environmental concerns, individuality, and social and cultural change through magic and magic-tinged science. Worldwide chaos is explained as part of the *Grimm* universe through Wesen (fantastical creatures), leading to a more united view of humanity and equality of human experience. Lindsay suggests that *Grimm* gives its American audience a form of societal unity through historic folklore and a fictional explanation for the struggles Americans perceive to be happening within their own society as well as in other parts of the world.

Based on Jane Orton's fieldwork conducted in Tibetan cultural areas of the Indian Himalayas, her chapter "Himalayan Folklore and the Fairy Tale Genre" explores Himalayan understandings of what defines a fairy tale in contrast to the Western understanding of the term. In parts of the Himalayas, a distinction is made between "lakshung" (fairy tales) and "kyakshung", which are shorter stories, the kind one might tell over tea. In light of the proposals to record and disseminate many of these stories using new media, folklore scholar Orton examines these genre definitions and investigates the various contexts in which these stories are told.

Jason Harris, an instructional assistant professor at Texas A&M University, analyses in his chapter Bill Willingham's popular *Fables* and *Jack of Fables* comics, which use fairy-tale pastiche and syncreticism based on the ethos of comic book crossovers to redeploy and subvert previous approaches to fairy-tale characters. Tension between Willingham's subordination of fairy-tale characters to his libertarian ideological narrative and the traditional folkloric identities drives the storytelling momentum. Harris demonstrates in his work that Willingham's portrayal of the Big Bad Wolf, Snow White, Rose Red, and Jack challenges assumptions about gender, heroism, narrative genres, and what comprises a fairy tale. Emerging from negotiations between tradition and innovation are fairy-tale characters who defy constraints of folk and storybook narrative, mythology, and metafiction.

Thanks to the scholarly articles of this Special Issue, we not only gain different, innovative insights into how today's media is changing the face of the fairy tale, we also learn about the manifold ways in which fairy tales pervade and influence contemporary popular culture. Just as authoritative as tales told through oral storytelling modes, fairy-tale adaptations of the 21st century in "old" and "new" media reflect the sociocultural conditions in which they were made. The nature of the fairy tale should thus be understood as a complex but ever-changing, fluid one, which allows for the fairy tale's constant mutability and reinvention. It is the hope of the editor that this Special Issue will contribute in fresh and stimulating ways to the overarching discussion in fairy-tale scholarship surrounding the significance of the fairy tale for society as it migrates into new times and places.

Conflicts of Interest: The author declares no conflict of interest.

References

1. *Grimm.* Created by Stephen Carpenter, David Greenwalt and Jim Kouf. National Broadcasting Company (NBC), 2011–present.
2. Haase, Donald. "Television." In *Folktales and Fairy Tales: Traditions and Texts from around the World*, 2nd ed. 4 vols. Edited by Donald Haase and Anne Duggan. Santa Barbara: ABC-CLIO, 2016, pp. 1007–11.
3. *The Huntsman: Winter's War.* Directed by Cedric Nicolas-Troyan. Perfect World Pictures/Roth Films, 2016.
4. *Snow White and the Huntsman.* Directed by Rupert Sanders. Roth Films, 2012.
5. *Hansel & Gretel: Witch Hunters.* Directed and written by Tommy Wirkola. MTV Films/Gary Sanchez Productions/Studio Babelsberg, 2013.
6. *Shrek.* Directed by Andrew Adamson, and Vicky Jenson. Pacific Data Images, 2001.
7. *Shrek 2.* Directed by Andrew Adamson, Kelly Asbury, and Conrad Vernon. Dream Works Animation/Pacific Data Images, 2004.
8. *Shrek Forever After.* Directed by Mike Mitchell. Dream Works Animation/Pacific Data Images, 2010.
9. *Shrek the Third.* Directed by Chris Miller and Raman Hui. Dream Works Animation/Pacific Data Images, 2007.
10. *Into the Woods.* Directed by Rob Marshall. Walt Disney Pictures/Lucamar Productions, 2014.
11. *Maleficent.* Directed by Robert Stromberg. Walt Disney Pictures/Roth Films, 2014.
12. *Frozen.* Directed by Chris Buck and Jennifer Lee. Walt Disney Pictures, 2013.
13. Bacchilega, Cristina. *Fairy-Tales Transformed? Twenty-First-Century Adaptations and the Politics of Wonder.* Detroit: Wayne State University Press, 2013.
14. *Pan's Labyrinth* (El laberinto del fauno). Directed and written by Guillermo del Toro. Tequila Gang/Estudios Picasso/Telecinco Cinema/Sententia Entertainment/Esperanto Filmoj, 2006.
15. *Over the Garden Wall.* Directed by Patrick McHale. Cartoon Network, 2014.
16. Lüthi, Max. *The Fairytale as Art Form and Portrait of Man.* Bloomington: Indiana University Press, 1984.
17. *Puella Magi Madoka Magica.* Directed by Akiyuki Shinbo. Shaft and Aniplex, 2011.
18. *Once Upon a Time.* Created by Edward Kitsis and Adam Horowitz. American Broadcastin Company (ABC), 2011–present.
19. *Mad Men,* Created by Matthew Weiner. American Movie Classics (AMC), 2007–2015.
20. *Game of Thrones.* Directed by David Benioff, Alan Taylor and Daniel Brett Weiss. Written by David Benioff, George R.R. Martin and Daniel Brett Weiss. Home Box Office (HBO), 2011–present.

Himalayan Folklore and the Fairy Tale Genre

Jane Orton

Abstract: Based on fieldwork by the author conducted in Tibetan cultural areas of the Indian Himalayas, this paper explores Himalayan understandings of what defines a fairy tale, in contrast to the Western understanding. In parts of the Himalayas, a distinction is made between *"lakshung"* (fairy tales) and *"kyakshung"*, which are shorter stories, the kind one might tell over tea. In light of the proposals to record and disseminate many of these stories using new media, this paper seeks to examine these genre definitions and investigates the various contexts in which these stories are told.

Reprinted from *Humanities*. Cite as: Orton, J. Himalayan Folklore and the Fairy Tale Genre. *Humanities* **2016**, *5*, 50.

1. Introduction

The Western fairy tale genre has long been the subject of attempts by scholars to be defined, and the concept has proved to be a slippery one. Recent scholarship [1] has even questioned whether some of the most famous European fairy tales can be classed as such. It is very difficult to define exactly what a fairy tale is, but fairy tale expert Jack Zipes links their development to "oral folk tales, which contain wondrous and marvelous elements" ([2], p. 2). Vladimir Propp's *Morphology of the Folktale* [3] attempts to describe fairy tales according to their component parts and Max Lüthi [4] surveys fairy tales in contrast to related genres.

Around the globe, a similar distinction exists between fairy tales and other kinds of stories, but there is no consensus about how to differentiate between these various narratives. At the same time, stories from outside of the West are being digitised and disseminated in both old [5] and new [6] media. Often, these stories are not organised along the lines of traditional genre distinctions, but according to particular objectives: narratives containing animals are collected for use in conservation, for example, regardless of whether they are fairy tales, fables or other kinds of narratives [5]. These new groupings, along with their availability to scholars made possible by new media, provide an opportunity to reassess the limits of various narrative traditions.

When researching folk tales in Spiti, a cold mountain desert in the northern Indian Himalayas, I would ask participants if they could tell me any stories about the area and was sometimes told that they did not know any stories. They did, however, know a fairy tale (*lakshung*). When I asked what the difference was between a fairy tale and other stories, I was told that the fairy tale was a story about someone having powers, whereas a *kyakshung* was a shorter story, often told while having tea.

This paper presents one such example of a *lakshung*, collected by the author in Spiti in August 2015.[1] Features of the European fairy tale, as identified in scholarship, will be contrasted with those of this tale, with the aim of broadening the Western understanding of fairy tales and shedding new light on genre definitions.

2. Results

In an interview [7] with Dawazangmo, a resident of Spiti, the following fairy tale was obtained:

> Once, there was a King named Baladewana and a Queen named Kunzangma. When they were married for a long time, they had still no children. They prayed and the goddess came, holding a dhu (shell) and in the other hand tha (prayer beads). She said,
>
> "You will have a child who will be very brave and indeed a kind man."
>
> They had a child and named it Dhondova. After three years, the Queen died. The king was worried about bringing up the child, so he married a commoner. Her name was Panmachen. After the marriage, the goddess came again and said that they would have a child who would make chortens. They had a child called Chungo Doyon.
>
> After a few years, the children were very close, but the mother was jealous of the first child inheriting the kingdom. She went East and found old men and women talking, saying that the younger child would get nothing. She went South and found young people saying the same. She went North and youngsters were also saying the same. She went West and found small children making thrones from stones—one big and one small. They said the big one was for the older brother and the small one for the younger brother.
>
> "I have to do something," she thought.
>
> She pretended to be ill and called the king. The king offered to do anything for her, so she asked for her son to inherit the kingdom and he agreed. They exiled the older brother. During the night, the brothers were braiding their hair (chuti). The younger brother tied his braid to his

---

[1]   The findings of this study are the results of 40 unstructured interviews conducted in Spiti in July and August 2015. The interviews were conducted in Spitian, a language closely related to Tibetan, and translated into English with an interpreter present. Transcripts of English translations of the stories referenced here can be obtained from the author of this paper.

older brother. The older brother cut his hair and left. When the younger brother woke and found his older brother gone, he went after him.

Tsalma (food given at birth) was given to the older brother. The younger brother followed and they shared the tsalma. They boiled leather and ate it. The younger brother felt thirsty and fainted. The older brother took him to the waterfall and went away.

If men have power, they can change into a monkey (sheu). The younger brother changed into a monkey because he had died and had the power to change. He lived there and ate fruit from the trees. He ate half of the fruit and left half for his brother.

The older brother went far away and saw lungta (wind horse). He called out, "Father!" There was a monk in the house who recognised him as a son from a previous life. He took him inside.

The older brother was a talented horse-rider, superior to others; other children wondered about him and were jealous. There was a meeting and it was decided that the brother should be thrown into the lake. When they came to the monk's house, the monk used his power to hide the brother in the horn of an ibex. The villagers came and were angry. They said they would make lā (spirit) burn red under the fire and threatened to burn the monk with it. The monk was hiding and the older brother came out and offered to go with the villagers. The villagers took him.

The Princess of that place (to which he was taken), Lechewalden, came and took him with her. She tied her hair to his, but the brother also cut his hair and jumped into the lake. He found many people and animals thrown into the lake. He was a reincarnation of a god, so he revived all the people in the lake and came back. He went to the monk and called, "Father." The monk did not know who he was and said,

"I have no child."

However, he (the monk) opened the door. He was shocked and fainted.

The older brother, the monk and the revived people all went to the waterfall and saw the monkey. As the older brother stepped three steps, so did the monkey. But the monkey was afraid of the monk. The older brother went and saw the fruit gathered by the younger brother. He took the younger brother into the village by the lake and was made King because of the Princess.

The brothers decided to visit their parents. The mother of the younger brother was ashamed of herself (nubda). She sank into the ground with shame. The younger brother was made King of the first kingdom.

3. Discussion

It is not the aim of this paper to provide a definitive classification of Himalayan fairy tales. Rather, by highlighting features commonly associated with Western fairy tales that can be found in Dawazangmo's *lakshung*, and by noting important differences between these tales and the way that they are transmitted, this paper seeks to challenge and deepen Western genre definitions.

3.1. Features of the Western Fairy Tale in the Lakshung

Fairy tales, argues Zipes [2], are a type of appropriation of the wonder folk tale. Zipes mentions several features of the wonder tale:

> Rarely do wonder tales end unhappily. They triumph over death. The tale begins with "once upon a time" or "once there was" and never really ends when it ends. The end is actually the true beginning. The once upon a time is not a past designation but futuristic: The timelessness of the tale and lack of geographic specificity endow it with utopian connotations—utopia in its original meaning designated "no place", a place that no one had ever envisaged. We form and keep the utopian kernel of the tale safe in our imaginations with hope." ([2], p. 4).

Dawazangmo's *lakshung* exhibits the features of Zipes' wonder tale. The ending is a happy one, with both brothers being made kings of their respective kingdoms. Death is triumphed over, with the younger brother living as a monkey after his death and the people of the lake being revived. The *lakshung* also exhibits the common beginning Zipes associates with the wonder tale ("Once, there was a King named Baladewana and a Queen named Kunzangma ... "). It could also be said that the end "is actually the true beginning" in the sense that the story ends at the beginning of the brothers' reigns over their respective kingdoms. Moreover, the tale is not geographically specific.

Further, Zipes [2] summarises Propp's [3] functions of the wonder tale, giving them his own emphasis as follows:

1. The protagonist is confronted with an interdiction or prohibition that he or she violates in some way. Often the protagonist commits an error or seeks to improve his or her social status by embarking on a journey. One way or another the protagonist is commissioned—sent on a mission.

2. Departure or banishment of the protagonist, who is either given a task or assumes a task related to the interdiction and prohibition, or to the desire for improvement and self-transformation. The protagonist is assigned a task, and the task is a sign. That is, his or her character will be marked by the task that is his or her sign.

3. The protagonist encounters: (a) the villain; (b) a mysterious individual or creature, who gives the protagonist gifts; (c) three different animals or creatures who are helped by the protagonist and promise to repay him or her; or (d) three different animals or creatures who offer gifts to help the protagonist, who is in trouble. The gifts are often magical agents, which bring about miraculous change.

4. The endowed protagonist is tested and moves on to a battle and conquers the villain or inimical forces.

5. The peripety or sudden fall in the protagonist's fortunes is generally only a temporary setback. A wonder or miracle is needed to reverse the wheel of fortune. Sometimes a fairy, hermit, wise man or woman, or magically endowed human or animal will intervene to benefit the protagonist.

6. The protagonist makes use of gifts (and this includes the magical agents and cunning) to achieve his or her goal. The result is (a) three battles with the villain; (b) three impossible tasks that are nevertheless made possible; and/or (c) the breaking of a magic spell.

7. The villain is punished or the inimical forces vanquished.

8. The success of the protagonist usually leads to (a) marriage; (b) the acquisition of money; (c) survival and wisdom; or (d) any combination of the first three ([2], pp. 3–4).

Dawazangmo's *lakshung* may be said to exhibit the first function in the sense that both brothers—the principal protagonists in the story—embark on a journey: the older brother first leaves the kingdom and the younger brother goes after him. The second function can be seen in the fact that the older brother's character (brave and kind) is exhibited not just in the prophesy of the goddess, but also during his journey (for example, his offer to go with the villagers when the monk was threatened). The third function can be seen in both the gift of *tsalma* and the hospitality of the monk. The fourth function can be seen in the older brother's showdown with the villagers and the fifth and sixth can be seen in his revival of the people in the lake. The seventh function is satisfied when the mother of the younger brother sinks into the ground with shame. Finally, the eighth function is satisfied when the older brother is made king because of the Princess.

Max Lüthi [4] identifies elements of the fairy tale's style that can also be seen in Dawazangmo's *lakshung*. The fairy tale hero "is not astonished by miracles and magic; he accepts them as if they were a matter of course" ([4], p. 46). Moreover, in Lüthi's view, there is no detailed description in the fairy tale ([4], p. 50); in the *lakshung* also we are given no detail about the appearance of any of the characters. This, argues Lüthi, "gives the European fairy tale its clarity and precision" ([4], p. 50), which is added to by the isolation of the characters, for example in the separation

12

of two brothers. Such a separation of brothers can also be seen in the *lakshung*. In Lüthi's fairy tale, there is a tendency towards extremes and contrasts ([4], pp. 50–51), which can be seen in the death of the younger brother before he is reborn as a monkey. Lüthi writes that fairy tales show a preference for solid, man-made objects ([4], p. 51); this is possibly seen in the *tsalma* given to the older brother and the *tha* held by the goddess, although natural objects are also important (the *dhu* and the ibex horn). Inner journeys become outwardly visible in Lüthi's fairy tale ([4], p. 51); in the *lakshung*, both brothers eat food given at birth and the younger brother is reborn as a monkey. There is a delight in (often word-for-word) repetition in fairy tales, according to Lüthi ([4], pp. 53–54). This is seen in the *lakshung* in the mother's journey ("She went East/South/North/West and found ... "). Finally, danger is averted at the last possible minute ([4], pp. 56–57), which could possibly be seen in the *lakshung*, in the older brother's coming out as the monk is threatened and in hiding.

A preliminary survey of features of the fairy tale in the work of Zipes, Propp (via Zipes) and Lüthi suggests that the *lakshung* shares many of the characteristics of its European counterparts. However, this survey is not exhaustive, and it can be argued that the Western conception of the fairy tale is itself an evasive one.

3.2. The Fairy Tale as an Indistinct Genre

We have seen that Dawazangmo's *lakshung* shares many features that scholarship associates with the Western fairy tale. However, it should be noted that the distinction between the Western fairy tale and other genres is not absolutely distinct. In European literature, fables contain fairy tale motifs or vice versa. As Propp ([3], p. 5) points out, animal tales contain elements of the fantastic, and animals play a large role in fantastic tales. Moreover, Zipes classes Hans Christian Andersen's "The Ugly Duckling" as a fairy tale, although it could also be seen as a fable. He writes,

> Placing one's faith in God is an undercurrent in Andersen's most famous fairy tale "The Ugly Duckling" (1844). Although there are no Christian references in this narrative, Andersen uses the tradition of animal tales to demonstrate that there is such a thing as intelligent design. The duckling must have faith to overcome all the obstacles in his life so that he can triumph in the end. As in the traditional tales in which animals, insects, and plants speak and come to life, Andersen conveys didactic morals. They are not always religious... They stand in the tradition of Aesop's fables and reflect Andersen's notions of 'survival of the fittest' ([2], p. 124).

Hans Christian Andersen's fairy tales fall into the literary (rather than oral) tradition; having been written for children by a single author, they differ significantly from the oral tales collected in Spiti. However, the possibility of classifying these tales in different ways illustrates the potential genre overlap in the Western tradition.

It may be that "a scientific exactness [for classifying narratives] . . . does not in fact exist" [8]. Indices that identify folk narratives through tale types, such as that by Antti Aarne and Stith Thompson, have been a valuable tool of analysis for folklorists. Uther [8] points out that the Aarne-Thompson system cannot possibly document all oral and written folk narratives of the world, pointing to the fact that "the tale type index is structured according to genres and arranged according to themes . . . While we can see from the history of folktale classification that all these various genres can suitably be placed in the tale type index, there are other folk narratives that do not fit in its thematic divisions." Uther's revision of the Aarne-Thompson catalogue includes the miscellaneous type, which allows for heterogeneous types or those tales that are difficult to clarify.

In the Himalayan context, one story presented to me by Tashi Tandup as a *kyakshung* [9] could plausibly be called a fable due to its moral message, although the protagonist is not an animal:

> Khira Gompo Dorje was a hunter in Tibet. He used to bring a leg of whatever he had hunted to a monk. One day, he went to the monk and saw all the bones of the animals he had hunted—they nearly filled the room. He felt sorry in his heart for all the death he had caused. He decided to commit suicide and threw himself off a cliff. Immediately, he attained Enlightenment and flew away. The monk thought,
>
> "I have said lots of mantras and meditated a lot."
>
> So the monk threw himself off a cliff—but instead of attaining Enlightenment, he died. The moral is: it matters what is in your heart, not who you are.

Thus, in this region of the Himalayas, as in the European tradition, fables are not synonymous with animal tales. In the same way, animals often play a role in fairy tales, for example the monkey in Dawazangmo's *lakshung*. However, the distinction between *lakshung* and *kyakshung* (first made to me by Dawazangmo, but independently confirmed by other interview participants) is a common one, and seems to rely in part upon the context in which these tales are told. More research on this matter is needed, but tales presented to me as *kyakshung* have included saints' legends [10], local legends [11] and etiological stories [12].

Writing of the European tradition, Steven Swann Jones ([13], p. 9) highlights a fundamental feature that distinguishes the fairy tale from other genres: "While these other genres of the folktale are reasonably mimetic—that is, they depict life in fairly realistic terms—*fairy tales depict magical or marvelous events or phenomena as a valid part of human experience.*" Jones acknowledges two other genres that include

14

non-realistic elements: the fable and the tall tale. However, Jones points out that, in the fable, the non-realistic personification of animals is "a literary device for isolating and portraying human foibles, not as an ontologically or philosophically accurate representation of the phenomenal world. Similarly, in the tall tale, the marvelous events are considered artistic exaggerations, storytelling 'lies' ... " ([13], p. 10). It is only, according to Jones, in the fairy tale that we are expected to accept these magical elements at face value.

It is true that in Dawazangmo's *lakshung*, these marvelous elements are accepted at face value (the power of the younger brother to change into a monkey, the power of the monk to hide the older brother in the horn of an ibex and the power of the older brother to revive the people in the lake are all examples of this). In another *lakshung* told to me by Lobsang Tenpa [14], houses are magically erected by the gods and "anything is possible." However, if we are to classify Tashi Tandup's story as a fable, we must reject the assertion that fables do not ask us to accept magical elements at face value. One might argue that the hunter's ability to fly could be seen as a literary device to illustrate human foibles when contrasted with the monk's failure to do so. However, the animal personification of Jones' example plays a very different role: here, we are only asked to accept the anthropomorphism at face value before we hear a story of "otherwise realistic human behavior" ([13], p. 10). In Tashi Tandup's tale, the marvelous ability to fly plays a pivotal role in exposing the monk's folly. We also see instances of the magical and protective powers of animals (in this case, the yak) in Spiti in local legends [11] and etiological stories [12]. In this case, the distinction between *lakshung* and *kyakshung* cannot rest on the presence or absence of elements of the marvelous. This is not due to the absence of the marvelous in *lakshung*, but rather to the presence of it in the *kyakshung*.

3.3. Fairy Tales and Old Media

We should remember that, before the advent of new media, the European fairy tale underwent a transformation at the hands of old media. The development of the fairy tale from oral folk tales into the written literary genre in Europe must be seen in context. Lüthi points out that the written recording of fairy tales was influenced by particularities of the culture and time in which they were recorded. He writes:

> It must now be clear that the Grimm brothers did not retell the fairy tales exactly as they heard them. On the contrary, they carefully edited them, simplifying or embellishing them according to their poetic inclinations or pedagogical intentions ... Naturally, they were not completely independent of the spirit and the taste of their times ... ([4], p. 28).

Moreover, Giambattista Bastile, who compiled the 50 fairy tales of the Pentamerone "did not retell the fairy tales exactly as he heard them; he fashioned them to his taste. It was the taste of the baroque era" ([4], p. 29).

In addition, the author's personal situation and character play a role in the development of the fairy tale genre as it shifts from the oral to the literary tradition. As Zipes writes,

> The more the literary fairy tale was cultivated and developed, the more it became individualised and varied by intellectuals and artists, who often sympathized with the marginalized in society or were marginalized themselves. The literary fairy tale allowed for new possibilities of subversion in the written word and in print . . . ([2], p. 7).

Zipes is not alone in his assertion that fairy tales must be seen in their historical contexts. Warner [15] criticizes Bettelheim's Freudian analysis of the fairy tale, arguing, from a feminist perspective, that his argument ignores historical influences on the fairy tale genre, especially when dealing with cases such as that of the wicked stepmother. She writes, "This archetypal approach leeches history out of fairy tale. Fairy or wonder tales, however farfetched the incidents they include, or fantastic the enchantments they concoct, take on the colour of the actual circumstances in which they are or were told" ([15], p. 213).

When trying to extrapolate features of the Western fairy tale to produce genre definitions, we should remember that the fairy tale has undergone an evolution within the context of European cultural history, and has been influenced by those individuals who have elected to collect and record these tales. Therefore, it would be rash to assume that fairy tales from around the globe must meet the criteria arising from the study of the European form to be deserving of the name. As we have seen, Himalayan fairy tales may share many of the features associated with the European fairy tale, but perhaps we should appeal to the concept of family resemblance (rather than distinctness of form) when discussing genre definitions in both cultures.

4. Conclusions

There is a distinction between the fairy tale and other genres in Himalayan culture, and a superficial reading may justify the claim that these genre distinctions include similar features to those found in the Western tradition. However, this claim must be qualified to reflect several considerations. Firstly, the genre distinction between fairy tales and other genres in the West is not always a clear one. We see examples of fairy tales that can also be classed as fables, and motifs commonly associated with one genre regularly appear in other genres. Secondly, the written form of the Western fairy tale was influenced by specific historical and even personal circumstances. We cannot expect to see such circumstances reflected in the style of their Himalayan counterparts. In addition, although a strong written literary tradition exists in the Himalayas, this is not the same as an endeavour to collect fairy tales per se, as attempted by the likes of Bastile, Perrault or the Grimms. As a result, a large part of the distinction between *lakshung* and *kyakshung* rests on the context in which they are told (longer stories that require more time, as opposed to shorter stories to be told over tea). This in itself merits further investigation: to what extent can we draw genre distinctions according to the context in which narratives are deemed appropriate to be told? In the light of proposals to animate, record and digitally disseminate fairy tales along with Himalayan stories from other genres, it is possible that exposure to new media may change the face of the Himalayan fairy tale. Moreover, the resulting accessibility of these tales to Western scholars can broaden our global understanding of the fairy tale genre itself.

Conflicts of Interest: The author declares no conflict of interest.

References and Notes

1. Johan de Mylius. "'Our time is the time of the fairy tale': Hans Christian Andersen between Traditional Craft and Literary Modernism." *Marvels & Tales* 20 (2006): 166–78.
2. Jack Zipes. *When Dreams Came True: Classical Fairy Tales and Their Tradition*. London: Routledge, 2013.
3. Vladimir Propp. *Morphology of the Folktale*, 2nd ed. Austin: University of Texas Press, 1968.
4. Max Lüthi. *Once Upon a Time: On the Nature of Fairy Tales*. Bloomington: Indiana University Press, 1976.
5. Lynne R. Baker. "Links between Local Folklore and the Conservation of Sclater's Monkey (Cercopithecus sclateri) in Nigeria." *African Primates* 8 (2013): 17–24.
6. The International Institute for Tibetan and Buddhist Studies GmbH. "Folktales-Maerchen." Available online: http://www.tibetinstitut.de/folktales-maerchen.html (accessed on 29 February 2016).
7. Dawazangmo. Interviewed by Jane Orton. Unstructured interview. Kibber, 7 August 2015.
8. Hans-Jörg Uther. "Classifying folktales." Available online: http://www.folklorefellows.fi/?page_id=915 (accessed on 22 May 2016).
9. Tashi Tandup. Interviewed by Jane Orton. Unstructured interview. Chicham, 5 August 2015.
10. Phunchock Namgyal. Interviewed by Jane Orton. Unstructured interview. Kibber, 8 August 2015.
11. Lukse. Interviewed by Jane Orton. Unstructured interview. Ki, 13 August 2015.
12. Takpa Tanzin. Interviewed by Jane Orton. Unstructured interview. Ki, 13 August 2015.
13. Steven Swann Jones. *The Fairy Tale: Magic Mirror of the Imagination*. London: Routledge, 2002.

14. Lobsang Tenpa. Interviewed by Jane Orton. Unstructured interview. Chicham, 10 August 2015.
15. Marina Warner. *From the Beast to the Blonde: On Fairy Tales and Their Tellers*. London: Random House, 2015.

"After Ever After": Social Commentary through a Satiric Disney Parody for the Digital Age

Kylie Schroeder

Abstract: "If you've ever wondered why Disney tales all end in lies," then ask YouTube artist Paint—aka Jon Cozart. He has created a video for YouTube.com that re-imagines what happened after four of Disney's leading ladies' "dreams came true." Continuing a tradition that is as old as the tales he sings about, the artist combines characters and melodies that have become culturally ubiquitous since the media domination of the Disney Corporation with an interpretation of the material that tries to make sense of the world in which it exists. Continuing the criticisms of post-modernism and feminist theory, Cozart challenges the "happily ever afters" that have become the stock endings for the genre. Through comedic satire he creates parodied storylines that bring four animated princesses out of their Disney realms and into the real world where they must deal with environmental destruction, racism, and colonialism, among other issues. The use of a video-sharing site such as Youtube.com not only allows for the expanded distribution of fan-created material, but it also directly addresses a wider audience than traditional oral story tellers could possibly reach: the Internet. This case study looks at the ways in which the global recognition of Disney culture allows for the creation of social commentary through familiar and beloved characters, while an increasingly digitally-connected world impacts the capabilities and understanding of both the creator and the viewers of the material. While far from being a new phenomenon, the reinterpretation of fairy tales takes on content and a form that reflects the increasingly globalized and digitized world in Cozart's Disney parody.

Reprinted from *Humanities*. Cite as: Schroeder, K. "After Ever After": Social Commentary through a Satiric Disney Parody for the Digital Age. *Humanities* **2016**, 5, 63.

1. Introduction

"If you ever wonder why Disney tales all end in lies," then you are not alone. In 2013 YouTube artist Paint, named Jon Cozart, created a musical parody that asks this very question and responds with a catchy and humorous but slightly shocking series of answers. The medley was published on the popular video-sharing site, where it has been watched over 61 million times since its publication. The video, titled "After Ever After," reimagines four self-aware Disney princesses (Ariel, Jasmine, Belle, and Pocahontas) in our turbulent reality and explores—or perhaps exposes—the author's version of what has taken place since their "happily ever afters."

This formulaic ending for protagonists of the fairy tale has been pervasive in the genre, especially since the domination of the Walt Disney Corporation began in 1937 with the film *Snow White and the Seven Dwarves* [1], and as part of children's print literature before that time. The development of postmodernism and feminism in recent decades has resulted in an audience that is less willing to accept that standard and unsatisfying conclusion[1]. Even prior to this criticism, there has been a long history of fairy tale revisions for a variety of reasons. A combination of fairy tale scholarship, new media and amateur media studies, folklore, and cultural studies adds to the analysis of this form of fairy tale revision which reflects the globalized and digitized world in which Cozart's video was created. While there has recently been a surge in fairy tale retellings through television shows, movies, and books to meet this contemporary demand, the unique access and sharing capabilities of YouTube.com allow individuals to create and broadcast their own material to a world-wide audience from the comfort of their own homes. This is the setting in which "After Ever After" has achieved massive popularity. The following case study is one example of the ways in which fan-based material has evolved and is broadcast to its audience.

Cozart parodies the plots of four animated Disney movies with recognizable music from the original films. Not only is this compilation artistic, humorous, and extremely catchy, but it satirically critiques Western society—politics, environmentalism, racism, colonialism, and more—through familiar characters. Cozart's perspective as the creator is that of a young, American male, but his audience is expanded by the content of his parody and the platform through which the material was produced. This case study of Cozart's first "After Ever After" video examines the use of Disney heroines as spokespersons through which Cozart presents a digital parody that also functions as social, historical, political, and environmental commentary. According to noted scholar Jack Zipes, fairy tales "never really end when [they] end" ([4], p. 10) and Cozart is one of many who takes advantage of this and make use of "the end" as a new beginning. In doing so, he retains some aspects of "classic Disney" while subverting much of the sense of wonder that gives the original genre its name. I will review work that has been done in relevant areas of study, present the content of the video, analyze a number of choices made by the author in the creation of the text, and discuss the video as part of the tradition of fairy tale revisions with its role in digital media. Cozart is hardly the first person to

---

[1] For a more extensive discussion see Cristina Bacchilega's work [2,3].

create this kind of commentary, but I believe the format and function of the text are worth closer examination.

2. Literature Review

This article has drawn from the works of scholars in folklore, media studies, cultural studies, and other disciplines. Each has the potential to inform the others and can be used in combination to build a better understanding of this case study. Fairy tales have permeated many disciplines and have accrued theoretical, literary, feminist, and psychoanalytical analyses stressing social issues such as race and gender representation. From the history and development of the genre to its use in the digital age, fairy tales remain a relevant topic in both academic and vernacular spheres. Scholars have also looked at the way in which commodification has affected those tales and how fans interact with them—especially with the development of technology.

Diverse work has been done in the field of fairy tale studies which focuses on the function of the genre and its relevance—throughout history and in contemporary society. Scholarship has clearly documented the use of folk and fairy tales to respond to the world in which they exist through the evolution of oral tales into print literature and later into diverse forms of media. They have become what Jack Zipes calls a "cultural institution" [4]. In his numerous publications, Zipes has looked at the ways in which the genre has been used and manipulated throughout its history. Along with the analysis of the fairy tale tradition, there has been much critique of the genre. One of the most significant developments in recent years is that of post-modernism and feminism from both scholars and authors within the genre. In *Post-Modern Fairy Tales: Gender and Narrative Strategy* [3], Cristina Bacchilega provides an analysis of contemporary fairy tale "transformations" through the lens of folklore and literature studies. Bacchilega has also written specifically on feminist fairy tales. Other authors who have explored these theoretical critiques include Kay Stone, Donald Haase, and Marina Warner. These critiques look at the biased and generally patriarchal worldview that is present in the tales, as well as the distrust of the tales' relationship with "truth." Another source of analysis is the commodification of fairy tales, which has perhaps been influenced most by the rise and reign of the Disney Corporation.

Janet Wasko has focused on the power of the Disney name and its associated products, identifying its unique and recognizable style which is combined with a cultural importance that "cannot be emphasized" enough [5,6]. On a more focused note, scholars such as Kay Stone [7] and England et al. [8] have looked at the role of the Disney princess, while Joel Best and Kathleen S. Lowney inspect the impacts of the Disney reputation for better and for worse [9]. The writings of other scholars including Kristian Moen [10] and Johnson Cheu [11] have also influenced this analysis. While it may seem as though mass production of a fixed text would inhibit the re-tellings of the tales in question, fans have "enthusiastically embrace[d] favored texts and attempt[ed] to integrate media representations into their own social experience" ([12], p. 18).

Henry Jenkins's *Textual Poaching*, written in 1992, remains applicable in the age of digital culture [12]. Jenkins explores fan culture and the ways in which people interpret and reproduce material that is related to a subject of their interest, from fan fiction to filk (fan folk music). Jenkins writes as both a fan and an academic and looks specifically at the ways in which fans of television shows appropriate material. They "reread them in a fashion that serves different interests" and turn the activity into "a rich and complex participatory culture" ([12], p. 23). While this text was published in the early 1990s, the practices described are still active today, though they have continued to evolve with technology. These fandoms are generated around a shared interest in popular culture, and while Jenkins points out that some of these groups have negative connotations associated with membership, a sense of community is found within the fandom. Jenkins writes that "fans possess not simply borrowed remnants snatched from mass culture, but their own culture built from the semiotic raw materials the media provides ([12], p. 49). *Textual Poaching* focuses mainly on case studies of fan-composed stories, film compilations, and songs. These forms continue to be relevant in the digital age and their formats have adapted to accommodate the evolving technology.

Since the infiltration of the Internet into daily life—particularly in the Western world—there has been an increase in scholars looking at the impact of the content that appears there. Of particular interest to this study is the work that has been done with "user-generated content," or UGC, especially in the context of amateur-produced media [13]. John Quiggin calls UGC "a distinctive feature of the internet" and the edited work of Hunter et al. examines the social, cultural, and legal perspectives associated with amateur media [13]. This can be seen as a direct extension of the fan-created culture discussed by Jenkins; however, the form, content, and process have been adapted to the 21st century.

Drawing a connection between the former areas of study is a fairly new area of research: digital folklore. In *Folklore and the Internet*, Trevor J. Blank has combined the work of folklorists pursuing the previously under-studied area of lore that develops in a digital space [14]. He addresses the neglect of scholarship focused on the Internet and the volume provides a variety of topics that highlight the prevalence of folklore in digital spaces. In his introduction, Blank quotes folklorist Alan Dundes: "Technology isn't stamping out folklore; rather, it is becoming a vital factor in the transmission of folklore and it is providing an exciting source of inspiration for the generation of new folklore" [14]. One such digital space that combines user-generated content with fan-interpreted variations of commodified fairy tales is YouTube.com.

3. Case Study

The four-minute video entitled "After Ever After-DISNEY Parody" [15] opens to four horizontally arranged frames of the same young man, dressed in four different colored t-shirts and standing against four colored backdrops (Figure 1). He is Jon Cozart: YouTube username "Paint." Cozart's channel was created in December 2005 (10 months after YouTube's launch), and in the 10+ years that he has been active, the channel has accrued 3,329,665 subscribers and he has produced over 25 videos. His YouTube channel indicates that "After Ever After" is his most popular video, with over 61,500,000 views in the three years since its publication [15].

After Ever After - DISNEY Parody

Figure 1. Frames 1–4 from left to right [15].

As the video begins, the Cozart in each frame maintains a fairly passive expression and makes eye contact with the camera. After a moment of silence, all of the Cozarts sing to the tune of "When You Wish Upon a Star" (which is also the melody that accompanies Disney's iconic castle logo before the beginning of the corporation's films): "If you ever wondered why/Disney tales all end in lies/here's what happened after all their dreams came true." This is the first piece of the six-section compilation, and it functions as the introductory narration to the video. Cozart presents a problem that has been noted in scholarship with the rise of feminist theory and post-modernism and offers an explanation as to why—that the "happily ever after" we are given by the classic films is not the truth. The narrators tell their audience that they are about to get a glimpse behind the curtain that Disney lowers at the end of each movie. The speaker then switches from the third person—talking about those with the dreams—to speaking in the first person and takes on the roles of four Disney princesses in order to share their stories.

For the sake of clarity, when discussing the author I will reference Cozart and will the attribute actions of the performer to "Cozart-as" followed by the specific character name. When discussing the words and actions of the fictional character that is speaking, I will use feminine pronouns and the character's name on its own. Finally, when I refer to the background vocalists who are responsible for harmony and secondary characters, I will refer to "Cozarts" in the plural.

The first "ever after" to which the audience is introduced is that of Ariel from the 1989 animated feature film *The Little Mermaid* [16]. Frame 2 expands slightly and Cozart-as-Ariel holds up a small sign with the princess's name and related imagery (Figure 2). He and his counterparts, who function as vocal back-up and background dancers, sing to the tune of the movie's song "Under the Sea"; however, instead of the original lyrics that celebrate the wonders of living in the ocean, Cozart has parodied the original song with an environmentally-focused theme.

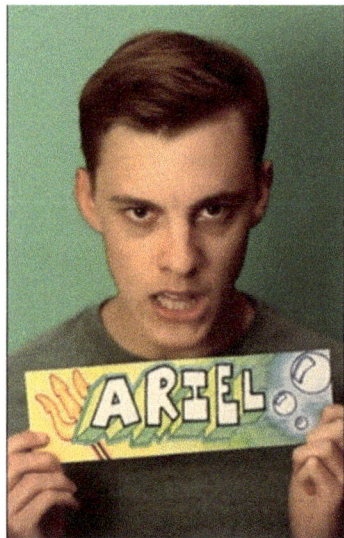

Figure 2. Cozart-as-Ariel. [15]

"I loved being princess down in this beautiful ocean blue/But mermaids are going missing, they end up in someone's stew/So just try to put yourself into somebody else's gills/You're killing my ecosystem with fishing and oil spills/Thank you BP[2], thank you BP/The British are killing, oil is spilling, now I can't see...My Eyes!/Chinamen feast on Flounder's fins/Plus the Japanese killed all my whale friends[3]/Oceans are browning, I think I'm drowning thanks to BP/You suck!"

Ariel's frame shrinks and the next Princess to sing is Cozart-as-Jasmine from *Aladdin* (1992) (Figure 3) [17]. She—still Cozart in the first person—shares her fears with the audience to the melody of "Prince Ali".

Figure 3. Cozart-as-Jasmine.

"Hey, I'm OK, but I'm slightly scared/My husband's a mark for the War on Terror[4]/Aladdin was taken by the CIA/We're not Taliban, you've got the wrong man in Guantanamo Bay/Prince Ali, where could he be, drowning in wawa[5]/Interrogation from the nation of the "free"/Bin Laden's taken the fall, we're not trained pilots at all/Jafar went crazy and no one put up a fuss/We're for freedom, Genie can vouch for us[6]/Bush

---

2   On 20 April 2012, a drilling rig named *Deepwater Horizon* exploded and sank into the Gulf of Mexico. It is considered to be the biggest accidental oil spill in history of the industry. At the time of this video's production cleanup was still taking place [18,19].
3   In reference to media outrage against harmful fishing practices.
4   The United States declared an international military campaign called the "War on Terror" after the World Trade Center bombings of 11 September 2001.
5   In reference to waterboarding.
6   Expected referential knowledge that Aladdin was responsible for freeing the Genie from his servitude.

was crazy, Obama's lazy, al-Qaeda's not in this country/Set free my Prince Ali!"

Frame 4 diminishes and the third enlarges: Cozart-as-Belle (*Beauty and the Beast,* 1992) is taunted by the Cozarts in the three minimized frames (Figure 4) [20]. Belle sings to the opening song of the movie ("Belle") and tells the audience:

Figure 4. Cozart-as-Belle. [15]

"This town's gone wild since I married Adam[7]/They think I'm going straight to hell/But the charges laid on me of bestiality/Could wind up getting me thrown in a cell /No, I'm overrun by mad men/I hear they plan to burn me at the stake/They legit believe I'm Satan/And now I hear that PETA's[8] gonna take my beast away."

The final Disney heroine to contribute to the musical parody is Pocahontas from the 1995 animated feature film of the same name [21]. The original movie ends when her love interest sails away from Virginia. Her song, in the style of "Colors of the Wind," remembers that:

"After John Smith traveled back to England/I helped my people cultivate the fields/More English, French, and Spaniards came to visit/And they

---

[7]   The Beast's human name.
[8]   People for the Ethical Treatment of Animals.

greeted us with guns and germs and steel[9]/They forced us into unknown lands of exile/They pillaged, raped, and left us all for dead/So now I'm far more liberal with a weapon/When I separate their bodies from their heads/Have you ever held the entrails of an English guy? Or bit the beating hearts of Spanish men?/Can you shoot an arrow in some French guy's eyeball? Can you paint with the red colors in these men?/I can murder if I please cause I'm dying of disease/I can paint with the red colors in these men." (Figure 5)

Figure 5. Reaction to Pocahontas' violent solution to colonialism. [15]

The sixth and final piece of the compilation features all four Cozart-as-princesses harmonizing with a thematic phrase from their respective section of the medley. "Thank you BP," mingles with "where's Prince Ali?" "Bestiality" is added by Cozart-as-Belle and finally Cozart-as-Pocahontas chimes in "I've got STDs[10]." The video ends with the six-note melody that accompanies Disney's castle logo at the end of the films' credits. In this way, Cozart's creation is framed by Disney musical rhetoric.

In this case study, there are a number of elements that contribute to the complex construction of the video. In order to discuss the power behind the parody, it is essential to explore the chosen format, content, and characters through which Cozart

---

[9] *Guns, Germs, and Steel: The Fates of Human Societies* is a 1997 non-fiction book by geographer and physiologist Jared Diamond that won the Pulitzer Prize in 1998 [22].

[10] Sexually transmitted diseases.

relates his message. While there are many facets of Cozart's video that would benefit from discussion, this paper will focus on its form and function by examining three choices made by the creator: the format of the "text"[11], the question "why Disney (and Disney princesses)," and the use of satirical parody in the case study.

4. Analysis

Cozart's "After Ever After" is one of many fairy tale re-writes that have taken place throughout the history of the genre. Jack Zipes states that "[d]uring its inception, the fairy tale distinguished itself . . . by both appropriating the oral folk tale [specifically, the wonder tale] and expanding it" ([4], p. 7) Zipes also notes that "the words that are selected in the process of creating the tale allow the speaker/writer freedom to play" with the material in a new way ([4], p. 7). The intention of this analysis is to examine three different aspects of the video that impacted the form and function of Cozart's creation.

While the supplemental information included in the case study was meant to provide context for the parody and the original material, I would like to acknowledge my role as an interpreter of Cozart's work. "After Ever After" is available to anyone with an Internet connection and as such will be seen and understood through an innumerable number of personal experiences. While I have tried to make use of relevant scholarship, my analysis and discussion are influenced by my personal worldview. This being said, I would like to offer possibilities for interpretation—not the singular intended meaning. An interview with Jon Cozart has also shaped my analysis of the material. I want to mention that meaning can be found regardless of authorial intent, and this does not lessen its importance to those for whom the meaning exists.

4.1. Digital Media as a Storytelling Tool

Without a doubt, the digital format of this video influences the capabilities of the creator and allows for the production style that is featured in the parody. The genre of online video offers an interesting mix of possibilities that can be compared to oral storytelling and those that are portrayed through mass media (i.e., movies, television, etc.). The web has been a forum for creative expression since its introduction to the public in the 1980s; in *Amateur Media*, John Quiggen reflects that "ever since the emergence of the internet, those affected by its ever-growing reach have tried to make sense of the new ways of doing things made possible by this technology" ([13], p. 27). YouTube.com is the number one website for user-generated content and its capabilities for free mass distribution allow amateurs to upload content that

---

[11]   Used here in the broad sense, referring to the video as a text.

is widely available to anyone with access to the Internet [13]. In her chapter on the digital salon, Helen Pilinovsky echoes Jenkins in distinguishing between the "original story" and the adaptations that are created for profit [13]. The fan-created medium is separate, though there are some who have crossed the line between amateur and professional activities through their creation of UGC. Other YouTubers that have gone viral with a similar style of production include Todrick Hall, who creates Disney-inspired mash-ups and pop culture music covers, Pentatonix, an a Capella group who have achieved commercial success, and Nick Pitera, known for his one-man music numbers and movie interpretations in which he sings all vocal parts. Cozart's video is a combination of these: he presents an a Capella, Disney-themed, one-man quartet that has been reinterpreted through satire.

The videos themselves are quite intricate, as the digital format allows the artist to create a one-man quartet[12]. "After Ever After" features Jon Cozart, four times over in four separate frames. Not only does he portray the four princesses but he also provides the narration, the background vocals and harmonization, percussive sounds, and additional characters responsible for inserting comments into the songs. These frames, all individually and painstakingly recorded and edited into a single compilation, are choreographed in such a way that the characters seem to be interacting with one another. There is also the additional artistic challenge of recreating the meter, melody, and rhyme of the original songs while altering the content and voice of the characters. Aside from the satiric message that is shared, the video can—and should—be appreciated for its artistry. While a single oral performer can portray different characters and actors in a movie can interact with one another, Cozart mediates between the two through digital media and interacts with himself as he portrays different characters. This is an example of how, through the use of digital media, a single performer is not limited to a solo. In an interview with the artist, Cozart shared that he wanted people to know how much time and effort went into the creation of the final product. Jenkins discusses the drive for "technical perfection" in fan-created work ([12], p. 247) and Cozart clearly reflects this interest.

YouTube as a platform is also an interesting choice for storytelling in a digital format because of its accessibility and prevalence[13]. Not only does it impact the creator's production abilities but it also influences the audience of the video. In an article on digital storytelling as a teaching tool, Dreon, Kerper, and Landis reflect that the "unprecedented access to technology has changed the way ... 'digital natives' communicate, interact, process information and learn" ([23], p. 4). The authors state

---

[12] Variations of this trend are seen elsewhere on YouTube and in popular culture; e.g., Todrick Hall, Nick Pitera.
[13] Referring to those with technological capabilities and Internet access.

that "the viral video is the cultural currency of today's youth" ([23], p. 7) and, clearly, Cozart is a practiced money-changer. When asked why he chose the platform of YouTube to share his creations, Cozart responded that "[t]he barrier of entry is so, so low—at least it was when I started making videos 10 years ago. I've always loved the idea of a kid in his room making something for millions of people" [24]. Anyone with access to the Internet is capable of creating a YouTube account, and an account is not required to view media on the site. As opposed to oral storytelling, YouTube does not provide a live audience or a live performance; however, this does not mean that they are any less interactive. The site allows comments and actions such as voting a clip up or down. "After Ever After" currently has 126,787 comments and a total of 1,243,343 votes (1,226,955 "likes" and 16,388 "dislikes") [15]. When asked about fan response, Cozart stated that while he does not react to negative comments, he "[does] take the audience's time seriously [and] never want[s] to present something that's wasteful of someone's day" [24]. This comment displays a perceived relationship and an accessible venue for audience response and interaction with the text and its creator. Not only does the digital format allow for unique styles of video to be produced, posted, and responded to, but the influence of digital culture has had an impact on globalization and access to current events. This allows Cozart to reference events that are taking place around the world, for people watching around the world. This access to global happenings—or simply the power of a Google search—makes the content of the video relevant and accessible to potential audiences.

4.2. Why Disney (and Disney Princesses)?

One of the important aspects of the wonder tale is the identifiable characters who are linked to certain activities, tasks, and settings [25]. In her essay "Some Day My Prince will Come: Female Acculturation through the Fairy Tale", Marcia K. Lieberman states that "[o]nly the best known stories, those that everyone has read or heard, indeed, those that Disney has popularized, have affected masses of children in our culture" (in [26], p. 15) The Disney Corporation has introduced stock characters through the mass commodification of characters in movies, books, songs, and other media. According to Best and Lowney, "[v]irtually all Americans—and much of the world's population—have been exposed to Disney's products" and in the public mind, the Walt Disney Corporation has come to be associated "with decent, family-oriented entertainment" ([9], pp. 445, 433). Not only is the brand perpetuated through films and other media (radio, theater, television, live-action movies), but it is also prevalent in merchandising, educational material, and theme parks. In her analysis of the function of the Disney Princess, Do Rozario states that "Disney's popular image and global profile ... makes the Disney Princess in effect the 'princess of all princesses'" ([27], p. 34). Even when the corporation branched out to produce more mature content under different companies, the "Disney name [was] preserved for animated features ... aimed at children" ([9], p. 436). According to a 2003 article in *USA Today*, "fairy tales were considered the big-screen domain of Disney animation" in Hollywood [28]. In fact, some scholars suggest that Disney has effectively taken the place of "traditional" fairy tales, as the brand is so pervasive in North America and around the globe [7,9]. The films used by Cozart were all produced between 1989 and 1995, in a period that England et al. refer to as the "middle" Disney princess movies [8] and Do Rozario attributes to "Team Disney," about 20 years after Walt Disney's death [27]. Janet Wasko notes in detail the brand's dominance in the entertainment industry [5,6]: in her book *Understanding Disney*, Wasko defines the trope of "classic Disney" as closed fantasies with "distinct beginnings and usually happy endings, moral tales, [a] structured story line, light entertainment" along with individualism and optimism, innocence, and the presence of music, humor, and anthropomorphized animals and inanimate objects to move the plot along [5].

Zipes points out in his book *The Enchanted Screen: The Unknown History of Fairy Tale Films* that there are many filmmakers who have made use of fairy tale material, but is critical of the shadow that Disney casts over other reinterpretations [29]. In some ways, Disney has become canonical when it comes to speaking of fairy tale films, or according to the research of Kay Stone, fairy tales in general [7]. The domination of the fairy tale seems to have created a static representation and general understanding of the fairy tale as it became mass-produced popular culture; however, Cozart's video is a clear example that people are still using fairy tales to deal with issues and are using the digital connections that currently exist to inform and export their retellings. Zipes (among other scholars) takes issue with the ubiquitous nature of Disney culture, and while he definitely makes a point that the tales have been slotted into a Disney form, this case study shows that people are trying to say what they need to say with the material that is available to them, and that which will reach a large audience in the case of an artist such as Cozart.

4.3. The Function of Parody and Satire in "After Ever After" as Social Commentary

The style of the text—catchy Disney tunes sung with over-animated expression and performed with choreography—is starkly contrasted by the content of the lyrics. In creating this video, Cozart has taken Disney princesses, whose movies are clearly recognized as family friendly, and given the characters distinctly anti-Disney qualities. Instead of being happy with their endings, they react in an angry or concerned way. In the case of Pocahontas, the reaction is one of a violent nature. By removing these women from an idealized fairy tale setting and placing them in our reality, the contrast becomes that much more effective as satiric parody.

Satire and parody are two distinct genres, though they can work together to achieve different purposes. Kreuz and Roberts reference Beckson and Gantz in their definition of satire as "the ridicule of a subject to point out its faults" ([30], p. 100). Likewise, they reference Holman and Harmon in their definition of parody: " ... imitation, intended to ridicule or criticize" ([30], p. 102). When used as a rhetorical device, satire requires knowledge outside of the text and parody is bounded by the text. Cozart's satirical parody assumes that the audience is familiar with not only the Disney movies (plots, characters, songs) but also has a general knowledge of historical and contemporary events. According to Kreuz and Roberts, "[w]hen readers encounter texts, they bring to these works prior knowledge about the text in general. Expectations about the type of text being read are one component of this prior knowledge" ([30], p. 97). The fairy tale is a well-known genre that implies a certain set of actions, and especially in the case of Disney, an expected outcome. Therefore, the use of satire and parody on a genre such as this is able to subvert those expectations through the drastic shift between the known plots of the tales and the lyrics that Cozart has composed, which contain seemingly anti-Disney themes. In an analysis of "fairy-tale collisions" Zipes asserts that "it has become impossible for serious artists to accept the traditional structures and 'goodness' of fairy tales in a globalized world that has gone haywire" ([31], p. 136). The development of UGC with roots in amateur media allows for the visibility of "serious artists" who operate from a non-commercial space.

5. Discussion

Without a doubt, "After Ever After" retains many pieces of the tradition that has been commodified and commercialized by Disney. While utilizing these elements, Cozart also creates a medley of anti-wonder tales. Just as the narrator of a fairy-tale can reveal his or her position based on the choices that he or she makes, the material is also left up to the interpretation of the viewer. Oral tales, told face to face, often communicate specific esoteric meanings to the audience. However, the YouTube audience is much broader than that of a traditional oral tale. In a way that is similar to another piece of mass-produced media, there is one original version available. There are restrictions to a deeper understanding of the parody: language, knowledge of current and historical events, and familiarity with the Disney brand. In this audience, individuals are allowed to make different levels of connection within the video and to the world outside of it.

In her book *Fairy Tales Transformed? Twenty-First Century Adaptations & the Politics of Wonder*, Cristina Bacchilega discusses artist Dina Goldstein's series *Fallen Princesses*, in which "[Goldstein] imagines fairy-tale heroines in 'modern day scenarios' and replaces the 'happily ever after'" with hyper-realism [2]. I see Cozart's work expanding on this type of subversion by not only bringing the princesses into the modern world, but by using them as representatives to speak about issues that are larger than themselves through parody and satire. Zipes also mentions Goldstein's work as one of many examples of "fairy tale experimentation" through mediums including photography and painting that he classifies into two categories: "remaking and recreating classic tales" and "conflicted mosaics." The former refers explicitly to widely recognized tales with the intent of offering "startling critique ... that urge[s] ... viewers to rethink what they know about the tales," while the latter "draw[s] on an assortment of fairy tale fragments to evoke a sense of wonder" and are "fairy tales unto themselves" ([31], p. 137). "After Ever After" falls into Zipes's first category—though admittedly the tales are canonically Disney—and draws on historic and contemporary "reality" from the worldview of the artist. He is able to reference issues around the globe—from an admittedly Western, if not more specifically American, point of view, while relying on the assumption that his audience will be familiar with both the Disney and the popular culture references, and thereby benefit from the retelling. While Zipes looks at examples of photography, painting, and stained glass among other forms of what might be considered "high art", he does not give much attention to amateur art; he mentions live performance [31], but does not explore examples in detail. However, his conclusions about subversive art are applicable to Cozart's performance: they "unquestionably represent a discontent with the way their actual realities are configured" and reveal "piercing truths of [the artists'] imaginative visions that compel us to re-create traditional narratives and re-think the course our lives have taken" ([31], p. 155).

The three types of satirical commentary in "After Ever After" can be classified as environmental, social, and historical. I have identified these categories based on the main themes that prevailed throughout the video. They are not mutually exclusive and some of the sections feature more than one of the aforementioned genres of commentary. The topics cover a range of issues from pollution and harmful environmental practices to Islamophobia, an unfortunately prevalent theme in today's media and global relations. While Belle's lyrics seem slightly out of context with the social commentary of the other princesses, as they are related to accusations of bestiality and witchcraft, this can be seen as a criticism of the persecution of strong, intelligent women or perhaps the passing of judgement on non-traditional relationships (inter-racial, same-sex) that have been and continue to be a topic of discussion. Again, I would like to stress the influence of personal interpretation, in which the satire suggests an idea—taboo relationships and external judgment—through humor and familiar characters; however, individual viewers are able to assign relevance based on their personal experiences.

In their Disney "happily ever afters," Ariel is transformed into a human and marries Prince Eric while Jasmine chooses to wed Aladdin instead of being forced into an arranged marriage. Belle falls in love with the Beast, which transforms him into Prince Adam. Finally, Pocahontas saves John Smith from harm at the hands of her father, facilitates peace between the invading Englishmen and her tribe, and watches as Smith sails away to Britain. Not only does Cozart disregard these endings, but he uses relevant historic and current events that are connected to the familiar characters. Instead of anonymous (and non-anthropomorphic) sea life being affected by the sinking of the *Deepwater Horizon* and harmful fishing practices, Ariel's friends are being killed. Cozart's Pocahontas embodies perhaps the most contrary of these plot devices, showcasing her lack of regret in meeting colonization with violence. Kay Stone criticizes Disney for their "portrayal of a cloying fantasy world filled with cute little beings existing among pretty flowers and singing animals" [7] and Cozart's depiction of these princesses is about as far away from their fantasy worlds as they could possibly get. While the video retains enough of the original to make the connection clear—characters, melodies, iconography—he drastically subverts the events they must face. This dissonance can be shocking but it also inspires thought about the issues raised. The satiric setting of the video allows anachronistic connections to be established.

Disney movies have received criticism for the changes that have been made for the commercial value of some of their feature films. Pocahontas, in particular, involved cultural consultants in an attempt to combat this criticism, but the movie is still quite ahistoric in its attempt to fit into classic Disney structure. While Cozart does utilize historic events, the satire is not limited to accuracy. For example, Cozart's Pocahontas reflects the tragedy of colonialism on many American Indian peoples, but uses the stock figure to speak about the experience as it relates to a wider group. Regardless of historical or movie accuracy, the text has been altered to make a maximum impact through its satirical content.

Through the use of recognizable and well-loved Disney heroines, Cozart's dark and satiric but unapologetically catchy parody invites the audience to see the world through the eyes of popular fairy tale heroines. These parodied lyrics bring up social and environmental commentary that is currently relevant and would be relevant to the Disney figures if they were inserted into our world. Beloved characters could be dying from pollution or would be discriminated against due to ethnic heritage. While there is definitely a level of shock value in the video, the lyrics also make the audience consider "what if?" the hyper-real situations were true. What if Ariel and Flounder washed up on a beach, dead and covered in black oil slick? Would Princess Jasmine face hate, discrimination, and stereotyping simply because she is an Arab woman? Might Belle be at risk of bodily harm due to the one that she loves? Would Pocahontas resort to blood-fueled rage to deal with the atrocities that resulted from colonization? Are we, as a society, ready to take responsibility for these kinds of consequences? And if it seems horrific through the experience of a fictional character, what is the reality for the populations that the princesses are representing? These are the questions posed through Cozart's satire. These are the thoughts that the satire inspires in "After Ever After" and Jon Cozart uses the medium of digital media to share these ideas through the World Wide Web. Due to the individual and participatory nature of digital media, and the diverse audience to whom access is available, there is not a single or definitive way to interpret the content of the video, but it is open to endless possibilities.

YouTube functions as a digital kind of participatory culture in which interactive action can take place between individuals who have never met face to face. In some respects, this seems like a return to the reinterpretation associated with oral transmission. Quiggen states that as a result of this being a "[c]entral part of everyday life, the dichotomy between participants and observers has broken down" ([13], p. 28). This is facilitated through the comments and voting of the videos, but UGC can also generate another wave of responses. It is interesting to note that there have been several re-makes of Cozart's video since its publication on Youtube.com which have also been posted on the site. These have included a live costumed interpretation while Cozart's voice(s) play over a speaker system [32] and another YouTube user recreated the video with Disney-inspired costumes and her own vocals [33].

6. Conclusions

Scholars, authors, and artists have extensively examined historic, postmodern, and feminist fairy tale revisions, but Cozart is pushing the criticism farther through the popular medium of YouTube.com. Compared to early Disney females such as Snow White and Aurora, the characters of Ariel, Jasmine, Belle, and Pocahontas are more autonomous than the first group of princesses: In their films, Ariel and Pocahontas save the lives of their respective love interests. Jasmine and Belle disregard the rules of their societies. Stover claims that this "'new wave' of princess films ... transformed the damsel into a heroine of sorts" ([34], p. 3). Still, they exist within patriarchal societies in which love and a man define their happy ending. Cozart's video explores the contrast between Disney's ideals and the world today in a format that reflects globalization and technological advances in the same way people have reacted to fairy tales since they were more socio-geographically bounded. The take-over of Disney appears to some to have left a mass-produced idea of what a fairy tale should be. This has overshadowed other fairytale interpretations in popular and fringe culture, though more authors are attempting what Zipes calls "de-dizneyfication." Still, Cozart shows through this case study that Disney can be a powerful satiric tool with a wide reach, and uses this to his advantage in the creation of fan-based material. After a period of static fairy tales in pop culture, this video is one example of a re-imagining of the material that is popping up and it is allowed because of globalization. Zipes convincingly argues for the de-dizneyfication of the fairy tale, but one cannot deny its popularity and potential for impact.

A sequel was created by Cozart featuring four new princesses and their various problems in the "real world." It has amassed over 44 million views since its publication in June of 2014. In future work, I would be interested in examining the increasingly proactive nature of the females included in the satire as well as the recent addition of translations of the video and live performances that take place. Clearly, the manipulation of fairy tales has not stopped or been confined solely to that of corporate production: YouTube allows for the creation of user-generated content, increases visibility and participatory culture, and inspires even more re-interpretation.

Acknowledgments: The author would like to sincerely thank Claudia Schwabe, Lynne McNeill, Lisa Gabbert, Jon Cozart, Geneva Harline, Shannon Branfield, Andrea Blaser, Bethany Hanks, and all those who have contributed to the improvement of this article.

Conflicts of Interest: The author declares no conflict of interest.

References and Notes

1. *Snow White and the Seven Dwarves*. Directed by David Hand. Burbank: Walt Disney Productions, 1937.
2. Cristina Bacchilega. *Fairy Tales Transformed?: Twenty-First Century Adaptations & the Politics of Wonder*. Detroit: Wayne State University Press, 2013.
3. Cristina Bacchilega. *Postmodern Fairy Tales*. Philadelphia: University of Pennsylvania Press, 1997.
4. Jack Zipes. "The Changing Function of the Fairy Tale." *The Lion and the Unicorn* 12 (1988): 7–31.
5. Janet Wasko. *Understanding Disney: The Manufacture of Fantasy*. Cambridge: Polity Press, 2001.
6. Janet Wasko, Mark Phillips, and Eileen R. Meehan, eds. *Dazzled by Disney?* London: Leicester University Press, 2001.
7. Kay Stone. "Things Walt Disney Never Told Us." *The Journal of American Folklore* 88 (1975): 42–50.
8. Dawn Elizabeth England, Lara Descartes, and Melissa A. Collier-Meek. "Gender Role Portrayal and the Disney Princess." *Sex Roles* 64 (2011): 555–67.
9. Joel Best, and Kathleen S. Lowney. "The Disadvantage of a Good Reputation: Disney as a Target for Social Problems Claims." *The Sociological Quarterly* 50 (2009): 431–49.
10. Kristian Moen. *Film and Fairy Tales: The Birth of Modern Fantasy*. London: I.B. Tauris, 2013.
11. Johnson Cheu, ed. *Diversity in Disney Films: Critical Essays on Race, Gender, Sexuality and Disability*. Jefferson: McFarland, 2013.
12. Henry Jenkins. *Textual Poachers: Television Fans and Participatory Culture*. New York: Routledge, 1992.
13. Dan Hunter, Ramon Lobato, Megan Richardson, and Julian Thomas, eds. *Amateur Media: Social, Cultural and Legal Perspectives*. London: Routledge, 2014.
14. Trevor J. Blank, ed. *Folklore and the Internet: Vernacular Expression in a Digital World*. Logan: Utah State University Press, 2009.

15. Paint. "After Ever After—DISNEY Parody." *YouTube*, 2013. Available online: https://www.youtube.com/watch?v=diU70KshcjA (accessed on 1 April 2016).

16. *The Little Mermaid*. Directed by Ron Clements and John Musker. Burbank: Walt Disney Feature Animation, 1989.

17. *Aladdin*. Directed by Ron Clements and John Musker. Burbank: Walt Disney Feature Animation, 1992.

18. Richard Pallarty. "Deepwater Horizon Oil Spill of 2010." *Encyclopedia Britannica Online*, 2016. Available online: https://www.britannica.com/event/Deepwater-Horizon-oil-spill-of-2010 (accessed on 22 July 2016).

19. BP—United States. "Deepwater Horizon accident and response." 2014. Available online: http://www.bp.com/en_us/bp-us/commitment-to-the-gulf-of-mexico/deepwater-horizon-accident.html (accessed on 22 July 2016).

20. *Beauty and the Beast*. Directed by Gary Trousdale and Kirk Wise. Burbank: Walt Disney Feature Animation, 1991.

21. *Pocahontas*. Directed by Mike Gabriel, and Eric Goldberg. Burbank: Walt Disney Feature Animation, 1995.

22. Jared Diamond. *Guns, Germs, and Steel: the Fates of Human Societies*. New York: W. W. Norton & Company, Inc., 1997.

23. Oliver Dreon, Richard M. Kerper, and Jon Landis. "Digital Storytelling: A Tool for Teaching and Learning in the YouTube Generation." *Middle School Journal* 42 (2011): 4–10.

24. Jon Cozart. Personal communication with author, 15 February 2016.

25. Jack Zipes. *Why Fairy Tales Stick: The Evolution and Relevance of a Genre*. New York: Routledge, 2006.

26. Jack Zipes. *Don't Bet on the Prince: Contemporary Feminist Fairy Tales in North America and England*. New York: Routledge, 1987.

27. Rebecca-Anne C. Do Rozario. "The Princess and the Magic Kingdom: Beyond Nostolgia, the Function of the Disney Princess." *Women's Studies in Communication* 27 (2004): 34–59.

28. Susan Wloszczyna. "A Fairy-Tale Bending." *USA Today*, 19 September 2003. Available online: http://usatoday30.usatoday.com/life/movies/news/2003-09-16-fairytale_x.htm (accessed on 1 February 2016).

29. Jack Zipes. *The Enchanted Screen: The Unknown History of Fairy-Tale Films*. New York: Routledge, 2011.

30. Roger J. Kreuz, and Richard M. Roberts. "On Satire and Parody: The Importance of Being Ironic." *Metaphor and Symbolic Activity* 8 (1993): 97–109.

31. Jack Zipes. *The Irresistible Fairy Tale: The Cultural and Social History of a Genre*. Princeton: Princeton University Press, 2012.

32. Victoria Martin. "After Ever After Live at UMass Dartmouth (Better Quality)." *Youtube*, 2013. Available online: https://www.youtube.com/watch?v=XRYxEhWneSg (accessed on 1 April 2016).

33. Brizzy Voices. "After Ever After (Jon Cozart Disney Cover)." *Youtube*, 2014. Available online: https://www.youtube.com/watch?v=AbHDkOmIB0Q (accessed on 1 April 2016).
34. Cassandra Stover. "Damsels and Heroines: The Conundrum of the Post-Feminist Disney Princess." *LUX: A Journal of Transdisciplinary Writing and Research from Claremont Graduate University* 2 (2013): 1–10.

"All That Was Lost Is Revealed": Motifs and Moral Ambiguity in *Over the Garden Wall*

Kristiana Willsey

Abstract: Pointedly nostalgic in both its source material and storytelling approach, *Over the Garden Wall*'s vintage aesthetic is not merely decorative, but ideological. The miniseries responds to recent postmodern fairy tale adaptations by stripping away a century of popular culture references and using motifs, not to invoke and upset increasingly familiar fairy tales, but as an artist's palette of evocative, available images. In privileging imagery and mood over lessons, *Over the Garden Wall* captures something that has become vanishingly rare in children's media: the moral ambiguity of fairy tale worlds.[1]

Reprinted from *Humanities*. Cite as: Willsey, K. "All That Was Lost Is Revealed": Motifs and Moral Ambiguity in *Over the Garden Wall*. *Humanities* **2016**, *5*, 51.

Three drops of red blood on white snow, against an ebony window frame. Three dresses the color of the sun, the moon, and the stars in the sky. Rough hemp necklaces, swapped in the night for the gold chains of the giant's children. These familiar motifs leap to mind, not just because we know them from various versions of Snow White (ATU 709), Donkeyskin (ATU 510B), and Mollie Whuppie (ATU 327B), but also because they are rich in sensory detail, marked by vivid colors and textures. Motifs are the still, constant centers of oral narrative, pins holding together the loose weave of emergent performance. Storytellers, particularly in literary and cinematic adaptations, build detailed, emotionally complex worlds around these minimalist, memorable images, arranging motifs like a kaleidoscope to convey ever-changing social, political, and ideological values.

Fairy tales are transforming and transformative texts; like their characters, they break rules, shape-shift, and change the world. But as the canon of familiar fairy tales has narrowed, cementing much-mediated versions of the stories as singular and authoritative, fairy tales become less fluid, and motifs become less mobile. They begin to function less like building blocks of endlessly variable narratives, and more like puzzle pieces that must be put together in the right order to reach a given message or moral: Appearances can be deceiving, so be patient with your beastly

---

[1] This article has been adapted and expanded from two conference papers, presented at the 2015 Western States Folklore Society meeting, and the 2016 International Conference for the Fantastic in the Arts, and benefited from the thoughtful comments and suggestions of audience members, discussants, and my fellow panelists.

lover. Don't stray from the path. You have to kiss a lot of frogs. Someday, your prince will come. Playing against these well-worn scripts, a wave of postmodern parodies—the *Shrek* franchise (2001–), *Ella Enchanted* (2004), *Happily N'Ever After* (2005), *Hoodwinked!* (2006) and so forth—struck a chord with audiences, but also helped to further the moral simplification of fairy tales, naturalizing clichés even as they subverted them.

Unlike the majority of fairy tale films and television shows of the last decade, Patrick McHale's Emmy Award-winning animated miniseries *Over the Garden Wall* (2014) does not disrupt or critique fairy tale norms. Rather than trading on the familiarity of iconic characters, images, or plot points to tell an old story with a fresh twist, McHale instead tells an original fairy tale in a pointedly old-fashioned way. Favoring traditional hand-drawn animation, a literary and artistic pedigree that skews heavily pre-20th century, and an emphasis on narrative closure that is becoming uncommon in an increasingly serialized and sequel-driven marketplace, the miniseries is tonally and stylistically distinct from the rapid-fire reference-based humor of *Shrek* and company. Though the show's vintage aesthetic drew the most attention, *Over the Garden Wall*'s nostalgia is not purely decorative, but ideological. The miniseries responds to the ironic self-awareness of recent postmodern fairy tale adaptations by stripping away a century of popular culture associations and using motifs, not as a kind of narrative shorthand, but as an artist's palette of evocative, available images. In privileging imagery and mood over lessons, *Over the Garden Wall* captures something that has become vanishingly rare in children's media: the moral ambiguity of fairy tale worlds.

1. Old Stories for New

The miniseries opens in medias res, as brothers Wirt (Elijah Wood) and Greg (Collin Dean) find themselves in a dark wood where the straight way is lost. In the show's most overt reference to Dante's *Divine Comedy*, the brothers' psychopomp through the place called the Unknown is a bluebird named Beatrice (Melanie Lynskey). The brothers are stalked by a shadowy antagonist, The Beast (Samuel Ramey), and helped by a gruff Woodsman (Christopher Lloyd) who both hates the Beast and serves him. Wirt and Greg encounter a colorful cast of characters, and in each of the ten 11-minute, self-contained episodes, learn about themselves and this strange world. It isn't until the final two episodes that the full impact of the brothers' adventure is revealed: Greg and Wirt are drowning on a Halloween night gone wrong, and their struggle to return home from the Unknown is a spiritual journey back to the land of the living.

Instead of making the strange familiar, the show makes the familiar strange, offering a fairyland that is all the more uncanny for being close to home. The series locates its fairy tale world, not in the classic castles and cottages of European tradition, but in an American rural past. Scenic shots of golden maple leaves, pumpkin patches and wild turkey ensure that the "dark wood" of a mythical afterlife is readily identifiable as New England in the fall. Riverboats, log cabins, single room schoolhouses, husking bees, and a folksy, turn-of-the-century musical score underline an Americana ambiance that evokes Carl Sandburg's *Rootabaga Stories*, L. Frank Baum's *Oz* books, Mark Twain's "local color" writing, and the literary legends of Washington Irving. The music, provided by LA-based nouveau-gypsy band The Petrojvic Blasting Company, is a mixture of parlor music, ragtime, folk and jazz, while the show equivalents of the angel and the devil, the Queen of the Clouds and the Beast, are both voiced by renowned opera singers (Deborah Voigt and Samuel Ramey, respectively). Like the miniseries itself, the songs are original, but "antiqued", in the manner of Susan Stewart's "distressed" genres [1]; they are designed to sound and feel like songs you already know, or almost remember.

Much of the critical reception focused on the "Grimmness" of the show, in reference to both the macabre concept, and the show's muted, autumnal color palette—particularly compared to the candy-colored, vinyl-textured digital worlds of recent children's animation. In fact, the series is most like Grimms' fairy tales, not in its tone or subject matter, but in what it seeks to accomplish. Like the *Kinder- und Hausmärchen*, *Over the Garden Wall* might be called a "purifying" project: an attempt to strip away decades off accumulated fairy tale scripts and uncover (or invent) an "original" story. Richard Bauman and Charles Briggs describe how the modern era was characterized by practices of purification and hybridization, in which language was alternately decontextualized to free it from social and political connotations, and then recontextualized to fit an emerging model of modernity that aimed to "restore [texts] to their 'simple' 'pure', 'integral' and 'complete' form" ([2], p. 216). The Grimms' editorial practices, Bauman and Briggs explain, produced fairy tales that looked and felt authentic precisely because they blended multiple texts and voices so subtly.

Similarly, McHale's miniseries purifies fairy tale motifs of a century of popular associations[2] and recontextualizes them within a world of earlier, more obscure references. *Over the Garden Wall* is a love-letter to classic animation, rife with visual allusions to 19th and early 20th century artists and illustrators: In the episode "Schooltown Follies", Greg and Wirt attend school with animals in period dress, styled on the illustrations of 19th century New York children's book publishers

---

[2] Even the modern frame story is ambiguously set, with no pop-cultural references to help viewers determine whether Wirt and Greg are children of 2014, or 1984. A mix-tape plays a prominent role, but Wirt's crush tells him she doesn't have a tape player, perhaps because Wirt (like his creators) is prone to somewhat anachronistic forms of self-expression.

the McLoughlin Brothers.[3] "Songs of the Dark Lantern" incorporates a character modeled on Betty Boop in an homage to the pioneering animation of Max Fleischer, while the episode "Babes in the Wood", which depicts Greg traveling to Cloud City in his dreams, nods to turn-of-the-century American cartoonist Winsor McCay's "Little Nemo in Slumberland." The title "Babes in the Wood" itself is a reference to the traditional broadside ballad, and foreshadows the episode's plot: discouraged from their fruitless search for the way home, Wirt and Greg lie down in the snow, cover themselves with leaves, and nearly freeze to death. Greg is lifted up to Cloud City (as the "babes" are lifted bodily into heaven, in some of the softened versions of the ballad or pantomime) and meets singing "reception committee[s]" of angels and animals in a scene straight out of MGM's 1939 film *The Wizard of Oz*. Greg rescues his new friends by bottling the blustery villain, the North Wind, in a nearly wordless slapstick scene clearly influenced by Disney's "Silly Symphonies." But as *Salon* television critic Sonia Saraiya notes, "You don't need to know the referents in 'Over the Garden Wall' to understand the story; it draws on such deeply rooted archetypes that it feels like a lost tale produced from the depths of childhood" [3]. Viewers might take pleasure in identifying potential allusions,[4] but the miniseries is not a puzzle-box of pop-culture asides, with "Easter eggs" for viewers to track down. In the same way that "Herder, the Grimms, Schoolcraft, and Boas […] pioneered techniques of textual hybridization in which written texts came to mirror as transparently and authentically as possible a set of primordial oral, traditional texts that they purported to recontextualize," ([2], p. 312) *Over the Garden Wall* paradoxically produces a sense of originality and authenticity by the depth and variety of its literary and artistic intertexts.

2. Singular Storytelling in a Transmedia Market

Of course, the miniseries is not a literary text approximating an oral tradition, but a televisual narrative nostalgic for an earlier era of media consumption. Just as the Grimms' *Kinder- und Hausmärchen* emerged from the rise of modernity—the "rough storm" that sweeps through the harvest and makes traditional oral literature feel rare and precious—*Over the Garden Wall* is a reaction to both the most recent wave of postmodern fairy tales, and to what some media studies scholars [5,6] are calling the post-television era. As a stand-alone miniseries, *Over the Garden Wall* feels quaint or even twee to audiences accustomed to fairy tale adaptations spun off,

---

[3] "Lullaby in Frogland" paints "McLoughlin Bros" on the side of a riverboat, in one of the few examples of influence explicitly acknowledged within the show itself. Most of the allusions I (and others) discuss are referenced in interviews, or on McHale's Twitter and Tumblr feeds.

[4] See in particular the four-part series beginning with "'By the Milk-Light of Moon': Myths and Meanings of 'Over the Garden Wall'" by io9 user alliterator [4].

serialized, syndicated and merchandized. *Guardian* reviewer Brian Moylan observes wryly that, "between its aesthetic and the Americana invoked by the original songs, it's like this cartoon was made for those who buy artisanal pickles at the Brooklyn flea market. It has that same sort of fetishisation of the past that many who know the meaning of the word hipster do as well" [7]. Many critics remarked on the "artisanal" or "small-batch" nature of the show;[5] McHale explains in an interview with various journalists that, "It's sort of a difficult show to make. The amount of musical variety, and we're using real instruments for all the music, not synths; the backgrounds are so complicated; and the animation quality we wanted it to be a little bit higher, and that's just not something that we can really sustain for a long ongoing series" [9]. With its vintage aesthetic and well-digested references, the miniseries is a wistful attempt to preserve, not just a particular kind of story, but a kind of storytelling.

Over the Garden Wall is a traditionally broadcast, family-oriented television miniseries in an era of open-ended, multiplatform digital narratives. McHale originally conceived *Over the Garden Wall* as a holiday "special", something of an anachronism in a world where DVR and Netflix has made the idea of audiences tuning in together obsolete. Scant weeks earlier, various news sources [10] had announced the end of an era—the last remaining network to air Saturday morning cartoons had rearranged their programming, ending a weekend tradition that held strong from the 60s through the 90s. With the advances of digital streaming, as well as more narrowly defined target ages and demographics, Saturday morning cartoons became obsolete; anything can be watched any time now. But with its Halloween-themed story and richly drawn fall color palette, *Over the Garden Wall* drew meaning from its timeslot, such that subsequent viewings on other platforms feel like encore performances. The series originally aired two eleven-minute episodes a night over 5 nights, from November 3rd through the 7th of 2014. Though available as a digital download through iTunes and Amazon, the release date and staggered broadcast schedule acted as a small rebellion against the death of "event television".

While other programs embrace the participatory potential of transmedia storytelling, anchoring strands of narrative worlds across a wide swath of platforms, "*Over the Garden Wall* feels like a small, carefully crafted world that might disappear as soon as the episode ends" [3]. Henry Jenkins defines transmedia storytelling as the distribution of a work of media across multiple platforms, each of which tells part of the story or offers a different perspective on a single ongoing text, such that "to fully experience any fictional world, consumers must assume the role of hunters and gatherers, chasing down bits of the story across media channels" ([11], p. 21). Since

---

[5] For a breakdown of the cultural politics behind the critical reception of the show, see Erin Horáková's review in *Strange Horizons* [8].

Over the Garden Wall has had a rich afterlife through fanfiction and fanart, as well as a limited-issue graphic novel, it is not exempt from what Jenkins calls "convergence culture" [11]. But nevertheless, it remains staunchly, committedly low-fi. When asked in a *Nerdist* podcast [12] about continuing the story, McHale makes it clear that "it's a self-contained story, with a definite end." The idea of a narrative that *ends* has begun to feel unexpectedly retro. A recent article for the *Guardian* ("Unfinished business: How Disney and Marvel killed happy ever afters" [13]) laments that the feedback loop of online fandoms has kept beloved film characters from riding off into the sunset; stories can never be satisfactorily resolved as long as they are still profitable. "What has changed", Nicholas Barber argues, "is that viewers are no longer being given—to quote Frank Kermode or Julian Barnes—the sense of an ending [. . .] to many of us, that fairytale fantasy was one of cinema's most attractive aspects." While sequels, spin-offs and novelizations are nothing new, storytelling in a transmedial moment can render a text inescapable; each platform begins where the others leave off until the narrative world rises three-dimensionally around us.

Perhaps Jenkins' "hunter-gatherers", viewers picking up the pieces of a discontinuous narrative, are a natural extension of the viewing habits fostered by fairy tale pastiche, in which fans take pleasure in skillfully tracking fairy tale characters and motifs scattered across increasingly overlapping narratives. *Over the Garden Wall* is both original (not retelling any recognizable fairy tales), and self-contained (not explicitly incorporating or commenting on fairy tales beyond itself), qualities that have become unusual during the rise of what we might call the fairy tale "expanded universe". This style of narrative unites a variety of literary and cultural traditions under a single umbrella and tries to reconcile the complicated web of relationships this produces—characteristic examples are Bill Willingham's graphic novel series *Fables*, ABC's *Once Upon a Time*, or the Hallmark miniseries *The 10th Kingdom*. In *Fables*, for instance, narrative economy collapses any and every Prince Charming into one philandering prince, while the Snow White of ATU 709 must also be the sister of Rose Red in ATU 426. Similarly, in *Once Upon a Time*, Rumplestiltskin is sufficiently beastly to stand in for Belle's love interest. Conversely, *Over the Garden Wall* is its own world, free of any reference to recognizable characters or specific story arcs. Like their audiences, 21st century fairy tales occupy a world that is becoming both larger and smaller: Cinderella isn't confined to her own tale type anymore, but she also can't leave her castle without tripping over Sleeping Beauty, Red Riding Hood, or Rumplestiltskin. The scattering of plot points and story arcs across media platforms, though practically making a narrative larger, can have the effect of making the world feel smaller, crowded with stories we now know too well. The miniseries' singular, self-contained format is one answer to the sprawling, open-ended narratives of the web, which are endlessly refreshable in a way that both excites and exhausts.

3. The Incredible Shrinking Fairy Tale Canon

The pre-20th century aesthetic cultivated by McHale's miniseries evokes an old fairy tale recovered or restored, an appealing prospect to audiences convinced that the fairy tale genre has been thoroughly measured and mapped. As the opening narration intones, "Somewhere, lost in the clouded annals of history lies a place that few have seen—a mysterious place, called the Unknown, where long-forgotten stories are revealed to those who travel through the wood" [14]. The appeal of "reveal[ing]" stories "lost" or "long-forgotten" proved as potent in 2012 as in 1812: when a cache of stories from 19th century folklorist Franz Xaver von Schönwerth was discovered in an archive in Germany, the idea of authentic fairy tales lost for centuries struck a chord with the public and began trending on Twitter [15]. It fell to scholars to temper the excitement with reminders that we are not actually lacking in obscure fairy tales (and these particular fairy tales were not completely unfamiliar). In an interview for fan site *The Mary Sue* [16], Maria Tatar points out, "Our fairy-tale repertoire is not as expansive as it could be. At times it feels as if we ferociously repeat the same stories: "Cinderella", "Snow White", "Little Red Riding Hood", "Sleeping Beauty", and "Jack and the Beanstalk". When each year sees multiple film treatments of Snow White or Sleeping Beauty, it may seem as though we have exhausted our fairy tale canon, when it has instead been artificially narrowed by the popular and commercial desire to hear the same stories over and over again.

As the fairy tales we tell become more standardized and less varied, the definition of "fairy tale" continues to shrink, to fit within this moving target. The critical charge of popular "twisted" fairy tales takes for granted that the genre being humorously exploded is static and natural. In other words, it presumes and even invents the canon it critiques, a process Susan Stewart called "artifactualization": "there is no natural form here, but a set of documents shaped by the expectations that led to their artifactualization in the first place" ([1], p. 106). In order for a parody to work, the new twist has to reproduce the earlier text, often with a narrative efficiency that simplifies and naturalizes it. Though films like Dreamworks' *Shrek* and (Disney's answer to Shrek), *Enchanted* (2007) received critical praise for subverting staid fairy tale conventions, Cristina Bacchilega and John Rieder suggest that both films ultimately conform to more rules than they break:

> [W]hile the parodied rescue scenes [of Shrek] draw on a satirical demystification of fairy tale formulas and motifs already active in popular culture, the effect is merely humorous and transient because the alliance of fairy tale and romance still ends up shaping the stories' closure and emotional power ([17], p. 31).

The image of a prince rushing to rescue a princess in a tower is humorously deconstructed in the opening frames of each film, but every fresh iteration of the joke further reinforces the narrowing scope of the fairy tale canon.

As our stock of familiar stories shrinks, the work those stories do is distributed more heavily on a small number of highly visible motifs, which act as a means of simplifying and packaging stories. Jeana Jorgensen has described the fragmentation and recombination of familiar motifs as "fairy tale pastiche", particularly in commercials in which advertisers use a lost slipper or red hood to efficiently invoke a fairy tale and its associated meanings [18]. Building on this, Cristina Bacchilega connects the parodic use of fairy tales to the iconicity of well-known motifs, observing, "what is new here, as I see it, is not the reproduction of isolated fairy tale symbols and images in new contexts, but that their reutilization in branding 'new' products often rests on the marketability of mixing and parodying these iconic bits" ([19], p. 111). These are motifs that can never be experienced on their own terms, their meaning is always "in the second degree" [20], less a part of the story we consume than asides, reminders of what texts to read this new story *through* or *against*.

Decontextualizing motifs from familiar narrative arcs and their burden of associations, *Over the Garden Wall* is free to break fairy tales down to their constituent elements and assemble a new story. *Over the Garden Wall* is rich in familiar fairy tale motifs used in unfamiliar ways: in the opening sequence, Greg leaves a trail of candy to mark their path, like the trail of breadcrumbs (R135.1) in Hansel and Gretel (ATU 327, also 431). In another episode, Wirt and Greg take shelter from a storm in the home of a witch, who declares she can smell them when she comes home, in the manner of the Giant of ATU 328A, Jack and the Beanstalk. Greg is a "wise fool" who challenges the Beast by completing a series of impossible tasks: he brings the Beast the golden comb and silver thread demanded—a honeycomb and a spiderweb—and uses forced perspective to catch the sun in a china cup (motif H1023.22). Like the Ferryman of ATU 460/461, the Woodsman is compelled to cut down the mysterious Edelwood trees to keep his lantern lit, and can only be free of his burden if he finds another to take his place (motif H1292.8). The Beast, we eventually learn, keeps his soul outside of his body, as in ATU 302, the Giant Without a Heart. But the fairy tale motifs are never entirely what they appear, frustrating or foiling expectations about the internal logic of fairy tales. In the first episode, Greg frees a bird caught in a branch and is rewarded with her help (motif B364.1), but the struggle was staged by Beatrice herself, who plays off the children's knowledge of fairy tale rules to lead them into a trap. Greg accomplishes all of the Beast's impossible tasks, but they are only a pretext to distract him from the growing cold—it was never a victory. "I beat the Beast", he tells his brother weakly, while the Edelwood tree grows around him.

Conversely, in the version of fairy tale canon condensed and artifactualized through repeated remediation (especially on the part of Disney, which is now incestuously mining its own already narrow canon in an ambitious slate of upcoming live action remakes), a kiss breaks a spell, kindness to animals is rewarded, and witches bearing gifts should not be trusted. Meanwhile, stories of disenchantment through decapitation (motif D711) as in Madame D'Aulnoy's "The White Cat" or Andrew Lang's "The Seven Foals", have fallen out of vogue for some reason. In some versions of ATU 425, burning the beast's skin restores his human form (D793.2); in other versions it backfires and throws the lovers further apart. Some witches take your children for stealing from their gardens (ATU 310), but in some stories the order is reversed—the witch in Tatterhood (ATU 711) tells the queen what to eat to conceive a desperately wanted child. In fact, fairy tale rules are less widely agreed upon than recent pop culture adaptations might lead viewers to expect. Describing his functions for the wonder-tale, Vladimir Propp reminded us that, though Interdiction and Violation are paired functions, "A command often plays the role of an interdiction. If children are urged to go out into the field or into the forest, the fulfillment of this command has the same consequences as does violation of an interdiction not to go out into the forest or out into the field" ([21], p. 27). Structurally, this is perfectly sound, but for the social or psychological analyses according to which fairy tales are often interpreted, the idea that obeying the rules and breaking the rules are all the same troubles tidy assertions about the moral agenda of fairy tales.

4. The Shock Effect of Beauty

As a small number of fairy tales are adapted, expanded, reworked and interwoven, familiar motifs become a means to invoke a set of canonical fairy tale rules and codes to push back against. But as John Frow notes, "Texts—even the simplest and most formulaic—do not *belong* to genres but are, rather, uses of them" (qtd. in [17], p. 27). McHale treats the genre, not as a box to break out of, but as a toolset of evocative, available images with which to build new stories. *Over the Garden Wall*'s success lies in its recognition of what makes fairy tales so mobile and resilient: morals are culturally and historically contingent, but the emotional and sensory impact of blood on snow, death trapped in a sack, or a comb that becomes an impenetrable forest can be recontextualized to serve a number of narrative roles. In prioritizing mood, tone, and imagery to achieve a vintage aesthetic, McHale echoes the approach of 18th and 19th century scholars who used a text's poetic force, particularly its capacity to seize the imagination, as a measure of age and authenticity. By this (ideologically loaded) metric, a genuine work of folk narrative or poetry would be "emotional, vivid, figurative, spontaneous, without artifice" ([2], p. 147). In the same vein, *Over the Garden Wall* uses fairy tale motifs, not to invoke and upset familiar stories, but in the way oral narrators use them, as resonant images—what Max Lüthi [22] called the "shock effect of beauty".

The notion of fairy tales as fundamentally lessons, buried in poetry, has been spurred by the popular success of psychological interpretations of fairy tales—Bruno Betelheim's Freudian approach in *The Uses of Enchantment*, the Jungian analyses of Joseph Campbell in *Hero With a Thousand Faces* and Clarissa Pinkola Estés in *Women Who Run With the Wolves*. But it makes equal sense to read from the other direction and say that fairy tales are fundamentally poetry, buried in lessons. Fairy tales can be made to incite action, instill values, or invite judgment, but before they can do any of those things, they must strike on the mind. Lüthi's analysis of "Beauty and its Shock Effect" observes that fairy tales model the powerful, narrative-driving impact of beauty for readers, who are caught in the beauty of the story just as the characters within the story are enchanted—literally stricken dumb or dead—by a portrait of a beautiful princess: "[The fairy tale] describes not beauty but its effect, and in accord with its characteristic inclination to the extreme, represents this effect as a sort of magic" ([22], p. 3). Thinking back on their early childhood reading experiences, Maria Tatar's students "find it challenging to try to show what children learn from the lesson that they identify in [Hans Christian Andersen's 'The Princess and the Pea']" only agreeing that it is about "sensitivity"—the focus is on the embodied sensation of the pea, bruising the princess' flesh through the layers of featherbeds ([23], p. 78). Describing the sensory immersion that makes early reading experiences so powerful, Tatar notes that, "the authors of children's books stockpile arsenals of beauty and horror to construct 'peak experiences'," that maintain their hold on readers well into adulthood ([23], p. 12). The imagery of fairy tales is minimalist but memorable, spare and sparkling, dipped in blood or gold.

If the "beauty" of princes and princesses, forests of gold and silver, slippers of fur and mountains of glass seems more reminiscent of rarified courtly tales than a folk narrative aesthetic, we can focus instead on the shock. Carl Lindahl's study of North American Jack tales finds that "beauty" in the traditional sense is less significant in mountain Märchen than violence: it is the intimate, visceral details of the story that form the template for oral storytelling. Lindahl cautions against privileging the study of structure over the poetic force of fairy tale imagery, noting that,

> The power with which Märchen images impress visual memories upon their listeners should lead us to question the idea that these tales survive solely because of their perfectly memorable structures. There is substantial evidence to the contrary. Rather than memorizing plots, tellers "see" their stories in their minds' eyes, hanging their memories of the tale on one or more spectacular images ([24], p. 85).

Similarly, Harold Scheub's study of oral narrative in southern Africa argues that analyses of storytelling have historically focused too abstractly on stories' morals, or too myopically on structuring, organizing and categorizing folk narrative, while neglecting the role of poetic features like image and rhythm. He writes, "the first ingredient of story, its basic building block, is image, most importantly fantasy image, which becomes a means of evoking emotions at the same time that it becomes a critical way of organizing those emotions" ([25], p. 29). Fairy tales can be used to convey messages and moral stances, but they are remembered as a series of rich colors and sharp contrasts, as thrills of excitement or horror. McHale's miniseries is assembled from narrative arcs kept deliberately brief and strange; the story seems to exist as a framework for the imagery, rather than the reverse.

5. Against Interpretation

Over the Garden Wall is a miniseries that knows how to hang the story on "spectacular" imagery, arguably at the expense of narrative coherence and characterization. Critiques of the show find that the miniseries is more concerned with surface than substance. *The New York Times* notes that "the stories are perilously thin", while *Variety's* review suggests that the show's rarified aesthetic trumps its plot: "there's less interest in how they complete their journey home than in just savoring the imagery of getting there, which should appeal to a rather narrow and refined palate" [26,27]. But the slight, enigmatic quality of the narrative is not a flaw, but a strategy. Fittingly, the show is driven by dream-logic: characters drop in and out of the brothers' journey, monstrous enemies often turn out to be friends in disguise, animals speak or sing unexpectedly, time and distance are vague. In what some critics viewed as weak storytelling or poor characterization, Wirt and Greg have little agency in their story. They react to this strange world, but rarely make decisions that drive the narrative, and when they do, the perspective often shifts to make that decision meaningless. In "Mad Love", for instance, Greg and Wirt (but mostly Beatrice) spend an episode attempting to rob a rich tea baron to pay their steamboat fare.[6] When Quincy Endicott gives them the money freely, Greg flings the coins into a fountain because, as he explains bitterly, "[he's] got no sense[/cents]" [14]. In "The Ringing of the Bell", Wirt tries to rescue a maiden from what he thinks is a cannibalistic witch, only to find (in an Angela Carter-esque twist) that it is the girl who is the monster. Acting as audience stand-in (particularly for the child viewers), Greg spells it out: "For some reason, I thought that old lady was the people-eater. But it was Lorna all along! It just goes to show you stuff" [14]. Typical for Greg, whose childish non-sequiturs provide much of the program's humor, it's a funny statement because it isn't clear what it does "go to show you". The episode thwarts the expected moral—that appearances can be deceiving—because in the end, there

---

[6]   The fare is 2 pennies, traditionally placed on the eyelids of the dead, foreshadowing the series reveal and the limbo-like nature of the Unknown.

are no heroes or villains. Lorna is an innocent monster, Auntie Whispers is a loving jailer, and Wirt's young hero is largely irrelevant to either of their stories. In a review for the speculative fiction magazine *Strange Horizons*, Erin Horáková argues that the show's minimalist plots and moral opacity are key to the series' appeal: "*Over the Garden Wall* posits that set answers are themselves poor things to pin your hopes on and let guide your actions: the Woodsman's false lanterns" [8]. Beyond a certain mood or feeling, it's difficult to know what message to take away from these spare, vivid stories—which is, I would argue, the point.

Essentially, *Over the Garden Wall* is faulted for the same psychologically thin, visually lush, morally ambiguous approach to storytelling that characterizes the folk narrative traditions it draws from. In a review for the *New Yorker*, Maria Tatar praises fantasy writer Philip Pullman's 2012 translation of the Grimms as "sheer story that, in the end, leaves the work of finding messages and decoding morals entirely up to us" [28]. Tatar sees Pullman's retelling as a response to the 200 years of popular and scholarly interpretations that have grown up around the *Kinder- und Hausmärchen* like Sleeping Beauty's briars: "Left cold by Freudian, Jungian, or Marxist readings of fairy tales as well as by feminist critiques and any of the usual orthodoxies, Pullman longs for what the poet James Merrill calls an 'unseasoned telling'—purged of dross, untainted by an overlay of piety, politics, or prudery". Tatar, of course, has spent a career unearthing the piety and politics beneath the Grimms' 'unseasoned tellings', but nevertheless recognizes in Pullman's nostalgic approach a kinship to the Grimms' own 19th century editorial practices. The "charged imagery" of fairy tales work best when their work is "elliptical, as the text works on us in its own silent, secret way" [28]. Similarly, the allusive, underdetermined morals of *Over the Garden Wall* allow viewers breathing room to experience the fairy tale on their own terms, rather than being instructed in how to read or use it. Ultimately, the miniseries reminds us that fairy tales do not "mean" anything on their own. What fairy tales do or say, the specific morals or social messages imparted by the stories, are less significant (and less durable) than *how* they say it: via the evocative, emotionally-laden motifs invested with fresh meaning by each storyteller and audience.

6. Conclusions

It is only when we are on the cusp of a new medium that we truly recognize the constraints and possibilities of the old—a kind of televisual estrangement. *Over the Garden Wall* is a story that, for all its vintage aesthetic, reflects a very contemporary anxiety about the kinds of stories, and venues of storytelling, being transformed beyond recognition by new media. As Donald Haase observes, "Whatever the paradigm shift in communication, the folktale becomes a vehicle through which the impact of this shift is observed and assessed" ([29], p. 222). McHale's fairy tale, aesthetically and formally, becomes a vehicle for commentary on the increasingly permeable, open-ended nature of both the post-television era, and postmodern fairy tale adaptations themselves. In response to the reduction and simplification of the fairy tale canon, which saw a small number of stories become more well-trodden and entangled, McHale crafts and curates a deliberately small world, less encumbered by the baggage of popular retellings and interpretations. Decontextualizing fairy tale motifs from the layers of associations that have made them recognizable and marketable allows motifs to function on their own terms, as the minimalist, memorable images that make fairy tales so powerful and protean. Though the cultivated quaintness of the miniseries might be dismissed as nostalgia for its own sake, *Over the Garden Wall*'s 19th century storybook visuals are more than superficial; they are a reflection of the show's investment in recovering or restoring a fairy tale world less predetermined and more morally opaque. *Over the Garden Wall* is a new story doing an old job, an original fairy tale that promises that, as the theme says, "all that was lost is revealed".

Conflicts of Interest: The author declares no conflict of interest.

References

1. Susan Stewart. *Crimes of Writing*. New York and Oxford: Oxford University Press, 1993.
2. Richard Bauman, and Charles Briggs. *Voices of Modernity: Language Ideologies and the Politics of Inequality*. Cambridge: Cambridge University Press, 2003.
3. Sonia Saraiya. "Making viral TV: How 'Too Many Cooks' and 'Over the Garden Wall' work their hypnotic magic." 14 November 2014. Available online: http://www.salon.com/2014/11/14/making_viral_tv_how_%E2%80%9Ctoo_many_cooks%E2%80%9D_and_over_the_garden_wall_work_their_hypnotic_magic/ (accessed on 9 May 2016).
4. Alliterator. "'By the Milk-Light of Moon': Myths and Meanings of 'Over the Garden Wall' Parts One through Four." Available online: http://observationdeck.kinja.com/by-the-milk-light-of-moon-myths-and-meanings-of-ov-1657185829 (accessed on 14 April 2015).
5. Amanda D. Lotz. *The Television Will Be Revolutionized*. New York: New York University Press, 2007.
6. Henry Jenkins. "Is This the End of Television As We Know It?" 22 May 2013. Available online: http://henryjenkins.org/2013/05/is-this-the-end-of-television-as-we-know-it.html (accessed on 14 April 2015).
7. Brian Moylan. "Over the Garden Wall: Slapstick for the kids, existential dread for the adults." *The Guardian*, 3 November 2014. Available online: http://www.theguardian.com/culture/2014/nov/03/over-the-garden-wall-slapstick-kids-existential-dread-adults (accessed on 14 April 2015).
8. Erin Horáková. "Over the Garden Wall." *Strange Horizons*, 30 November 2015. Available online: http://www.strangehorizons.com/reviews/2015/11/over_the_garden.shtml (accessed on 9 May 2016).

9.   Patrick McHale. "An Interview with the Folks behind Cartoon Network's *Over the Garden Wall*, Premiering Tonight! " *The Mary Sue*, 3 November 2014.

10.   Gail Sullivan. "Saturday morning cartoons are no more." *The Washington Post*, 30 September 2014. Available online: https://www.washingtonpost.com/news/morning-mix/wp/2014/09/30/saturday-morning-cartoons-are-no-more/ (accessed on 15 April 2015).

11.   Henry Jenkins. *Convergence Culture: Where Old and New Media Collide*. New York: New York University Press, 2006.

12.   Patrick McHale. "Exclusive: Patrick HcHale Talks Bringing Over the Garden Wall to Cartoon Network and Boom! Studios." Interviewed by Dan Casey. *The Nerdist*, 13 October 2014.

13.   Nicholas Barber. "Unfinished business: How Disney and Marvel killed happy ever afters." *The Guardian*, 9 February 2016. Available online: http://www.theguardian.com/film/2016/feb/09/unfinished-business-how-disney-and-marvel-killed-happy-ever-after (accessed on 15 March 2016).

14.   *Over the Garden Wall*. Directed by Patrick McHale. Cartoon Network, 2014.

15.   Victoria Sussens-Messerer. "Five hundred new fairytales discovered in Germany." *The Guardian*, 5 March 2012. Available online: https://www.theguardian.com/books/2012/mar/05/five-hundred-fairytales-discovered-germany (accessed on 26 June 2016).

16.   Maria Tatar. "The Mary Sue Interview: Fairy Tale Expert and *The Turnip Princess* Translator Maria Tatar." Interviewed by Carolyn Cox. *The Mary Sue*, 24 March 2015. Available online: http://www.themarysue.com/the-mary-sue-interview-maria-tatar/ (accessed on 15 March 2016).

17.   Cristina Bacchilega, and John Rieder. "Mixing It Up: Generic Complexity and Gender Ideology in Early 21st Century Fairy Tale Films." In *Visions of Ambiguity*. Edited by Pauline Greenhill and Sidney Eve Matrix. Logan: Utah State University Press, 2010, pp. 23–42.

18.   Jeana Jorgensen. "A Wave of the Magic Wand: Fairy Godmothers in Contemporary American Media." *Marvels & Tales* 21 (2007): 216–27.

19.   Cristina Bacchilega. *Fairy Tales Transformed? Twenty-First-Century Adaptations and the Politics of Wonder*. Detroit: Wayne State University Press, 2013.

20.   Gérard Genette. *Palimpsests: Literature in the Second Degree*. Lincoln: University of Nebraska University Press, 1997.

21.   Vladamir Propp. *Morphology of the Folktale*. Austin: University of Texas, 1968.

22.   Max Luthi. *The Fairy Tale as Art Form and Portrait of Man*. Translated by John Erickson. Bloomington: Indiana University Press, 1987.

23.   Maria Tatar. *Enchanted Hunters: The Power of Stories in Childhood*. New York: Norton and Company, 2009.

24.   Carl Lindahl. "Sounding a Shy Tradition: Oral and Written Styles of American Mountain Märchen." In *Perspectives on the Jack Tales and Other North American Märchen*. Edited by Carl Lindahl. Bloomington: Folklore Institute, 2001, pp. 68–98.

25.   Harold Scheub. *Story*. Madison: University of Wisconsin University Press, 1998.

26. Mike Hale. "In a World of Whimsy, a Perilous Journey Home." *The New York Times*, 2 November 2014. Available online: http://www.nytimes.com/2014/11/03/arts/television/over-the-garden-wall-a-new-cartoon-network-series.html (accessed on 14 April 2015).

27. Brian Lowry. "TV Review: Cartoon Network's 'Over the Garden Wall'." *Variety*, 31 October 2014. Available online: http://variety.com/2014/tv/reviews/tv-review-cartoon-networks-over-the-garden-wall-1201341506/ (accessed on 14 April 2015).

28. Maria Tatar. "Philip Pullman's Twice-Told Tales." *The New Yorker*, 21 Novermber 2012. Available online: http://www.newyorker.com/books/page-turner/philip-pullmans-twice-told-tales (accessed on 9 May 2016).

29. Donald Haase. "Hypertextual Gutenberg." *Fabula* 47 (2006): 222–30.

Baba Yaga, Monsters of the Week, and Pop Culture's Formation of Wonder and Families through Monstrosity

Jill Terry Rudy and Jarom Lyle McDonald

Abstract: This paper considers transforming forms and their purposes in the popular culture trope of the televised Monster of the Week (MOTW). In the rare televised appearances outside of Slavic nations, Baba Yaga tends to show up in MOTW episodes. While some MOTW are contemporary inventions, many, like Baba Yaga, are mythological and fantastic creatures from folk narratives. Employing the concept of the *folkloresque*, we explore how contemporary audiovisual tropes gain integrity and traction by indexing traditional knowledge and belief systems. In the process, we examine key affordances of these forms involving the possibilities of wonder and the portability of tradition. Using digital humanities methods, we built a "monster typology" by scraping lists of folk creatures, mythological beasts, and other supernatural beings from online information sources, and we used topic modeling to investigate central concerns of MOTW series. Our findings indicate connections in these shows between crime, violence, family, and loss. The trope formulates wonder and families through folk narrative and monster forms and functions. We recognize Baba Yaga's role as villain in these episodes and acknowledge that these series also shift between episodic and serial narrative arcs involving close relationships between characters and among viewers and fans.

Reprinted from *Humanities*. Cite as: Rudy, J.T.; McDonald, J.L. Baba Yaga, Monsters of the Week, and Pop Culture's Formation of Wonder and Families through Monstrosity. *Humanities* **2016**, 5, 40.

For popular culture, Baba Yaga affords a wondrous form to be appropriated with other forms in a Monster of the Week (MOTW) television show. An ambiguous Slavic figure, her origins stem from primeval sources in a Russian pantheon where she plays mythological and ritualistic roles of earth mother and death guardian ([1], pp. xxx–xxxiv; [2], pp. 8–31). With her iconic huge nose, iron teeth, and other ugly features, along with her mortar and pestle flying contraption, and her chicken-legged hut, she is distinctive and easily recognized. In Russian folktales including "Baba Yaga", "The Feather of Finist the Bright Falcon", "The Tsar-Maiden", and "Vasilisa the Beautiful", she may be known as a witch, grandmother, cannibal, examiner, and helper [1]. Never the protagonist of tales, she nonetheless may be both an antagonist and a helper, a threat to life and a benefactor of light. Her wonder, thus, is marked by being awful and full of awe.

Baba Yaga's presence has spread from Russia to the West since the nineteenth century. She may be thought of as a constellation of iconic features and ambiguous functions that together may coalesce and reconfigure in an array of genres, themes, modes, and media. Indeed, she has become a transcultural and intermedial figure associated with Mussorgsky's orchestral *Pictures from an Exhibition*, Ivan Bilibin's ubiquitous illustrations, and a wide array of popular, global products and productions from picture books to sneakers to punk rock to video games ([1], pp. xliv–xlv). An International Fairy Tale Filmography (IFTF) search brings up thirteen Baba Yaga films over the past seven decades, mostly Soviet, Russian, or Eastern Bloc productions, and two from the United Kingdom. This indicates that she maintains some bearing over space and time and adapts to various media and cultures.[1] Therefore, examining Baba Yaga's particular affiliation with the MOTW trope brings together folklore, fairy tale studies, narratology, media studies, adaptation studies, popular culture studies, psychology, and literary history and theory around the key issue of powerful traditional forms transforming.

For well over two centuries, intrigue over forms transforming has marked the emergence of modern scholarly fields, involving biology and poetics, as well as social sciences. Scholarly divisions such as literature, folklore, sociology, anthropology, art history, and humanities along with perceived divides of human expressivity, art, and knowledge between elite, popular, and folk cultures suggest that some forms transform due to sociocultural forces of colonialism and capitalism [3,4]. Given this history, folklore scholarship claims traditional forms and has emerged from antiquarian investigations and romantic nationalist inclinations [5–7]. Folklorists favor artifacts, songs, stories, manners, and customs learned and transmitted orally, by imitation, and in performance; these forms are widely shared yet still uniquely claimed by specific individuals and groups [8]. Questions of transformation especially have informed folk narrative research, and the tale has been a gateway for formal inquiry linking folklore with literary studies, anthropology, psychology, and linguistics [9–12]. Stephen Benson explains, "Folktales are intrinsically unstable" and thus lead to variability, "the basic constituent elements of a narrative can be manifest in a number of different versions" ([9], p. 22). Accounting for such variation with continuity leads to tale type and motif indexes, Propp's morphology of functions, and more linguistic-based narrative theories ([9], pp. 23–41). An impetus for this scholarship remains tracing and understanding the social work accomplished or constrained by such communicative forms and their transformations.

---

[1] The International Fairy Tale Filmography was accessed for a Baba Yaga origin search on 26 February 2016.

Adaptation studies and literary studies also traverse historical and contemporary lines of thought that involve cultural and media studies in concern about forms transforming and issues of variation and continuity. Gotthold Ephraim Lessing's *Laocoön* considers classical precedents of media adaptation, advocating that poetry and painting do not become conflated even though they may be considered together as "painting is mute poetry and poetry a speaking painting". He reiterates that criticism and art should distinguish among media although there will be shared forms ([13], pp. 4–5). For contemporary literary and cultural studies, Caroline Levine posits a broad definition of form to "mean all shapes and configurations, all ordering principles, all patterns of repetition and difference" in order to more effectively coalesce insights on a "new formalist method" ([14], p. 3). To avoid the conflation-of-media mistake Lessing critiques, Levine addresses the *affordances* of forms, borrowing from design theory to mean "the potential uses or actions latent in materials and designs", and she recognizes that all forms afford potentialities and portability ([14], pp. 6–7). We see Baba Yaga as a traditional form affiliated with folk narrative that has been appropriated by the MOTW trope to serve as a pop culture form, and we inquire into what this affords in terms of aesthetic and social potential.

Given that Baba Yaga's appearances on television remain quite limited, especially outside of the film rebroadcasts and animated shows on Soviet and Russian TV, it remains striking that there is a perceptible pattern. The few productions including Baba Yaga listed in the Fairy Tale Teleography and Visualizations (FTTV), so far, come from North America and Japan. Whether in an anime, supernatural drama, or children's mystery episode, this figure is associated with an antagonist in the MOTW trope, obviously so named because protagonists face a new monster each week. The wiki TVTropes attributes the MOTW label to the television show *The Outer Limits* [15] and its promise to bring viewers a new monster every week. A strict definition requires that the monster only appears in one episode and does not become part of an ongoing story arc although the temporality of weekly viewing affects the monster encounters [16]. The monster figure takes various forms over successive weeks with a recurring purpose to threaten the well-being of the protagonist, and even of the whole world. The threat catalyzes social relations in order to confront the monster's deformity and deviance, and more significantly to combat the will to subjugate and dominate. When Baba Yaga takes the monster position, the wondrous ambiguity that makes her both a helper and an antagonist in the tales lessens as her affordance for deformity and self-interest makes her another MOTW villain to be defeated.

Thus, the Baba Yaga figure is not organizing the MOTW trope, which has had at least as much to do with space aliens as traditional monsters since its inception, but rather it fulfills some key purposes that depend on her unique affordances even as they are transformed and flattened by the pop culture trope. Protagonists in the different series seek her defeat because she is traditionally ugly, powerful, and awful, which primarily means that she seeks control for her own self-serving benefit. This formation of Baba Yaga as sheer villain reduces the complexity and ambiguity of the folk narrative figure. Because producers have recognized the form affords the MOTW trope, Baba Yaga in association with the different weekly monsters invites consideration of monstrosity itself, a pop culture construct of who and what fits into the monster antagonist form and also of why monsters are threatening. Moreover, in the transformation of the strictly episodic MOTW format for ongoing story arcs, defeating the monster becomes aligned with constructing and maintaining relationships modeled on families. As a pop culture form that seeks a wide, loyal audience, the MOTW trope has come to feature protagonists and friends who build close relationships by regularly confronting monsters which, in the process, invites the MOTW viewers also to build close relationships with the fictional characters and with fans. Our recursive textual analysis and digital humanities topic modeling affirm that Baba Yaga emerges as a wondrous MOTW monster who, as a self-serving villain, affords social relations to formalize around families, both natal by blood and figural families of choice.

As a way to investigate the MOTW trope, we turned first to digital humanities methods; our purpose was to leverage a computer's computational capacities to take a step back and get a broader (yet paradoxically also more specific) view. Implementing scalable reading as an analytic tool can help identify patterns that lead to deeper insight into the tropes. We built a corpus to analyze by first identifying shows with a MOTW trope and compiling the data that episodes might provide. Aggregating patterns in the metadata and implementing textual analysis of the content of our corpus itself then incorporates the Baba Yaga figure from specific episodes into the affordances indicated through creating a MOTW monster typology and topic models (models which, in the abstract, might help explain some of the deeper, underlying composition of the trope). This research opens many questions and potentialities, but for this article it specifically provides details about how popular culture, with the MOTW trope, formulates wonder and families through monstrosity.Our corpus contains 18 different series, ranging from the full run of *The Outer Limits*, through the 1990s shows that revived the trope such as *The X-Files* [17] and *Buffy the Vampire Slayer* [18], to the most recent seasons of shows such as *Supernatural* [19] and *Dr. Who* [20]. Many of these shows had longer-than-average runs as far as TV series go, giving us 2168 episodes of television to explore. The dataset contains both descriptive metadata—episode plot summaries, character and actor names, and broadcast information—as well as textual content: in this case, subtitle files from each episode. That we investigated subtitles rather than scripts is significant; subtitle text only captures words spoken by a character (whether in dialogue or narration), and thus provides a focused snapshot of what was significant enough to be part of a conversation or audible framework in the episode.

Speaking is often important in these shows. Plots of MOTW episodes are usually portrayed as a Sherlock Holmes-ian mystery, where characters spend a great deal of time verbally discussing the monsters themselves as well as clues and twists. This holds true for both literal monster plots (such as in episodes of *Scooby Doo* [21] and the *X-Files*) and for metaphoric ones (such as episodes of *House* [22], where the doctors had to diagnose and treat a different disease each week, or episodes of *Criminal Minds* [23], where the FBI spent large chunks of screen time conversing about the monstrous weekly serial killer). With this paradigm in mind, we built a text corpus that combined each episode's dialogue with its metadata, and started to build computational models to explore how the monsters might be functioning across the specifics of a given series' theme or season arc.

Because the MOTW trope becomes a pop culture construct of who and what becomes a monster-antagonist, our first model was concerned with the various forms the monster could take across all these MOTW episodes. We built a "monster typology" by scraping together lists of monsters, folk creatures, mythological beasts, and other supernatural beings from Wikipedia, Freebase, and other online information sources. Trying to account for the forms that played the most prominent or recurring monster role, we searched through our dataset (both the subtitles and the metadata) and weighted appearances of monster types and names in the various episodes. For example, a monster antagonist reference appearing in an episode plot summary might get more weight than a passing reference in the subtitle text, but multiple repetitions of a name throughout a given episode would also be given greater weight. Our computer algorithms then ranked our weighted scores to determine which forms most commonly function as a monster of the week. The data shows that "demon" is the most commonly employed reference to a monster in our MOTW episodes, followed by "witch", the generic term "monster", and then "vampire".

It is important to acknowledge that our typological choices emphasize traditional monsters whereas technological or psychological monstrosity may not be identified given our search parameters. All monster types imply a belief system and ways of knowing and assessing dilemmas and threats to survival through a deviant human form. Gregory Schrempp observes that monsters in general are anthropocentric. He explains, "If we were capable of imagining an alien being that was entirely free of us—a 'totally other'—it would not be monstrous" ([24], p. 241). Monsters, to be identified as such, must have some human resemblance and deviate from something ordinary. This then implies that monstrosity involves some human deformation that threatens humanity although it certainly may implicate relationships and other life forms such as plants, insects, amphibians, animals, beasts, mechanical objects, and technological inventions as well. That "alien" appears in the more frequent monster types indicates that the extraordinary status leading to MOTW monstrosity may be extraterrestrial. But, most striking in the MOTW data is the preponderance of malevolent spiritual, supernatural beings taking the monster form that suggests a convergence of Christianity and earlier belief systems: demons, devils, witches, and vampires. The predominant appearance of these figures as MOTW monsters in our corpus may say something about a lingering satanic paradigm in pop culture.

While this overview of monster types is intriguing, we wanted our models to dig deeper into the data and explore the more complex narrative patterns underlying the seemingly formulaic monster confrontations. To do this, we employed topic modeling, a staple investigative tool of machine learning. Topic models are, at their heart, models of probability, where common clusters of words in a given text are grouped together to indicate which word groups, when present in a text, form a coherent "topic". As machines running the probability algorithms over a corpus of texts have no easy way to assign semantic labels to these topic sets, common topic model tools will instead return these word lists, allowing scholars to make sense of what the topics, or word clusters, might indicate about common narrative themes or conversation subjects.

Running the topic model simulations numerous times, slightly changing assumptions about how many possible topics to search for, what sorts of function words to include or exclude, and so on, we began to see patterns emerge across our corpus of MOTW episodes. There were strong signals of each show's basic premise; for example, one fairly large topic included words such as "alien", "ship", "planet", and "space". When we mapped the relationship between topic and show, we found this almost exclusively in sci-fi MOTW series such as *The X-Files* and *Star Trek* [25]. Other topics signaled television shows dealing with magic, religion, and so forth. However, four topics cut across all the shows, indicating a narrative cohesion that seems important for MOTW storytelling on television. The first of these demonstrates a common framework of setting or place with words such as "night", "police", "body", "found", and "clue". Such a topic provides tangible evidence for the claim that MOTW episodes employ crime and detective motifs even when not explicitly in a mystery genre. The second common topic continues to lay out major narrative themes across episodes; words such as "woman", "sex", "male", "rape", and "blood" are grouped together, revealing just how often MOTW television stories deal with violence, usually against women.

If these first two topics in our modeling illustrate common narrative modes of setting, theme, and a mystery and crime plot, the other two episode-spanning topics perhaps tie back to the MOTW trope's sense of narrative purpose. One of these topics employs words such as "father", "mother", "love", "house", "parents", "child", "friend", and "family". While it may be almost too obvious to label this topic as being about interpersonal (usually familial) relationships, functionally such a topic plays an increasingly vital role in these shows. Generally speaking, characters in the shows we are exploring are not family, and in fact usually are not even friends in the first few episodes. Rather, the various monster plots serve as a catalyst for actually creating the familial-like bonds with the monsters determining the controlling issues or exigence. While the formation of such bonds through trial and hardship is a television narrative trope that goes far beyond procedural MOTW episodes, it functions quite a bit differently in a show such as *Angel* [26] (where, even in later years with more serialization, week-to-week monsters act as MacGuffins to draw the makeshift "family" closer) than it does on heavily serialized monster shows such as *Lost* [27] (where an antagonist creature such as the smoke monster must eventually be explained, justified, and situated narratively in the larger series arcs, often to less-than-successful results). We see that the other most common thematic topic is quite similar, superficially, since terms such as "mother", "father", and "child" are also included. Although, the clustering algorithms here associate these familial labels with words such as "died", "gone", and "hard". In other words, this topic concerns the loss of a close human relationship and keys on the natal family impacted by the monsters' violence and subjugation. Unexpectedly, the topic modeling suggests that dramatic arc *and* episodic MOTW series concern themselves as much with close relationships as with monsters per se. Our data analysis confirms that Baba Yaga as a traditional figure associated with motherhood, danger, ugliness, old age, witchcraft, life, and death would serve well in the narrative components and concerns of MOTW series, especially those associated with strong will, threats, and relationships.

As popular culture producers and viewers appropriate the Baba Yaga form for the television trope, they associate a monster's will to dominate with Baba Yaga's specific constellations of supernatural strength and mythic powers and, thus, reformulate her traditional wonder as a form of sheer villainy. The traditional portability of these forms, which means transmission through person-to-person channels of imitation and performance, transforms into the portability afforded by the technologies and institutions associated with mass media. The shareable traditional forms associated with folklore that appeal to popular culture are being conceptualized as the *folkloresque* in recent work by Michael Dylan Foster and Jeffrey A. Tolbert [28]. Popular culture has an orientation toward entertainment, middle and lower social classes, production for mass distribution, and a profit motive; it is a field and subject of study, as well as a mode of expression. As Foster configures it, "Popular culture is a set of processes and products that exists within a commercial-industrial structure and are oriented toward financial remuneration" ([28], p. 7). A simple definition of the folkloresque, then, is that it is popular culture's "perception and performance of folklore" ([28], p. 5); in other words, the folkloresque involves ways that traditional forms transform when produced for mass consumption. When these forms transform as popular culture, they connect "to some tradition or folkloric source existing outside the popular culture context" ([28], p. 5). Wonder is something tradition affords popular culture in general and that Baba Yaga and traditional monsters afford the MOTW trope specifically.

While a MOTW episode is not a fairy tale and Baba Yaga is not only a fairy-tale character, the forms intermingle in part because they all afford access to wonder through shareable character traits, functions, plot moves, and themes. Cristina Bacchilega writes of wonder as an effect that "involves both awe and curiosity" and reiterates the fairy tale's primary affiliation with wonder ([29], p. 5). Marina Warner, introducing a collection of French wonder tales, states the case for wonder: "It names the marvel, the prodigy, the surprise as well as the responses they excite, of fascination and inquiry; it conveys the active motion toward experience and the passive stance of enrapturement" ([30], p. 3). Foster considers authenticity a major contribution of folklore to popular culture through the folkloresque because it implies the validation afforded by tradition itself ([28], p. 5). Yet, wonder should be considered folk narrative's greater affordance because it links the validation of tradition with potentiality. As Warner observes, "All the wonders that create the atmosphere of fairy tale disrupt the apprehensible world in order to open spaces for dreaming alternatives" ([31], p. xx). When Baba Yaga transforms into a folkloresque form in the MOTW trope, her traditional potentialities are drastically foreclosed as she remains only a villain, but as the monster form, she still catalyzes the threat that leads protagonists to assess and formulate new family relations.

A Baba Yaga indexes cosmic realities and potentialities of borders, beginnings, and endings, and her appearance in a MOTW episode affords the production a traditional formulation of the mysteries and challenges of life. Among other tale types, she is associated with "Hansel and Gretel" (ATU 327) in the story "Baba Yaga and the Kid", with "Beauty and the Beast" (ATU 425) involving an animal bridegroom and search for a lost husband in "Finist the Bright Falcon", and with "The Frog Princess" (ATU 402) involving an animal bride in "Vasilisa the Beautiful" [1]. Andreas Johns confirms that Baba Yaga is most at home in the folktale, "usually identified by its marvelous, fantastic elements" ([2], p. 44). Still, her affiliation with a Russian pantheon filters into her tale roles and presages her alliances with mythical gods and demi-gods from other cultures as well. Late eighteenth-century artists such as writer Mikhail Chulkov and editor Matthew Guthrie, according to Johns, consider a Baba Yaga to be a Slavic "underworld goddess" and Russian Persephone associated with death, winter, storms, blood sacrifice, and "represented in the form of a monster" ([2], pp. 16–20). In other situations, she is involved with birth, cycles of the sun and moon, and familiar with nature and creatures. Always fantastic and sometimes majestic, she associates with other dangerous, powerful beings such as Koschei the Deathless, dragons, tsars, even children and youth. According to Helena Gosilco, she "unites fundamental polarities in a circle or ring that images the cycle of life" ([32], p. 13). More than just a story character and villain, a Baba Yaga is a supernatural figure and even replicable as in some ATU 425 versions where the protagonist travels to three successive Baba Yagas in her quest for the lost groom. In the MOTW trope, protagonists investigate, confront, judge, and seek to contain or destroy such an extraordinary and deformed being because, for selfish purposes, such wonderful powers are going awry.

Given centuries of presence in tales and these rich, ambiguous mythical and tale associations, Baba Yaga, just by name, adds this form's supernatural affordance to *Soul Eater*, a manga created by Atsushi Ōkubo [33] and 51-episode anime [34]. Rayna Denison identifies some features that indicate this anime would achieve transnational reach in "its presentation of a group of young teen characters, in its gothic aesthetic style and in its generic positioning in the action and horror genres" ([35], p. 451). Notably, Denison does not associate success with the folkloresque deployment of myth and tale and the traditional epistemological, ontological, and cosmic systems that the Baba Yaga and other traditional forms bring to the series. Still, these traditional associations lie latent in the features Denison does identify, since gothic styles and action and horror genres also can take a folkloresque turn toward long-held, cross-cultural knowledge and belief expressed in recognizable traditional forms.

Baba Yaga, therefore, as a monster form in the anime affords these streams of traditional knowledge, belief, and world making to flow through the series, especially because a brief reference to her abode interacts with other traditional and pop cultural forms and their affordances. Created post-Harry Potter, the *Soul Eater* series features, both in manga and anime formats, a dizzyingly complex range of characters, monsters, social and interpersonal issues, and story arcs in a simple premise that students of the Death Weapon Meister Academy (DWMA), including teams of youth meisters and transforming humanoid weapons, must gather 99 evil souls and one witch in order to turn the weapon into a death scythe for use by the headmaster, Shinigami—Death himself [33,34]. The well-being of the world hangs in the balance.

Associated with the manga arc "Operation Capture Baba Yaga Castle" and an "Arachnophobia *vs.* DWMA" arc that concluded the anime series, the ambiguous Russian witch, death guardian, earth mother, donor, tester, and villain only appears in the castle name. Still, the folkloresque is at play because the familiar form of her iconic hut on chicken legs transforms here into a spider-like castle guarded by eight spider-leg towers with controlling Demon Tool Locks that protect the throne room. The capacity for replication applies as the domicile bearing Baba Yaga's name now has eight rather than two legs. The castle is named for Baba Yaga, and it houses the central antagonist, Arachne, who also in a folkloresque move plays a role in the series' transformed version of Greek mythology's Gorgon sisters. Arachne Gorgon, one of three powerful sister witches, is the targeted antagonist of this arc, founder of the Baba Yaga Castle hidden in an Amazonian river basin and leader of Arachnophobia, an eight-hundred-year-old group creating Demon Weapons and using the Book of Eibon, a Demon Book associated with a great sorcerer of knowledge, to fight Death [36].[2] Medusa retains her name and becomes the middle, rather than youngest, Gorgon sister, while her traditional siblings Stheno and Euryale are replaced in *Soul Eater* by Arachne and Shaula. By giving the story an eight-century backdrop and transnational as well as supernatural geographic realm, *Soul Eater* incorporates folkloresque traits that can be understood in part through the Baba Yaga allusion and MOTW trope although both allusion and trope are augmented through the complexities of manga and anime.

Inherently intermedial and ripe with adaptation, manga and anime also teem with popular culture. As Foster configures it, admittedly in blurry categories, pop culture implies "entertainment and frivolity" the culture of the "nonelite", elements of "mass production and mass distribution", which involves "*mass* media", and aspects of "consumer culture" ([28], pp. 6–7), emphasis in the text]. Anime has become big, transnational business. Denison's article attests to the financial stakes in the growing disputes over fan subtitling, distribution, or piracy [35]. Yet, the bent toward the commodified and widely popular need not inherently exclude the possibility of these forms involve artfulness and wonder. Specifically working through the implications for anime and art, Susan Napier surmises, "Animation in general—and perhaps anime in particular—is the ideal artistic vehicle for expressing the hopes and nightmares of our uneasy contemporary world" because it is a "fusion of technology and art" ([37], p. 11). She champions anime as a "narrative art form", as well as a compelling visual form ([37], p. 10). More directly to our interests and observations of forms transforming, scholars associate animation with metamorphosis itself—requiring and inviting fluid motion and change. Napier says, "The favorite object of transformation is clearly the body" ([37], pp. 35–38). *Soul Eater* in the concept of humanoid weapons incorporates such metamorphosis while manifesting multiple other transformations over the course of the manga and anime, not to mention another iteration in *Soul Eater Not!* [38], something of a prequel also written by Atsuchi Ōkubo. Baba Yaga in the televised MOTW episodes remains only

---

[2] Although *Soul Eater* was not included in our corpus, clearly some concept of demon, at least in translation, serves as a crucial identifier of powerful objects and beings in the series.

an antagonist, even if in *Soul Eater* it is only as a domicile named for her that must be overtaken.

As with many pop culture monsters and villains, and some historical ones as well, desiring omnipotence for self-gain and world domination becomes the great threat associated with the monster form in this series. Arachne becomes a target of the DWMA and of her sister Medusa and other witches because in her desire to become the Mother of All she captures and destroys witch souls [3]. Because Arachne and Medusa are sisters, this contest also plays out as sibling rivalry which is won by Medusa when Arachne and Baba Yaga's Castle are breached and eventually destroyed. In this story arc, we see that the topical affiliation of MOTW monsters with family, homes, friends, death, and loss remains salient. The other primary topics from our data analysis, of crime procedurals and violence, ramify as well in terms of the monster figure enacting evil intent and being met with violent confrontation. Other plot elements and backstory moments in *Soul Eater* turn on complex natal family relationships and on the development of familial bonds among friends as well. Anime resists the neatly packaged closure of many fairy-tale endings, still the anime final episode, in English "The Word is Bravery!" [39], resolves the well-being of the world, and as importantly for many fans, asserts the well-being of key characters and their relationships. Cosmic status is righted at the anime's close by the assertion of bravery over fear, which becomes a rite of passage for the main protagonist, Maka, and many of her associates. The monsters' desires to subsume control for themselves is dispersed toward the protagonists' growth, relationships, and future possibilities.

While popular culture transforms traditional forms into the folkloresque for the MOTW trope, these wondrous forms interrogate family formation through deformation and villainy. Focusing on childhood and gender ideologies, Bacchilega and John Rieder conclude that what is at stake in transformations of form that involve adaptation, narrative and media genre mixing is "a fight to control the energies of fairy tale wonder" ([40], p. 41). Distinctive tale elements do not melt unidentifiably into a pop culture mass when appropriated into television shows and the MOTW trope, and neither do those of myth, legend, and other narrative forms nor those of televisual genres. Levine's term very aptly asserts the ways these forms combine without dissolving in that "patterns and arrangements carry their *affordances* with them as they move across time and space" ([14], p. 6, emphasis is mine). Rather famously, Warner surmises that "on the whole fairy tales are not passive or active; their mood is optative—announcing what might be" ([40], pp. xx). This optative mood becomes an affordance of the Baba Yaga form in the MOTW trope, ironically, as the monster seeks its own purposes and to control future possibilities. The trope foregrounds investigation, confrontation, making a judgment, and dealing with monsters all as ways of handling wonder going awry.

Seeing how Baba Yaga shares her folkloresque aura through minimal indexing in *Soul Eater* leads to considering the effect on wondrous possibilities and family relations when more components come into play in a live-action supernatural drama. The Canadian series *Lost Girl* includes Baba Yaga in the fourth episode of season two [41]. This episode, titled "Mirror, Mirror", suggests that the plot requirements of a drama series reformulate the traditionally ambiguous Baba Yaga functions. While the episode contains familiar motifs from the fairy tales, such as girls required to do menial chores and Baba Yaga being involved with cannibalism and an oven, two major plot points come from other narrative and belief traditions. This *Lost Girl* episode signals the truth claims and reality experimentation linked with legend. Elliott Oring observes that legend "requires the audience to examine their world view—their sense of the normal, the boundaries of the natural, their conceptions of fate, destiny, and coincidence" ([42], p. 126). Monsters challenge the normal and natural, which is why they must be sought out and confronted in these shows because they not only challenge norms but usually overtly attack them, symbolically and literally. Defeating the monster Baba Yaga in all three episodes studied here becomes a badge of destiny because her self-interest blocks, or destroys, the well-being of others. In a way, every MOTW series involves legend because by asserting that monsters exist they interrogate a world view that sees them as fictional and imaginary. And every episode threatens wonder as the monster tries to foreclose possibility.

Legend is indexed in this episode by how Baba Yaga functions as an ancient possibility that becomes a reality that can be accessed, by magical means, from the real world. She is sought in this episode to curse an errant boyfriend and is invoked by a Bloody Mary-type chant, itself a legendary activity, involving a mirror. The mirror here has a more functional than symbolic role: more portal to a curse than indicator of beauty. This plays into how the legend affords key elements of the MOTW trope, investigation and a willingness to delay judgment. *Lost Girl* advocates these very traits through its basic premise that the protagonist, Bo (Anna Silk), is a succubus, in this case configured as a being who feeds off of humans through sexual activity and may destroy them. Here, the MOTW trope transforms from the basic iteration and allows monstrosity to be part of the protagonist while she and her friends confront the dangerous possibilities of their own differences and other monsters. The series develops a complex ontology of supernatural Fae beings that stems primarily from traditional belief systems, rather than inventing new creatures [43]. Related to our monster typology, succubi and many of the beings in the series are demons and must be discovered and understood for their supernatural traits while operating in a human world. The process of investigating and delaying judgment is invoked repeatedly in the series, and this evokes the experimental mode of legend's claims to truth.

This episode, thus, transforms traditional behaviors of a Baba Yaga by tilting her function toward legend more than the tale. In Russian fairy tales in English translation, Baba Yaga certainly is a threat to those who wander to her hut, and while she may be sought for a boon, just as Vasilisa is sent to obtain light ([1], pp. 170–82), she rarely is sought to act like a witch and put a curse on someone. Cannibalism is more of her threat in tales. Yet, in this episode Kenzi (Ksenia Solo), Bo's sidekick, offers to get Baba Yaga (Kate Lynch) to seek revenge for Bo's being jilted by Dyson (Kris Holden-Ried). Already, the plot summary reads something like a conversation among teens although the show is set among twenty-somethings and involves adolescent issues of sexuality, identity, and interpersonal relations on a ramped up scale of age, experience, and the supernatural. Being sought to curse errant boyfriends is presented in the episode as a well-known role for a Baba Yaga. Kenzi, whose actress is Latvian-Canadian, considers other spells and then picks Baba Yaga explaining, "Every young Russian dyevooshka is taught to fear the old witch who lives deep in the woods in a cottage...Occasionally she'll help chicks get revenge on a dude who's wronged them" [41]. Eventually, she enters a bathroom and chants, in Russian and English, to Baba Yaga and asks for Dyson to feel the pain of rejection he has inflicted on Bo. Writing his name in red lipstick on the mirror, she leaves just before the mirror smashes to the sink and a shadowy figure rasps, "As you wish". The bathroom mirror in the episode indexes Bloody Mary, which is a teenager's legend trip because it involves going to place, often a bathroom, and completing actions to summon her and test belief [44]. Bloody Mary usually reveals the future, attacks those who seek her, or fails to appear at all.

Having young adults seek Baba Yaga to solve a problem through a teenage divination legend acknowledges the weighty tasks of gaining maturity and the ongoing applicability, and folkloresque use in the show, of traditional knowledge to work through such dilemmas. But, Kenzi's problem-solving technique is problematic itself when Bo becomes marked by Baba Yaga, and Dyson is rejected by every woman he meets. Characters learn the hopeful and dreadful consequences of calling on Baba Yaga when she is more than a possibility. Kenzi consults her fortunetelling aunt to enter Baba Yaga's realm and ends up destroying her in the oven and freeing her friends and several other unfortunate young women from the evil witch. That characters cannot walk through the woods to Baba Yaga's cottage establishes the ontological shifting of the series, the importance of having overlapping worlds. This ontology is referenced in the opening title sequence, where Bo in a voiceover states, "I belong to a world hidden from humans. I won't hide anymore. I will live the life I choose" [41]. Like other supernatural drama series, characters learn to see and deal with otherwise unseen paranormal, mythical, and magical worlds within the human world [45]. In addition to cosmic confrontations to save that human world, the more quotidian task in *Lost Girl* is for the protagonist, and her friends, to navigate their worlds successfully which means, in this case, by independence, making choices, and building close relationships.

The treatment of Baba Yaga in this episode is not an homage or recasting of her ethnographic or narrative authority but rather a folkloresque opportunity to mix traditional expressions and knowledge and belief systems for necessary plot and character development (Disney makes similar choices in most of its fairy-tale films). Baba Yaga can be sought, in Russian, to curse a boyfriend; she can appear after the manner of the Bloody Mary chant. She can be treated like a legend while retaining traits of a fairy-tale witch. When characters surmise that Bo bears Baba Yaga's mark, given the premise of the show and its deployment of the folkloresque, it is predictable that she would be a real being capable of helpful or harmful acts and accessible across worlds. Yet, Kenzi asks in surprise, "Baba Yaga is real?" [41]. MOTW series portray that possibility, evoke that wonder. Yet, in this episode what seems to matter more than the supernatural overlay is that friends need to work through betrayal and restore their friendship using any means available—even a Russian witch.

As a definitive formulation of MOTW trope, Baba Yaga does not return to the series, which continued for five seasons and ended with a complex set of narrative possibilities and relationship issues to confront with its finale. Relationships matter a great deal here, and as the series came to a close in 2015, the choice that mattered most to many fans seems to have been which partner Bo would end up with. By the series finale, "Rise", there also are cosmically complicated natal family issues such as Bo being the daughter of Hades (Eric Roberts) and possibly joining him in world destruction, starting with dismantling Toronto [46]. There is even more family intrigue in the finale involving the birth of Bo's half-sister, the death of the baby's mother, and Kenzi's new role as the baby's caregiver [46]. Yet, on the website AfterEllen, Dorothy Snarker posts the major concern for the finale, "I want Bo with 'X'. I won't be happy unless Bo is with 'X'. Because that's what happens when you invest five years into a show–you care what happens to these characters" [47]. For a series that made life choice a central feature, sexuality an imperative, friendship a resource, family a cosmic challenge, and navigating human and supernatural worlds an important mandate, it is striking that romance and committed pairing would prevail in the end. At this memorable point in the series, the fairy-tale motif most heavily questioned and critiqued in the past four decades reemerges. For the finale, the legend issues of knowledge, normative boundaries, and destiny roil on—subordinated in fan desire for a highly anticipated happily ever after (HEA).[3] That's a pop culture formation of wonder and family through monstrosity worth noting.

Baba Yaga and the other monsters of the MOTW trope, as our textual analysis and topic modeling indicate, threaten and catalyze family relations. These relations involve dyadic pairs, parents and siblings, and familial bonds among close friends. This happens thematically and also corresponds with changing narrative mores on television. The family component fits the MOTW transformation from a disconnected weekly series of monster confrontations towards the serial narrative arcs favored by contemporary television. Other issues also are investigated and developed over long-arc serials, but the challenges of natal families and the possibility of new family formations stem from, and counter, the self-serving threats posed by the MOTW monsters. Both series involving Baba Yaga and the MOTW trope analyzed to this point aired in the early 2010s, and both incorporate components of complex TV storytelling theorized by Jason Mittell. He establishes a poetics of narrative TV complexity that deserves its own study in terms of these series, but for now, his basic definition is most salient: "narrative complexity *redefines episodic forms under the influence of serial narration*" ([49], p. 18, emphasis in the text). In the series analyzed here, this narrative poetics links with the folkloresque deployment of traditional knowledge and belief systems which we have seen include supernatural beings, narrative genres, tale motifs, and mythical world building, and destroying, strategies. The narrative arcs that involve Baba Yaga as the monster specifically formulate families as they confront and work through a monster's will to dominate and through individual character's and viewers' desires for close relationships and belonging.

We posit that the folkloresque adds welcome diversity and possibility to the realism of recent serial melodrama (although exploring the contiguities and possibilities of fantasy and reality works for realistic *and* fantastic television series). Unlike *Breaking Bad* [50] or *The Wire* [51], the recent series that include a Baba Yaga MOTW episode depend on beings who have existed over a long duration. The plots and themes of these shows are informed by ancient knowledge, and the episodes advocate learning by investigation, confrontation, and delayed judgment. These series lead to cosmic battles of good and evil in addition to featuring significant attention to character interaction and relationships. In other words, these series deploy a range of folk narrative genres and the folkloresque. With online streaming and other new technologies altering how viewers access, see, and incorporate watching television into their lives, industry analysts, producers, and viewers all want to know where this is going and if it still can be called television. Along with

---

[3]   Most fans approved of this HEA finale. A SpoilerTV poll [48] concludes that 271 voters, or 32% responding, found the finale Awesome; 14% great; 16% good; 17% OK, and 22% poor or awful.

the more recent trend toward complex narrative arcs, series deploying the MOTW trope still have at least some episodes with one major monster confrontation resolved before the episode's end. The MOTW series show that some things do stay the same while television production and viewing have been in remarkable flux over this period; the more things change, the more they can also stay the same.

Amid this flux, at least one uncomplicated MOTW series from the 1960s remains in rebooted, franchised production—the former Saturday morning kids' cartoon, Hanna-Barbera's *Scooby Doo, Where Are You?* [21]. Although new characters appear in later productions, the franchise centers on Scooby Doo, a Great Dane, and Fred, Daphne, Shaggy, and Velma, four teenagers who drive around in a groovy van, confront a monster each week, and solve mysteries. It is not so surprising that it would take over forty years for Baba Yaga to take her turn as a Scooby MOTW. There was a Cold War with the Soviet Union for half of those forty years. Baba Yaga tales were not retold in another classic of 1960s TV fairy tales—*Rocky and Bullwinkle's* "Fractured Fairy Tales", although that show did not shy away from Cold War issues [52]. The Baba Yaga form was not yet fitting somehow. According to the FTTV database, she doesn't appear in North American television until a 1999 episode of *Arthur* explored multicultural beliefs, possible realities, and storytelling assumptions in another children's animated show [53]. Whatever the political and cultural causes, it was only in the first iteration of the Cartoon Network's years that Scooby and the gang met Baba Yaga in *Scooby Doo! Mystery Incorporated* (SDMI), the eleventh televised configuration overall [54]. No spoiler here, she was not really a supernatural being but rather a person in disguise with a greedy motive, thwarted by the meddling kids and their huge, endearing dog.

With the *Scooby Doo* franchise, the monster is crucial to each week's mystery investigation, yet the monster gets unveiled as a conniving human and debunked in every episode, putting us again in the realm of legend as studied by folklorists. As Jan Brunvand has noted, making a truth claim is a defining feature of the genre [55]. Brunvand dedicated his first collection of urban legends, *The Vanishing Hitchhiker*, to "my students past and present, skeptics and believers alike" [56]. So when the monster's veracity becomes a point for both skeptics and believers, a MOTW series involves legend in its genre mix. *Soul Eater* makes no such truth claim but rather assumes a world where mythic beings and humans constantly interact. In all *Scooby Doo's* reboots and intermedial guises, including books, comics, live-action feature films, and games, the series follows a standard formula of mystery investigation about a disruptive monster. The investigation eventually unveils a human with a grudge or greedy plan who has perpetuated the offense. The world, in a cosmic sense, is never threatened by the monster, but the story scene is always challenged with some impending violation including commercial development, environmental degradation, and other personal gain of the perpetrator over community well-being.

Therefore, the transforming forms in this Baba Yaga episode, "The House of the Nightmare Witch", involve common motifs including the mobile hut on chicken legs and threatening behaviors with the distinctive *Scooby Doo* feature of the formulaic unmasking to show that this monster is merely a man [57]. As with other series, the monsters do the cultural work of bringing the folkloresque into the show because the monster implies some extraordinary aspect that often stems from traditional ways of knowing and many cultures.

The deployment of the folkloresque makes the cultural, and supernatural, differences foreign because in the MOTW trope the difference is deforming and threatening. This Scooby episode depends on foreign associations with a time and place where witches live in creepy huts in forests. That place is marked as Russian by explicit location at the opening of the episode, by feigned accents, clothing, Baba Yaga herself, and Faberge eggs. As the episode starts, Velma (voiced by Mindy Cohn) and a new character, Hot Dog Water (Linda Cardellini), are attempting to break into Baba Yaga's hut which happens to be displayed in a Russian museum. This implies the historicity of Baba Yaga if she and her hut can be put on display, but of course, this is debunked later in the episode when the Russian museum curator (Troy Baker) is revealed to have impersonated Baba Yaga in order to hide Faberge eggs in the hut and sell them on the black market. Debunking in the case of *Scooby Doo* always neutralizes the supernatural by explaining the monster with mundane, if nefarious, motives, and in the case of Baba Yaga, associates Russian culture with old-time images of huts, witches, and elaborate Faberge eggs created for defunct emperors. Not every MOTW episode makes such cultural commentary but it often is implied that cultural difference may be threatening or catalyzing of new relationships.

The break-in of Baba Yaga's hut is part of a serialized plot that distinguishes *SDMI* from other episodic franchise versions, showing that even the most formulaic series could be influenced by complex TV narrative trends. Velma is searching the hut to obtain part of a planispheric disk that, when completed, will reveal important information to Mr. E (Lewis Black), another new character in this particular series. Unlike the simple friendship shared through a focus on mysteries, this iteration develops relationship and character drama over the series involving Fred's (Frank Welker) missing birth parents, a love triangle that leads Daphne (Grey Griffin, also voice of Baba Yaga) to temporarily leave the Scooby gang, and romance between Shaggy (Matthew Lillard) and Velma. More than these relationship arcs, the dramatic plot arc is also highly folkloresque in that season two involves Babylonian mythology and cosmic forces that must be decoded and understood (rather than overtly battled as in the *Soul Eater* and *Lost Girl* series) to avoid global disaster. Like some MOTW series, *SDMI* also sets scenes in high school emphasizing the characters' adolescence. The serial supernatural and relationship arcs mix with the folkloresque, but not so well with the history and ethos of the franchise, and they mostly are dropped in the next iteration, *Be Cool, Scooby Doo!* [58], which is back to MOTW investigations. The series' own familiar narrative moves and character interactions suffice, and hold their own, against more complex storytelling.

Obviously, the formula of confronting, and debunking, a new monster every week remains central. The episodic nature of "The House of the Nightmare Witch", including the signature closing, asserts a lingering appeal for the recognizable and familiar through formulas. The simple interactions of the four main characters and Scooby Doo, even their typecasting as the pretty girl, handsome boy, smart girl, goofy guy, and talking dog allow for satisfying, memorable, and replicable storytelling and viewing. However, formulaic aspects have been a concern and a methodological and theoretical component of popular culture studies since the field emerged in the 1960s, about the time of this series and the MOTW trope itself. John G. Cawelti advocated attending to the formulaic as a methodological feature of popular culture because content-oriented studies tended to overgeneralization [59]. David N. Feldman critiqued and extended Cawelti's formulaic approach by emphasizing benefits of incorporating Russian formalist techniques in popular culture analyses [60].

Feldman advocates breaking popular narratives into their most basic parts called motifs, which is also what folklorists mean by the term, and labeling them either free (disconnected) from the final resolution or bound (connected) to it. He posits that the free and bound motifs are involved in a predictive method to better understand narrative because re-familiarization, or the final sorting of those motifs, may be a key to appreciating audience reception [60]. The play of free and bound motifs defamiliarizes audiences, if only temporarily, from a predictable, chronological story. Feldman explains that there then seem to be two ways to refamiliarize, one he calls "aesthetic" and the other "pragmatic" ([60], pp. 210–11). TV shows in series, setting aside franchises like *Scooby Doo*, and in specific episodes come to an end, and the aesthetic refamiliarization feels like a payoff if the free motifs have not totally overwhelmed those that turn out to be bound to the final resolution. Pragmatic refamiliarization, according to Feldman, involves how the final resolution resonates with life outside the story, with audience values, expectations, and relevance ([60], p. 211). According to Feldman's approach, refamiliarization may be the difference between the pleased and contented overall response to the *Lost Girl* series finale and the disappointed and dejected response to *Lost*. In the case of *Lost* there seems to have been a failure of both aesthetic and pragmatic refamiliarization; the innumerable free motifs did not resolve well with what turned out to be bound motifs, and expectations of many fans were dashed by the irrelevance of the finale after years of dedication to the series. It seems likely that the triumph of evil in a MOTW series would break the audiences' ability for pragmatic refamiliarization given the strongly folkloresque pull for good to win in the end. A *Scooby Doo* episode could end with a real monster who gets away, but fairy-tale, and MOTW, formula would be shattered. Viewers would be confused or disappointed, and fans may become distraught.

In regard to Baba Yaga and the MOTW trope, these three episodes connect an optative mode of wonder and a retributive mode of justice. The monster receives justice for executing self-serving desires and plans while protagonists are left in the end with new family formations and potentialities. Baba Yaga's crimes in these episodes all involve hurtful actions toward others for personal gain and include destroying other witches, betraying a friend, and selling national treasures. In the traditional tales, her demise is rarely so assured because she does not always violate such regulations and sometimes serves as helper. In the MOTW trope, her castle is unlocked and overrun; she is pushed in the oven or revealed as a fraud because of violating social regulations and seeking to trick and dominate others. The tale still exerts lingering power in the MOTW trope through its transformations as it mixes with myth, legend, and televised mystery procedurals, anime, and supernatural drama. Fairy tale remains crucial to these episodes in great measure because, as Feldman would put it, its traditional associations and folkloresque applications, its familiar forms, and well known plot arcs help writers, creators, producers, viewers, and fans get the free and bound motifs in place as these transforming forms suspend and meet audience expectations and relevance.

Katherine J. Roberts, in an astute study of fairy tale and case study law, explores how this happens. In part, she says it is because "'bad precedents' get retired", and stories that don't work "are left behind, much like cases which are overruled and fall into disfavor" ([61], p. 518). This disfavor seems to have happened with the serialized arc of *SDMI* which was jettisoned after two seasons. While *Lost Girl* fans needed to know Bo's life-long partner and wanted that HEA, Scooby fans need to wonder about the relationships among the gang and, obviously with all the reboots, continuously defer any conclusive endings (except those at the end of each episode). Coming up with new monsters each week is a daunting production task, so Baba Yaga presents a new precedent, as it were, because her stories have not been televised much outside of Russia and Slavic countries. But, audiences still gravitate toward monsters who violate social regulations and, thus, the monsters take the form of villains upon whom protagonists distribute retribution. Roberts observes that fairy tale "consistently seeks to uphold legal distinctions between legitimate and illegitimate acts of violence" ([61], p. 499). The monster's violence is illegitimate because consuming and self-serving while the protagonists' violence legitimately saves the group and society from harm.

In these MOTW series, the need for clarity prevails even though recovering the villain has been an important pop culture move recently. Providing an explanatory back story for a villain's anti-social tendencies, such as in *Maleficent* [62], happens regularly now and perhaps recapitulates the monster's backstory built into

72

Frankenstein [63]. So, if recent MOTW series assure Baba Yaga's demise more often than in traditional tales, perhaps creators and viewers do not know her well enough yet to treat her as more than just another monster. Roberts attributes much of fairy tale's polarized thinking to young audiences and the socializing role of tales, stating "fairy tales make it their primary business to punish the bad and reward the good, and to teach readers the boundary between the two" ([61], p. 511). These shows with adolescent protagonists aim toward society's nascent adults and reach both older and younger audiences as well, and with these Baba Yaga episodes draw stark distinctions that portray and punish her as bad. In her specific case in these episodes, monstrosity does seem to metamorphose into sheer retribution.

What then of wonder? The focus on retribution and relationships tells something about audience expectations and what remains relevant. Our topic analysis indicates concern in the dialogue of MOTW shows about crime and violence as well as interest in close relationships such as natal families, friends, and loss. Pat Gill's study of teen slasher films of the late twentieth century focuses on parental neglect and abandonment as a central factor in the disaster that comes upon the teens [64]. The *Buffy* movie in 1992 [65] exemplifies this parental non-involvement although the later television show corrects the oversight by giving her an involved single parent. The televised version even may have instigated the involvement of family relations with the monster confrontations. *Buffy the Vampire Slayer* [18] and *Angel* [26], created by Joss Whedon, are known for specifically working around the tropes' most strict episodic definition while regularly involving monsters. Relationships and the unfolding story take precedence in shows like this; as Whedon acknowledges, "Although we came out of it [Buffy] as a sort of monster-of-the-week format, it was clear that the interaction was the thing that most people were latching onto" ([66], p. 4) Paying homage to the 1960s MOTW children's mystery show, Buffy's friends even are known as the Scooby gang ([66], p. 12), a phrase that implies the hometown chumminess of teenaged friends and the possibilities of close relations built around nefarious purposes, whether conducting them or defending from them. More than just parental issues, which ramify into complex genealogies over generations in shows like *Soul Eater* and *Lost Girl*, these MOTW shows work through the association of wonder with families.

In these Baba Yaga episodes, when the monster threatens to subsume power to herself, this act instills awe in other characters that draws them together. This pro-social response, rather paradoxically, may come from a diminished sense of self evoked by experiencing something naturally or supernaturally grand according to the psychological research of Paul K. Piff. Several of his research team's studies demonstrate that "awe leads to more prosocial tendencies by broadening the individual's perspective to include entities vaster and more powerful than oneself" ([67], pp. 895–96). By definition and function, the monster already is more

73

vast and powerful than mere humans in at least some way. Baba Yaga's traditional form affords folkloresque access to natural and supernatural awe when transformed into the MOTW trope. In these episodes, the monster advocates self-aggrandizement when made aware of opportunities for more power, and wants to rule others and the world, but this leads the protagonists to confront such self-interest by seeking intimate prosocial relationships as partners and families.

This exploration and interrogation of close relations fits the impulse of wonder toward inquiry and awe, suggesting that these MOTW stories investigate, confront, delay judgment about, and seek to understand the possibilities of family itself. William A. "Bert" Wilson reminds us of the Robert Frost poem "The Death of the Hired Man" for insights into two ways of thinking about families and relations. There is in the poem a famous phrase uttered by Warren, the husband, "Home is the place where, when you have to go there/They have to take you in". Mary, the wife, tries to convince her husband to let their former hired hand stay with them because he is dying, and she responds, "I should have called it/Something you somehow haven't to deserve" ([68], p. 73). Wilson connects Warren's view of home with a biological, household view of family "held together by the bonds of blood, marriage, or adoption" while Mary's view gets linked to "those clusters of people we have come to call families, even though they are not bound together by consanguineal or affinal ties" ([68], pp. 73–74). This tension plays out in the poem as Warren queries why the hired man came to their house instead of his rich brother's thirteen miles away. The Arachne/Medusa battle of *Soul Eater*, the father Hades plot in *Lost Girl*, and the search for birth parents motif in *SDMI* bring natal family issues into the monster investigation and confrontation, illustrating the centrality of this topic.

Yet, these shows may be known more for the ways the characters bond with each other and their mentors through their schooling and monster hunting. Most of these close relationships are more healthy and supportive than the natal family dysfunctions. These relationship arcs create the "shipping" possibilities so appealing to fans and the friendship attachments developed over the weeks and years that make the characters themselves seem part of the viewer's family. Examining the Baba Yaga MOTW episodes indicates how the monster catalyzes the central topics from our data analysis that involve crime, violence, loss, and family. In terms of audience relevance, the relationship issues hit closer to home than the cosmic battles of good and evil ever will, we hope. These compelling narratives and storytelling frameworks invite production teams to incorporate traditional knowledge and belief systems into these series. So, it is the prescience of folk narrative that brings the folkloresque into the MOTW trope, and only the most basic possibilities with Baba Yaga have yet come into these productions. What is there now deepens and extends the potentialities of close relations by casting them in the midst of overlapping benign and malignant worlds that appear much like our own.

Acknowledgments: This research has been supported by SSHRC Partnership Development Grant 890-2013-17, Fairy Tale Cultures and Media Today. Additional support comes from two Brigham Young University (BYU) Mentored Environment Grants, awarded 2014–2015 and 2016–2017. Jill Rudyalso acknowledges a BYU Humanities Center One-Year Fellowship, with appreciation to Matt Wickman, director. She worked with Megan Armknecht and Sibelan Forrester on an earlier Baba Yaga and television study.

Author Contributions: Jill Rudy and Jarom McDonald envisioned the project; Jarom designed and performed the computations after compiling the monster typology and running the topic models; Jarom and Jill analyzed the data; BYU Office of Digital Humanities contributed analysis tools; Jarom wrote the section on the corpus; Jill wrote the introduction and all remaining sections.

Conflicts of Interest: The authors declare no conflict of interest. The founding sponsors had no role in the design of the study; in the collection, analyses, or interpretation of data; in the writing of the manuscript, and in the decision to publish the results.

Abbreviations

The following abbreviations are used in this manuscript:

MOTW	Monster of the Week
HEA	Happily Ever After
SDMI	Scooby Doo Mystery Incorporated!
BYU	Brigham Young University

References

1. Sibelan Forrester, Helena Goscilo, and Martin Skoro. *Baba Yaga: The Wild Witch of the East in Russian Fairy Tales*. Jackson: University of Mississippi Press, 2013.
2. Andreas Johns. *Baba Yaga: The Ambiguous Mother and Witch of the Russian Folktale*. New York: Peter Lang, 2010.
3. Gerald Pocius. "Art." In *Eight Words for the Study of Expressive Culture*. Edited by Burt Feintuch. Urbana: University of Illinois Press, 2003, pp. 42–68.
4. Henry Glassie. *The Spirit of Folk Art*. New York: Harry N. Abrams, 1995.
5. Regina Bendix. *In Search of Authenticity: The Formation of Folklore Studies*. Madison: University of Wisconsin Press, 1997.
6. Richard Bauman, and Charles L. Briggs. *Voices of Modernity: Language Ideologies and the Politics of Inequality*. Cambridge: Cambridge University Press, 2003.
7. Maureen McLane. *Balladeering, Minstrelsy, and the Making of British Romantic Poetry*. Cambridge: Cambridge University Press, 2008.
8. William A. Wilson. "Documenting Folklore." In *The Marrow of Human Experience*. Edited by Jill Terry Rudy. Logan: Utah State University Press, 2006, pp. 81–103.
9. Stephen Benson. *Cycles of Influence: Fiction, Folktale, Theory*. Detroit: Wayne State University Press, 2003.
10. Cristina Bacchilega. *Postmodern Fairy Tales: Gender and Narrative Strategies*. Philadelphia: University of Pennsylvania Press, 1999.

11. Jack Zipes. *Why Fairy Tales Stick: The Evolution and Relevance of a Genre.* New York: Routledge, 2006.

12. Marina Warner. *Once Upon a Time: A Short History of Fairy Tale.* Oxford: Oxford University Press, 2014.

13. Gotthold Ephraim Lessing. *Laocoön: An Essay on the Limits of Painting and Poetry.* Translated by Edward Allen McCormick. Baltimore: Johns Hopkins University Press, 1962.

14. Caroline Levine. *Forms: Whole, Rhythm, Hierarchy, Network.* Princeton: Princeton University Press, 2015.

15. *The Outer Limits.* Created by Leslie Stevens. American Broadcast Company, 1963–1965.

16. TVTropes. "Monster of the Week." Available online: http://tvtropes.org/pmwiki/pmwiki.php/Main/MonsterOfTheWeek (accessed on 26 February 2016).

17. *X-Files.* Directed by Chris Carter. Fox, 1993.

18. *Buffy the Vampire Slayer.* Directed by Joss Whedon. Fox, 1997.

19. *Supernatural.* Created by Eric Kripke. The WB, 2005; The CW, 2006.

20. *Dr. Who.* Directed by Waris Hussein. Written by Anthony Coburn. BBC, 1963.

21. *Scooby Doo, Where Are You?* Directed by Ken Spears and Joe Ruby. Written by Joe Ruby, Ken Spears and Bill Lutz. Columbia Broadcasting System, 1969.

22. *House.* Created by David Shore. Fox, 2004.

23. *Criminal Minds.* Created by Jeff Davis. Columbia Broadcasting System, 2005.

24. Gregory Schrempp. "Science and the Monsterological Imagination: Folkloristic Musings on David Toomey's *Weird Life.*" In *The Folkloresque: Reframing Folklore in a Popular Culture World.* Edited by Michael Dylan Foster and Jeffrey A. Tolbert. Logan: Utah State University Press, 2016, pp. 241–54.

25. *Star Trek.* Directed by Gene Roddenberry. National Broadcasting System, 1966.

26. *Angel.* Created by Joss Whedon and David Greenwalt. Fox, 1999.

27. *Lost.* Created by Jeffrey Lieber, J. J. Abrams and Damon Lindlof. American Broadcast Company, 2004.

28. Michael Dylan Foster, and Jeffrey A. Tolbert, eds. *The Folkloresque: Reframing Folklore in a Popular Culture World.* Logan: Utah State University Press, 2016.

29. Cristina Bacchilega. *Fairy Tales Transformed?: Twenty-First Century Adaptations and the Politics of Wonder.* Detroit: Wayne State University Press, 2013.

30. Marina Warner, ed. *Wonder Tales: Six French Stories of Enchantment.* Cambridge: Belknap Press of Harvard University Press, 2004.

31. Marina Warner. *From the Beast to the Blond: On Fairy Tales and Their Tellers.* New York: Farrar, Straus and Giroux, 1994.

32. Helena Gosilco. "Introduction, Part I: Folkloric Fairy Tales." In *Politicizing Magic: An Anthology of Russian and Soviet Fairy Tales.* Edited by Marina Balina, Helena Goscilo and Mark Lipovetsky. Evanston: Northwestern University Press, 2005, pp. 5–21.

33. Wikipedia. "Soul Eater (Manga)." Available online: https://en.wikipedia.org/wiki/Soul_Eater_(manga) (accessed on 2 March 2016).

34. Wikipedia. "Soul Eater (Anime)." Available online: https://en.wikipedia.org/wiki/List_of_Soul_Eater_episodes (accessed on 2 March 2016).

35. Rayna Denison. "Anime Fandom and the Liminal Spaces between Fan Creativity and Piracy." *International Journal of Cultural Studies* 14 (2011): 449–66.

36. Soul Eaterpedia Wiki. "Baba Yaga Castle." Available online: http://souleater.wikia.com/wiki/Baba_Yaga_Castle (accessed on 2 March 2016).

37. Susan J. Napier. *Anime: From Akira to Howl's Moving Castle.* New York: Palgrave, 2005.

38. *Soul Eater Not!* Directed by Masakazu Hashimoto. Written by Masakazu Hashimoto. Anime, TV Tokyo, 2014.

39. Soul Eaterpedia Wiki. "Episode 51." Available online: http://souleater.wikia.com/wiki/Episode_51 (accessed on 5 March 2016).

40. Cristina Bacchilega, and John Rieder. "Mixing It Up: Generic Complexity and Gender Ideology in Early Twenty-first Century Fairy Tale Films." In *Fairy Tale Films: Visions of Ambiguity.* Edited by Pauline Greenhill and Sidney Eve Matrix. Logan: Utah State University Press, 2010, pp. 23–41.

41. *Lost Girl.* "Mirror, Mirror." Season 2. Episode 4. Directed by Steve DiMarco. Written by Michelle Lovretta, Steve Cochrane and Emily Andras. Showcase, 2010.

42. Elliott Oring. "Folk Narrative." In *Folk Groups and Folklore Genres.* Edited by Elliott Oring. Logan: Utah State University Press, 1986, pp. 121–45.

43. Wiki. "Lost Girl: Creatures." Available online: http://lostgirl.wikia.com/wiki/Creatures (accessed on 5 March 2016).

44. Snopes. "Bloody Mary." Available online: http://www.snopes.com/horrors/ghosts/bloodymary.asp (accessed on 11 March 2016).

45. Lost Girl Wiki. "Season Five." Available online: http://lostgirl.wikia.com/wiki/Season_5 (accessed on 11 March 2016).

46. Claudia Schwabe. "Getting Real with Fairy Tales: Magic Realism in *Grimm* and *Once Upon a Time.*" In *Channeling Wonder: Fairy Tales on Television.* Edited by Pauline Greenhill and Jill Terry Rudy. Detroit: Wayne State University Press, 2014, pp. 294–315.

47. AfterEllen. "Lost Girl Season Five Recap." Available online: http://www.afterellen.com/tv/459619-lost-girl-recap-5--16-fae-thee-well (accessed on 7 March 2016).

48. SpoilerTV. "Lost Girl Series Finale Poll." Available online: http://www.spoilertv.com/2015/10/poll-what-did-you-think-of-lost-girl_26.html (accessed on 7 March 2016).

49. Jason Mittell. *Complex TV: The Poetics of Contemporary Television Storytelling.* New York: New York University Press, 2015.

50. *Breaking Bad.* Created by Vince Gillian. AMC Network, 2008.

51. *The Wire.* Created by David Simon. HBO, 2002.

52. *The Rocky and Bullwinkle Show: Fractured Fairy Tales.* Created by Jay Ward, Alex Anderson and Bill Scott. American Broadcast Company, 1959; National Broadcast Company, 1961.

53. *Arthur.* Directed by George Bailey. Public Broadcasting System, 1996.

54. *Scooby Doo! Mystery Incorporated.* Created by Joe Ruby and Ken Spears. Cartoon Network, 2010.

55. Jan Brunvand. "Truth Claims in Urban Legends." In *Encyclopedia of Urban Legends*, 2nd ed. Edited by Jan Brunvand. Santa Barbara: ABC-CLIO, 2012.

56. Jan Brunvand. *The Vanishing Hitchhiker: American Urban Legends and Their Meanings*. New York: Norton, 1981.

57. Scoobypedia. "The House of the Nightmare Witch." Available online: http://scoobydoo.wikia.com/wiki/The_House_of_the_Nightmare_Witch (accessed on 7 March 2016).

58. *Be Cool, Scooby Doo!* Created by Joe Ruby and Ken Spears. Cartoon Network, 2015.

59. John G. Cawelti. "The Concept of Formula in the Study of Popular Literature." In *Popular Culture Theory and Methodology*. Edited by Harold E. Hinds, Jr., Marilyn F. Motz and Angela M. S. Nelson. Madison: University of Wisconsin Popular Press, 2006, pp. 183–91.

60. David N. Feldman. "Formalism and Popular Culture." In *Popular Culture Theory and Methodology*. Edited by Harold E. Hinds, Jr., Marilyn F. Motz and Angela M. S. Nelson. Madison: University of Wisconsin Popular Press, 2006, pp. 192–213.

61. Katherine J. Roberts. "Once Upon a Bench: Rule under the Fairy Tale." *Yale Journal of Law and the Humanities* 13 (2001): 497–529.

62. *Maleficent*. Directed by Robert Stromberg. Written by Linda Woolverton. Walt Disney Pictures, 2014.

63. Mary Poovey. "'My Hideous Progeny': The Lady and the Monster." In *Frankenstein*, Norton Critical ed. Edited by J. Paul Hunter. New York: Norton, 1996, pp. 251–61.

64. Pat Gill. "The Monstrous Years: Teens, Slasher Films, and the Family." *Journal of Film and Video* 54 (2002): 16–30.

65. *Buffy the Vampire Slayer*. Directed by Fran Rubel Kuzui. Written by Joss Whedon. 20th Century Fox, 1992.

66. David Bianculli. "*Fresh Air* Interview with Joss Whedon: From NPR, *Fresh Air*, 9 May 2000." In *Joss Whedon: Conversations*. Edited by David Lavery and Cynthia Burkhead. Jackson: University of Mississippi Press, 2011, pp. 3–13.

67. Paul K. Piff, Matthew Feinberg, Pia Dietze, Daniel M. Stancato, and Dacher Keltner. "Awe, the Small Self, and Prosocial Behavior." *Journal of Personality and Social Psychology* 108 (2015): 883–99.

68. William A. Wilson. "Afterword: It All Depends on What You Mean by Family." *Southern Folklore* 51 (1994): 73–76.

Becoming the Labyrinth: Negotiating Magical Space and Identity in *Puella Magi Madoka Magica*

Sara Cleto and Erin Kathleen Bahl

Abstract: In the magical girl anime series *Puella Magi Madoka Magica*, middle-school girls receive the power and responsibility to fight witches in exchange for making a wish. The series has connections to many different genres and narrative traditions within the realm of folkloristics. However, the folkloric genre most relevant to the ethos and aesthetics of *Madoka* is that of the fairy tale. Drawing on Bill Ellis's concept of "fairy-telling" and scholarship on new media composition, in this paper we seek to investigate labyrinths as acts of embodied composing—not lairs of evil or destruction but rather creative material memory work that negotiates grief and despair. Many of the series' action sequences unfold in "labyrinths," the magical spaces controlled by witches. By composing a labyrinth, witches can simultaneously reshape their environment and create a powerful statement about identity through personalized performance in narrative spaces that they control. In particular, we argue that both the frameworks of "fairy tale" and "new media" give us useful analytical resources for beginning to make sense of the intricately complex phenomenon of *Madoka*'s labyrinths.

Reprinted from *Humanities*. Cite as: Cleto, S.; Bahl, E.K. Becoming the Labyrinth: Negotiating Magical Space and Identity in *Puella Magi Madoka Magica*. *Humanities* **2016**, *5*, 20.

1. Introduction

In the anime series *Puella Magi Madoka Magica* [1] (hereafter *Madoka*), a granted wish marks not a happily-ever-after ending but rather a complicated beginning. In the first episode, middle-school girl Madoka Kaname meets a cat-like creature named Kyubey[1] who offers to grant her and her friend Sayaka Miki any wish. In exchange, they must make contracts with him and become magical girls in order to fight witches, dangerous supernatural beings who spread curses and discord by mobilizing disruptive magical spaces called "labyrinths." As the storyline progresses,

---

[1] Romanization of Japanese names is never entirely consistent across fan communities; sometimes multiple variations occur and are intensely debated. In this article, we use the versions as they are spelled in the officially released English subtitles.

the girls discover that Kyubey was not transparent with them about the terms of their contracts. Although their wishes are indeed granted and they are given magical powers, magical girls eventually grow disillusioned with their task and succumb to despair, triggering their transformation into witches—meaning that in fighting the witches, they have really been fighting their own destinies all along.

Madoka has connections to many different genres and narrative traditions within the realm of folkloristics. The aesthetics of the labyrinth spaces draw upon the carnivalesque atmosphere of the festival, as do the performances that unfold within them. Figures drawn from historical legends, such as Joan of Arc and Cleopatra, appear in the final episodes of the series and are positioned on a continuum of magical girls, including the series' protagonists, throughout a reimagined history. Even myth is invoked as creation stories are explicitly unraveled and re-written at the series' conclusion. However, the folkloric genre most relevant to the ethos and aesthetics of *Madoka* is that of the fairy tale. Drawing on Bill Ellis's [2] concept of "fairy-telling" and scholarship on new media composition, we seek to investigate labyrinths as acts of embodied composing—not lairs of evil or destruction, but rather creative material memory work that negotiates grief and despair.

2. The Anime

The official *Puella Magi Madoka Magica* storyworld [3] is spread across several kinds of new media genres, including anime, manga, movies, and merchandise, along with numerous unofficial media formats such as fanfiction, fanart, and discussion forums. Our analysis will focus on the *Madoka* anime series, consisting of 12 episodes which originally aired in Japan in 2011 and were released in the U.S. via both online streaming and DVD in 2012 [4,5]. Over the course of the series, Madoka, who is reluctant to make a wish and become a magical girl, and Sayaka meet three girls who have already made contracts: Homura Akemi, Mami Tomoe, and Kyoko Sakura. Though they frequently clash with one another, they form uneasy alliances and battle witches together, but casualties are high. By the last two episodes, only Homura and Madoka remain, prompting Madoka to finally contract with Kyubey and become a magical girl with unique, unprecedented power.

Madoka not only features magical girls but is also an example of the "magical girl" genre of anime, which includes other series such as *Sailor Moon*, *Cardcaptor Sakura*, *Prétear*, and *Princess Tutu*. This series draws from many common elements of the genre, such as: middle-school-aged girls; an apparently average, somewhat inept heroine who reveals or receives magical powers; extended transformation scenes; and color-coded magical state costumes.However, *Madoka* also works within and against the magical girl genre, deliberately interrupting and subverting its conventions [6–8]. For example, Mami, the friendliest and most reliable of the magical girl characters, dies an unexpected and gruesome death during an early witch-battle, marking a distinct tonal shift in the series and shocking early audiences [9–11]. Additionally, the arrival of a small white catlike animal who possesses knowledge of magical powers and frequently appears in the main character's bedroom evokes the guardian-cats Luna and Artemis in the iconic magical girl anime *Sailor Moon* [12]. For the sailor scouts, these animal-like guardians serve as benevolent guides in helping the heroine discover and use her powers. However, Madoka and her friends eventually discover that Kyubey is part of an alien species that harvests the energy from magical girls' degeneration into witches in order to counteract the effects of cosmic entropy. These departures from genre convention draw attention to the question of narrative power: who can determine their own role within the narrative, and who can make their story stick? In a storyworld populated by bodies in flux and multiple timelines, the battle for narrative control and self-determination is paramount.

3. The Labyrinth

Many of the series' action sequences unfold in "labyrinths," magical spaces controlled by witches. Each witch possesses her own labyrinth, a disorienting maze both defensive and offensive—the labyrinth protects a witch's body from unexpected attacks, as a magical girl must survive and navigate the labyrinth before reaching the witch that resides at its center. It is a space in which the witch's will is externalized and made manifest, a personal, performative arena where combat between witch and magical girl takes place. The labyrinths themselves are highlighted by a marked shift in animation style—bold colors, collage-like layers, unusual textures, and erratic movements differentiate labyrinth sequences from the rest of the series, emphasizing their status as magical, otherworldly spaces with their own conventions and realities.

Despite the labyrinths' intensely personal nature, they are also public and confrontational. Although only magical girls can see witches, anyone can wander into a labyrinth, leaving them perpetually open to invasion and infiltration. Each labyrinth is composed of assorted objects and symbols, which vary depending on the personality of the witch that constructs it. In addition to the objects that fill the shifting paths of the labyrinths, each has at its center some kind of arena modeled after a public space. There are concert halls, formal gardens, and makeshift theatres—spaces in which communities traditionally come together for entertainment or celebrations. Labyrinths are personal and public, individual and yet reflective of community needs, echoing the material spectacle of festival[2] in their composition and function.

---

2   For further discussion of folklore and festival, see Noyes's *Fire in the Plaça* [15] and Foster's *Pandemonium and Parade* [16].

While *Madoka*'s labyrinths seem uniquely disruptive, they have precedence in other contemporary fairy-tale and new media narratives. Jim Henson's *Labyrinth* (1986) [13] and Guillermo del Toro's *Pan's Labyrinth* (2006) [14] both feature adolescent female heroines who encounter magical, morally questionable male figures as they pursue their labyrinthine quests. Although neither heroine is responsible for the physical construction of the labyrinth in her respective film, in both cases the young girls' wishes and imaginations play key roles in each labyrinth's creation, a connection that is strengthened in *Madoka*'s witches' labyrinths.

In *Madoka*, the possession and construction of labyrinths is a highly gendered phenomenon. Magical girls and witches are exclusively female. Kyubey explains that his race has specifically targeted adolescent girls because they believe that this population experiences emotions more powerfully than any other demographic that they have encountered. Kyubey and his race exploit the magical girl's emotions and their descent into despair, harvesting the girls' expelled energy for the greater good.

This sharp, gendered demarcation is at odds with other aspects of the series, which seem to self-consciously counter rigid gender binaries. This is perhaps most explicit through the depictions of Madoka's parents. Her mother, Junko, is a high-powered business woman who expertly applies makeup, works late hours, and occasionally comes home drunk. Tomohisa, Madoka's father, appears to be a stay-at-home parent; he cooks, tends to the house and the garden, and fondly takes care of his wife when she is inebriated. Junko and Tomohisa appear to have a very happy marriage; Tomohisa even has an extended conversation with Madoka about how greatly he respects his wife and her choices, even when they appear to be eccentric or unconventional. These roles within the family are foregrounded in the first episode of the series, suggesting the desirability of more flexible gender roles even as the magical girls are forced into rigid identity narratives with predetermined destinies—and thus drawing those destinies into question.

Labyrinths, though still associated with a rigid gender binary (as only girls can create them), can offer another, more individualized form of meaning-making and self-determination. They are nonlinear and often highly disorienting because they are explicitly drawn from disjointed fragments and redeployed as a kind of personality assemblage. However disorienting these labyrinths may be, a complex cohesion underlies their chaotic appearances. In English, a "labyrinth"[3] is distinct from a "maze" insofar as the latter is a space of puzzlement offering multiple pathways, while the former, no matter how circuitous the route, ultimately leads to one destination ([17], p. 23; [18], p. 8). Additionally, in recent times, the practice of

---

[3] Our choice here to focus on the English word "labyrinth" as a translation for the original Japanese 結界, *kekkai*, is based on both the official English subtitled and dubbed anime episodes.

"walking the labyrinth" has gained popularity as a method of spiritual healing and self-integration in both secular and religious contexts [17,19–21]. Both perspectives shed light on how a labyrinth may be viewed as a powerful tool for creating internal cohesion amidst external confusion and disarray. By composing a labyrinth, witches can simultaneously reshape their environment and create a powerful statement about a complex, yet integrated identity through personalized performance in narrative spaces that they control. In particular, we argue that both the frameworks of "fairy tale" and "new media" give us useful analytical resources for beginning to make sense of the intricately complex phenomenon of *Madoka's* labyrinths.

4. Fairy Tales

"Fairy tale" is a contested term, and within fairy-tale studies definitions are frequently revised or redevised. Stith Thompson characterizes these stories as tales "involving a succession of motifs or episodes. [They move] in an unreal world without definite locality or definite creatures and [are] filled with the marvelous. In this never-never land, humble heroes kill adversaries, succeed to kingdoms and marry princesses" ([22], p. 8). More recently, scholars have emphasized the affordances of the fairy tale as a genre over its distinctive contents. Jennifer Schacker and Christine Jones suggest "that the idea of the fairy tale might be better understood as an open-ended, playful way of engaging social and political issues in a form that defies the constraints of realist fiction rather than as a *fixed* discursive form that corresponds to a set of narrative rules" ([23], p. 488). For the purposes of our exploration of fairy-tale space, the classic assessment from J.R.R. Tolkien is particularly apropos, as Tolkien grounds his definition in "the nature of Faërie: the Perilous Realm itself," a magical space in which the marvelous can unfold. For Tolkien, a fairy tale "touches on or uses Faerie, whatever its own main purpose may be: satire, adventure, morality, fantasy. Faerie itself may perhaps most nearly be translated by Magic—but it is magic of a peculiar mood and power" and "the magic itself...must...be taken seriously, neither laughed at nor explained away" ([24], p. 10). In *Madoka* "Faerie" finds a corollary within labyrinths, otherworldly spaces created and deployed by witches. In these magical realms, witches and girls battle for dominance, and magical identities are constructed and performed in ways that would be impossible in realistic or everyday space.

The influence of the Western fairy tale is pervasive within the genre of anime, as well as the related genre of manga. Fairy-tale characters and tropes are taken up and entextualized within new narratives, often with uncanny results as the familiar motifs become strange in their redeployment and ambiguity. Both the fairy tale and the narrative tradition of manga and anime "are ways of opening the participants' minds to the unknown, to asking questions about the way things are, and to tolerating the absence of conclusive answers" ([2], p. 21). The defamiliarization of these stories can result in innovative retellings and reconstructions. As Bill Ellis observes, "Western fairy tales often play an explicit part in these narratives in a form that is less influenced by Western cultural norms. For this reason, elements that are intrinsic to the genre of the fairy tale become more visible when we see how Japanese authors read and reinterpret these narratives, not as all-too-familiar stories but as exotic and novel ways of reimagining universal human dilemmas" ([2], pp. 21–22). Decoupled from the conventions that frequently govern them, these Western fairy-tale tropes can be redeployed to create revisions and new tales informed by the fairy-tale genre but distanced from generic expectations.

Furthermore, the genres of the fairy tale and anime complement each other thematically. Fantasy-based anime frequently emphasizes "the ubiquity of chaos and discord" in "labyrinthine" worlds populated by characters "beset by apparently insurmountable obstacles" ([25], p. 161). Yet, the fairy-tale dimension present in such series "serves to imbue the quest with a tenacious sense of hope. Through the contrast and conflation of a dystopian world and fairy-tale aesthetics, and even fairy-tale optimism, the anime accomplishes a synthesis of reality and fantasy of eerie and, at times, truly disquieting intensity" ([25], p. 161). While not all fairy tales feature happily-ever-after endings, their association with optimism and success persists, and this atmosphere of possibility, even positivity, can contribute much needed levity to those anime (such as *Madoka*) that feature apocalyptic landscapes.

5. New Media

Like "fairy tale," "new media" is a contested term with many possible definitions; in digital media studies, for example, "new media" composing blends into discussions of "multimodal," "multimedia," and "digital" composing [26–28]. In this study, we rely on Wysocki's definition of new media in order to focus on creative expressions that draw attention to (rather than efface) their materiality: for our purposes, "'new media texts' [are] those that have been made by composers who are aware of the range of materialities of texts and who then highlight the materiality...Under this definition, new media texts do not have to be digital; instead, any text that has been designed so that its materiality is not effaced can count as new media" ([29], p. 15). Expanding the concept of "new media" to emphasize materiality over digitality allows us to consider *Madoka* not only in terms of extradiegetic "new media," but also "new media" on the level of diegesis—that is, how the characters within the story use the material resources around them to make meaning in a way that foregrounds the expressive media they use.

From the perspective of the magical girls in *Madoka*, the labyrinths are disorienting, confusing, non-linear, unintelligible, and perilous places—and therefore considered as unproductive and even evil. However, looking at these spaces through the lens of new media rhetoric and composing, we can see how those same ambiguous qualities also offer possibilities for interpretation as creative spaces of learning, discovery, and agential identity composing. For example, these labyrinths in many ways bear resemblances to a *Wunderkammer* (plural *Wunderkammern*), which Delagrange treats at length in her work on visual rhetoric, new media, and embodied composing [30,31]. Delagrange defines *Wunderkammern* as "cabinets or entire rooms in which naturally occurring and man-made artifacts were collected, collated and catalogued" ([31], "Revision"). As stages for arranging, displaying, and engaging curiosities of all kinds, a *Wunderkammer* serves as a space of both material and intellectual engagement; it is "an object-to-think-with that constructs an uncanny bridge between the mental and physical; it engenders wonder, a productive aporia between not-knowing and knowing" ([30], "Mental/Physical"). Likewise, a witch's labyrinth is a collection of objects meaningful to her life and identity in some way, carefully yet confusingly arranged and organized; it is an "uncanny" *aporia*, a space of puzzlement, both strange and familiar all at once ([32], p. 8) that challenges the ordinary sense-making strategies of those who try to navigate it.

As an "object-to-think-with," a labyrinth might additionally be viewed as rhetorical memory-making work enacted via new media objects. Turkle's collection *Evocative Objects* engages objects as "active life presences" with the power to "catalyze self-creation" ([32], p. 9), simultaneously "uncanny" and "rich with creative possibility" ([32], p. 8) in their ability to serve as identity-fashioning resources at key moments in an individual's development. Whittemore notes how the classical rhetorical technique of *ars memoria* employed imagined spaces as memory aids, whether walking through familiar spaces to remember talking points ("walking mnemonic") or observing scenery while sitting in the center of a theater ("memory theater") ([33], p. 6). It is interesting to note, as we will see in our case studies, that the witches' labyrinths foster both kinds of memory-making activities and spaces; the magical girls walk through half-familiar corridors in seeking out the witch, while the witch herself typically sits in the middle of a theater-like space at the center of the labyrinth. Like a *Wunderkammer*, Whittemore observes that these memory-spaces served as "both tools for learning and tools for finding," and comments that the most effective memory organization systems might not be file cabinets but rather "streetscapes and theaters" ([33], p. 6). These perspectives—uncanny spaces, evocative objects, memory-work, and learning through exploration—help us to reframe the witches' labyrinths not as evil spaces of absolute destruction, but as ambiguously, richly creative spaces for crafting identities and working through memories with the help of meaningful objects.

6. New Media Fairy-Telling

In analyzing *Madoka's* labyrinths as creative acts of new media composing, we borrow a term generated by Bill Ellis in his analysis of another magical girl anime (*Princess Tutu*). "Stretching our usual language," Ellis notes, "we could say that *Princess Tutu* is not about fairy tales at all but about *fairy-telling*, the ongoing tradition of generating new versions of old tales and inventing entirely new tales out of bits and pieces of existing ones" ([2], p. 231). Fairy-telling is both a critical and a creative act; one that involves "understanding the cultural grammar that governs fairy-telling and the gender conventions it makes visible, and gaining the skills to create new myths, ones that we can genuinely call our own" ([2], p. 236). In the witches' performances of memory-work—arranging "bits and pieces" of their lives, fairy tales, and the surrounding environment—their labyrinths become new tales, new interpretations of the world, the tellings of which are foregrounded in the hyper-materiality of their expression. In other words, the labyrinths can be viewed as acts of new media fairy-telling.

We apply these frameworks—fairy tale and new media together—to our close readings and analyses of three particularly significant witches' labyrinths that appear in *Madoka*: those of the witches Gertrud, Oktavia von Seckendorff, and Walpurgisnacht. Drawing from Ellis's definition of "fairy-telling" as the ongoing tradition of generating new versions of old tales and inventing entirely new tales out of bits and pieces of existing ones ([2], p. 231) and Wysocki's definition of new media composing as foregrounding a communicative act's materiality [29], we can look at the witches, in making their labyrinths, as powerful composers drawing on material objects from a fairy-tale repertoire and the stories of their lives in an act of creative embodied expression and identity-fashioning memory work.

7. Case Study 1: Gertrud

The first labyrinth to appear in the main timeline[4] belongs to a witch named Gertrud.[5] After an intimidating confrontation with their new classmate Homura, Madoka and Sayaka run from her and stumble into the labyrinth. They are disoriented and do not understand where they are or why their environment is changing so dramatically and rapidly. "Where did the exit go? Where are we?" Sayaka cries as gates and chains erupt into the concrete hallway through which they are running. The hallway quickly disappears behind an overlay of giant butterflies and windows floating unanchored in the air. In alignment with Sayaka's panicked question about the disappearance of the exit, this is a landscape that offers no

---

[4] Homura's magical girl powers include the capacity for time-travel, which she uses again and again in an attempt to save Madoka from death. Her actions create a succession of related timelines in the series. In this article, we have confined our discussion to the main timeline for the sake of clarity.

[5] The name Gertrud does not appear in the 12-episode television series, but in the extended media associated with the *Madoka* world more broadly, she has been identified through the rune-like characters that appear in her labyrinth. We will refer to this witch as Gertrud for clarity.

avenue of escape—the chains and gates suggest entrapment and claustrophobia, and the windows are not only too high to reach but they are empty, revealing the landscape behind them instead of offering an exit into another space. As they try to make sense of their surroundings, with still more disconnected images flashing by, Madoka exclaims, "There's something wrong—the path keeps changing!" The name "labyrinth" is apt—like *Wunderkammern*, these are not spaces with clear trajectories, but rather dynamic, circuitous spaces that actively direct the traveler's movements rather than being passively moved through themselves.

In addition to more recognizable images and motifs including briars and roses—symbols intrinsic to many classic European fairy tales including Sleeping Beauty and Beauty and the Beast—there is a profusion of images that resist recognition or interpretation. Chief among these are animate cotton balls with thick black mustaches that laugh and dance over a garden bed, behind the roses and briars, and then dart unmoored across the screen before gathering around Madoka and Sayaka and chanting at them. The words of their chant are in untranslated German, unintended to render legible meaning for Japanese or English audiences. Even if the production company deliberately chose not to subtitle or dub the chanted words, in the midst of a capably, clearly dubbed series, the effect is of opaqueness and unintelligibility. As the chanting grows louder, the cotton-ball faces suddenly bare their teeth, and slashing scissors appear among the convulsing chains, heightening the threat of danger, and even dismemberment.

In the midst of this crescendo of sound and visual threat, the chains begin to break and fall to the ground, and a bright light surrounds the girls. From a newly made, clearly marked path, another magical girl, Mami, appears, holding her soul gem[6], which emanates a bright, clear light, slicing through the chaos of the labyrinth and exerting creative control over its materials. As the girls greet each other, Gertrud's labyrinth, which has been subdued by Mami's appearance, begins to revive and thrash around the girls with renewed energy, reestablishing narrative dominance over her space. Mami promptly steps away from the other girls and engages her transformation sequence, in which her school uniform is replaced by her customized magical girl costume. At the end of her transformation, Mami stands on top of a large pile of Gertrud's accumulated objects, physically dominating the space. From this vantage point, she materializes a massive array of guns and fires them towards the heart of the labyrinth, forcing Gertrud to retreat, along with her labyrinth. The other-world of the labyrinth wavers and disappears, leaving the girls once more in the bare hallway in which the encounter began.

---

[6] A soul gem is the source of a magical girl's power. When it darkens from power loss or its owner's grief, a magical girl transforms into a witch.

The next day, the girls encounter the same labyrinth—and this time, the witch herself as well. The witch has a head like a drooping rosebush, with a gelatinous body, butterfly wings, and roses scattered below her. As she and Mami battle, the witch ensnares her in a thick cord and dangles her high above her head. However, hyper-conscious of her role as a performer and her audience, Mami assures Madoka and Sayaka that she is fine, and laughs that "I can't let myself look uncool in front of my magical girl trainees." As the witch rushes at her, brandishing thorns and snapping scissors, golden ribbons rise from Mami's bulletholes and ensnare the witch in a tangle of yellow threads. While the witch struggles to free herself, Mami turns a swirling ribbon into an enormous gun and shoots her; the witch disappears in a swirl of golden light. Butterflies rise into the air as Mami drops to the ground with a bow, and the labyrinth evaporates around them. As Gertrud collapses, Mami punctuates her performance by materializing a cup of tea and calmly sipping from it. In defeating the witch, Mami literally takes her place at the center of the stage; her power to shape the story has prevailed, and the world crafted by the witch dissolves into nothingness.

The composition of Gertrud's labyrinth, despite its seeming chaos, draws heavily upon fairy-tale motifs from Beauty and the Beast (ATU 425), Rapunzel (ATU 310), and most particularly Sleeping Beauty[7] (ATU 410) [35]. Roses and gardening paraphernalia abound; the flowers and their briars appear again and again, in addition to the sinister cotton-plant faces, abundant butterflies, flowers, and tilled garden rows, and Gertrud's appearance as a vaguely humanoid rose bush with butterfly wings in her garden-arena heightens this impression. The cotton balls heighten a connection to Sleeping Beauty tales, as they are materials associated with spinning and spinning wheels. Furthermore, imagery of restraint and enclosure echo the iconic briars that surround Sleeping Beauty's castle in many famous versions of the tale [36,37]; the flowers and other garden objects are frequently crossed or intermingled with actual briars, along with chains, gates, and other obstructions. Gertrud decontextualizes and recombines these elements to mobilize her attacks on the magical girls that enter her domain, wielding roses and butterflies against Mami's guns in an act of creative fairy-telling.

Despite these gestures at meaning-making, Gertrud and her chosen objects are fundamentally opaque to her audiences—both the magical girls and the viewers of the anime. Gertrud's labyrinth is particularly resistant to interpretation because no information is provided about the witch that constructed it, the magical girl that she once was, or how these objects relate to her own narrative. While the other two case

---

[7]   For further discussion of Sleeping Beauty in Japan, see Jorgensen and Warman's "Molding Messages: Analyzing the Reworking of 'Sleeping Beauty' in *Grimm's Fairy Tale Classics* and *Dollhouse*" [34].

studies we examine in this article are discussed explicitly among characters within the diegetic world, Gertrud's space is an enigma that surfaces without warning, explanation, or backstory. The magical girls' reactions—their disgust with Gertrud's reimagined body and their confusion in the face of her labyrinth—are foregrounded, and so the anime's audience experiences disorientation with them. However, as the series progresses, context and backstory provide clues to reading a labyrinth, as well as insight into the personalities and the creativity that construct them.

8. Case Study 2: Oktavia

Because Sayaka's storyline gradually unfolds over the course of the series, the audience is able to interpret her labyrinth as a witch in the context of her memories and the symbols meaningful to her. The labyrinths are too complex to afford a one-to-one correlation between symbol and interpretation; their objects' richness lies in their ambiguity and ability to evoke rather than signify absolutely. Instead, we suggest that awareness of her personality and backstory allow a degree of transparency that was not accessible for Gertrud or the other witches that precede Sayaka's transformation.

When Kyoko finds her, Sayaka sits alone on a bench in a darkened train station. After an accelerating disenchantment with her magical girlhood and increasing dissatisfaction with her personal life, Sakaya is overcome by despair and transforms from a magical girl to a witch. As Kyoko looks on in horror, Sayaka's physical body falls into the emergent labyrinth, and the train station transforms into an ocean scene, crossed with trains, tracks, and flying wheels, and punctuated with staves and music notes. At the center of this chaos is a witch, identified by flashing rune-like letters as Oktavia von Seckendorff. The looming figure wears a dark blue cloak reminiscent of Sayaka's blue magical girl cape, with a pink bow, ornate ruff, and loudspeaker-like helmet; she has a brightly colored mermaid tail and is seated upon an array of knightly pennants. The remaining magical girls take Sayaka's vacant human body and flee the labyrinth, unwilling to harm their friend in her witch form.

In an attempt to save Sayaka, Kyoko and Madoka reenter her labyrinth, which first appears as a quiet brick hallway lined with rune-scripted concert posters. Deeper in, the next hallway is more ornate, with red-carpeted floors, gold-adorned pillars, and round glass screens playing hazy images from Sayaka's memories. Suddenly, the doors snap shut behind them; the screens go black, and Kyoko warns, "She knows we're here! She's coming!" As with Gertrud's labyrinth, the witch's approach is signaled not by any motion on the part of the magical girls, but rather by the entire labyrinth rushing toward them as a series of doors opening up into a spacious concert hall, emphasizing the collapse of distinction between witch and labyrinth, narrative and performance. The hall is lined from floor to ceiling with red seats; off to one side, the silhouette of a conductor directs an orchestra—completely comprised of violinists—with inexorable regularity. At the center of the hall is Oktavia, swaying from side to side in time with the orchestra, sword raised like a baton. The train imagery returns when the girls approach her; as the witch raises her sword, spinning train wheels (both metallic and musical) appear and loom threateningly above Kyoko and Madoka. Madoka is protected by Kyoko's barrier, but the witch circles around the hall, hurling wheels at the magical girl. Although the witch carries a sword, she uses it to direct the wheels rather than to fight with the blade; her will is equally materialized through her body and her assembled labyrinth.

In viewing the labyrinth as an act of creative expression, as a material network through which the witch's identity is distributed, Oktavia composes her labyrinth from elements clearly related to her own memories. The train imagery, for example, evokes a key location from her transition to despair; it was a conversation she overheard on a train that made her question and ultimately reject her fight to protect humanity. In particular, music plays a key role in relation to Kyosuke, the boy she loves. Sayaka becomes a magical girl to help him; her wish is for his hand to be healed after an injury so that he could play violin again. However, as in life, she remains on the edge of the music; in her labyrinth, she places herself in an ambiguous role between conductor and audience. Although she clearly orchestrates the entire scene, at the same time she is removed from the orchestra and even the conductor figurehead, a listener rather than a musician herself. The labyrinth expresses an active power over music that she never possessed in life; even without a violin in hand, the performance is still very much her own.

Because two separate incarnations of Oktavia's labyrinth are depicted in the series, they can be understood as two iterations of the same narrative act. The same elements, particularly train tracks, wheels, and music notes, are drawn from the witch's memory and recast across different landscapes within the labyrinth. In this sense, the witch's creation/performance of each labyrinth echoes the tension between continuity and change that govern the (re)telling of a fairy tale, during which some elements remain consistent while others adapt based on changing factors like audience, context, and locale ([2], p. 233). The elements that Oktavia uses to construct her labyrinth are drawn from her memories as well as from fairy-tale tropes, and she remixes these pieces to create multiple versions of her own memory-narrative.

Between the oceanic theme that resurfaces across different incarnations of the labyrinth, Oktavia's mermaid tail, bodies in flux, unrequited love, and an emphasis on music, the fairy tale of "The Little Mermaid" serves as a useful intertext for decoding this labyrinth. Written by Hans Christian Andersen [38], and further popularized by Disney with their cinematic retelling [39], the fairy tale has been recently revitalized in Japan with Hayao Miyazaki's film adaptation *Ponyo* [40]. The motifs from the fairy tale resurface disjointedly, echoing across Oktavia's body and the labyrinthine landscape. Her memories of the boy are given shape by figures within the labyrinth as well as the orchestra comprised only of his chosen instrument. Within her labyrinth, Oktavia uses the affordances of new media fairy-telling to reimagine the boy she loves and to recast their relationship through the material fragments of a familiar tale. In this way, remembrance and creative storytelling intersect to frame a space in which Oktavia can grieve and reestablish narrative control over her story.

9. Case Study 3: Walpurgisnacht

The final labyrinth we wish to examine is that of the witch Walpurgisnacht[8], the crucial point around which the entire series has circled. The series actually begins with an encounter with Walpurgisnacht, although only her silhouette and the pieces of her labyrinth are pictured without any explanation. It is not until episode ten, when the multiple timelines are revealed and the same images are repeated, that the audience recognizes Walpurgisnacht and realizes the extent to which her presence has shaped the narrative and the vast scope of her compositional power. Unlike the other labyrinths encountered thus far, the witch Walpurgisnacht does not simply incorporate pieces of the "real world" into the creation of her magical labyrinth space. Rather, she is so powerful as to project her labyrinth over the entire city, blurring the lines between real and magical worlds beyond distinction.

Because Walpurgisnacht's labyrinth interrupts the structural integrity of the real world, the city's inhabitants perceive her appearance as a series of natural disasters and retreat to evacuation shelters. Homura, the last surviving magical girl, stands alone looking out over the empty streets. Following a festival procession of fantastic creatures, lacy curtains part and ornate numbers count down from five to one, heightening the anticipation of a spectacle just about to begin. In many ways, though, the spectacle has long been underway; the same lacy curtains, which resemble Walpurgisnacht's skirt, opens the *Madoka* series at the beginning of the very first episode, implying that the direction of the narrative has been under Walpurgisnacht's control all along.

Like Gertrud, Oktavia, and the other witches, Walpurgisnacht's body is composite. She has the most humanoid body—rather than mobilizing rosebushes or animal bodies to mimic a human form, Walpurgisnacht has the appearance of a woman. She wears an elaborate, blue gown with exaggerated bell sleeves and a cascading, tiered skirt. On her head sits a formal headdress reminiscent of medieval European nobility; it tapers to two sharp points, suggesting horns or a crown. Her face possesses prominent red lips and teeth but no other discernible features. Her back and limbs are long and straight, suggesting a regal bearing. She resembles

---

[8]   In Germanic folklore, "Walpurgisnacht" is a night for a witches' gathering.

nothing so much as an evil queen, a figure popularized most by Snow White tales (ATU 709) [35], particularly the Grimms' version [30]. Appropriately, Snow White focuses on intergenerational conflicts between women, which might be mapped onto the struggle between the youthful magical girls and the more experienced witches. Walpurgisnacht's headdress and queenly, but monstrous, appearance also suggests a connection to the villain of another iconic sleeping maiden fairy tale, Sleeping Beauty—particularly her incarnations in Disney's films *Sleeping Beauty* (1959) [41] and *Maleficent* (2014) [42] (though the latter was released several years after *Madoka* aired). In these versions, the witch-like fairy wears a headdress with two sharp, prominent points shaped to resemble horns—and in *Maleficent*, she is revealed to actually possess horns, which the headdress later envelops. Walpugisnacht's resemblance to magically powerful, morally questionable fairy-tale queens establishes the scope of her ability, and imbues the stakes of the magical girls' fight against the witch with fairy-tale wonder and weight.

Despite her resemblance to these familiar fairy-tale figures, Walpurgisnacht's appearance is uniquely uncanny. Her torso rests not on legs but on a giant stack of gears that fits beneath her skirts. She hovers above the cityscape, her humanoid body inverted, her head tilted towards the ground. She occasionally emits eerie, high-pitched laughter, particularly when Homura attacks her with an incredible barrage of explosives. Half humanoid, half machine, Walpurgisnacht utilizes fairy-telling fragmentation to assemble a body and labyrinth that speak to multiple discourses of material and narrative power. Walpurgisnacht is by far the most powerful witch yet encountered in the series: instead of hiding within a labyrinth, she projects her will and personality onto the world around her, dovetailing with the fairy-tale motifs of feminine power that she has reappropriated. While the preceding witches in the series challenged the demarcations between body and labyrinthine materials, reality and labyrinth-space, Walpurgisnacht shatters the boundaries as she imposes her physical body and her mental desires into and onto everyday reality. Her resemblance to recognizable fairy-tale witches/fairies heightens the perception of her ability to interrupt orderly hierarchies and to threaten established discourses of meaning-making through her power to re-compose the world into her own labyrinth.

10. Discussion: Composing and Telling

The power to compose the world ultimately does not belong to Walpurgisnacht, however, but to Madoka. In order to save Homura from an endless cycle of irresolvable conflict, and all magical girls from becoming witches, she makes a wish to literally rewrite the laws of the universe: to erase all witches before they are born by taking all magical girls' despair upon herself—and thus erasing herself from the normal plane of existence altogether as she is undone by her own wish. We see the effect of her wish in undoing Walpurgisnacht; as the laughing witch floats through the city, debris still strewn across the skies and Madoka's pink arrows raining down around her, she starts to disintegrate piece by piece until only her gear half remains. By the time Homura returns to the "present" timeline, the witch's presence has been entirely erased.

From the angles of fairy-telling and new media composing, we can start to see the witches and their labyrinths in a new light. The witches are clearly dangerous, with the potential for considerable destruction—yet at their core they are not evil monsters, but rather grieving young women. Instead of insidious lairs, we might look at the labyrinths as creative attempts at healing, sense-making, and identity-fashioning in the midst of despair. This is not a passive despair, a helpless grief. It has a life, power, and vitality of its own, taking pieces of memory and rearranging them in combination with fairy tales and everyday objects—a grief that has given up so thoroughly on the old world that it creates a new one instead out of the shards and sparks of mourning. For the witches, their role in Kyubey's plans are complete; once they have completed the transformation, Kyubey has no further need for them, apart from serving as enemies for future magical girls, and they are narratively free to compose their own stories via their labyrinths without any apparent need of any further sustenance apart from their own powers.

Herein lies the paradox. Madoka wants to save magical girls from despair and hatred; however, following her universe-shattering wish, when magical girls exhaust their power or fall into despair there is still no hope of healing. They are simply erased, body and soul, as Mami explains: "Before the hope we wished for summons an equivalent amount of misfortune, we have no choice but to vanish from this world." As witches, the girls had power, creativity, individual expression, and embodiment in the midst of their despair, the power to shape the world around them with their assembled story-worlds; with Madoka's new system, however, even that ambiguous power and creativity is denied them, and they are literally wiped out of existence. In taking the magical girls' despair upon herself, Madoka has not saved them; she has trapped them further by ensuring their complete erasure the moment hope or magic fails, and sapping all creative embodied power from their grief. The cycle continues, there is no redemption, and the curses have merely taken a different form—what has been lost, though, are the power, material bodies, and individual creativity of the witches who were once magical girls. We do not suggest that the witches are unambiguously good—after all, their labyrinths are extremely destructive intrusions into the real-world cityscape, and the curses that they spread result in contagious despair and even death for those who encounter them. But we do wish to foreground the creative potential of their labyrinths, as well as the narrative possibilities that they can present.

Madoka's vision of a better world takes away the witches' feelings of despair, but erases the magical girls entirely in the process. Rather than saving them, she leaves them with even less agency; their ability to feel and exist is taken away altogether. We might use Cornell's three minimum qualifications of individuation, as applied by Fleckenstein ([43], pp. 243–44) to new media composing, in order to critique this ending. A legal ethicist, Cornell posits that laws working towards greatest agency for all individuals involved (especially women) must meet at least three criteria: bodily integrity; access to symbol systems; and protection of the imaginary domain, which she defines as "the space of the 'as if' in which we imagine who we might be if we made ourselves our own end and claimed ourselves as our own person" ([43], quoted p. 244). Madoka's new universe fails these three criteria through the complete erasure of magical girl subjects. Conversely, even in their despair, the witches maintain bodily integrity through continued physical existence (and even an expanded existence, in considering the labyrinths as extensions of themselves); they have rich symbolic access to "develop and explore a robust matrix of personae" in the act of "renarrating and resymbolizing" themselves ([43], p. 244); and they are able to inhabit a space of self-reimagining and refashioning within their labyrinths as protected imaginary domains. For all their other complicated resonances, from this perspective the labyrinths can be seen as—uncanny, disorienting, sinister, but also liberatory—spaces of fairy-telling and new media composing.

11. Conclusions

Just as *Madoka* deliberately subverts the magical girl genre, so might it also deliberately encourage us to read against the grain of its own ending—to be a magical girl, without the ability to experience the full range of human emotions, good and bad, may be temporarily empowering but ultimately leads to the total erasure of the self, both body and soul. Ellis notes that in Japanese fairy tales, powerful women were frequently portrayed as monsters such as mountain ogres—kin, in a sense, to the witches and evil queens of Western fairy tales ([2], p. 222). In this light, perhaps the ultimate evil is not to become a witch—grieving and beyond the bounds of normal human society, but still embodied and powerful—but rather to be a magical girl—destined for complete erasure once her magic runs out. Donna Haraway claims that it is better to be a cyborg than a goddess ([44], p. 46); in the end, perhaps it is better to become a labyrinth rather than disappear as a magical girl.

Author Contributions: Sara Cleto and Erin Bahl developed concepts, researched secondary materials, and wrote the article in equal parts. Sara Cleto contributed the sections on fairy tales, while Erin Bahl contributed the sections on new media, but the article was a collaborative process.

Conflicts of Interest: The authors declare no conflict of interest.

Abbreviations

Madoka   Refers to the anime series *Puella Magi Madoka Magica*

References

1. *Puella Magi Madoka Magica*. Directed by Akiyuki Shinbo. Tokyo: Prod. Shaft and Aniplex, 2011.

2. Bill Ellis. "The Fairy-telling Craft of *Princess Tutu*: Metacommentary and the Folkloresque." In *The Folkloresque: Reframing Folklore in a Popular Culture World*. Edited by Michael Dylan Foster and Jeffrey A. Tolbert. Logan: Utah State University Press, 2016, pp. 221–40.

3. Marie-Laure Ryan, and Jan-Noël Thon. *Storyworlds across Media: Toward a Media-Conscious Narratology*. Lincoln: University of Nebraska Press, 2014.

4. Anime News Network. "Crackle, Hulu Also Stream Puella Magi Madoka Magica Anime." *Anime News Network*, 15 February 2012. Available online: http://www.animenewsnetwork.com/news/2012-02-15/crackle-hulu-also-stream-puella-magi-madoka-magica-anime (accessed on 6 February 2016).

5. Anime News Network. "Madoka Magica to Get English BDs Starting February 14 (Updated)." *Anime News Network*, 14 October 2011. Available online: http://www.animenewsnetwork.com/news/2011-10-14/ madoka-magica-to-get-english-bds-starting-february-14 (accessed on 6 February 2016).

6. Did You Know Anime. "Puella Magi Madoka Magica—Did You Know Anime? Feat. Kinenz." *YouTube*, 7 May 2015. Available online: https://www.youtube.com/watch?v=9ArGWxjYCnA (accessed on 6 February 2016).

7. Liz Ohanesian. "How Puella Magi Madoka Magica Shatters Anime Stereotypes." *LA Weekly.com*, 22 October 2012. Available online: http://www.laweekly.com/arts/how-puella-magi-madoka-magica- shatters-anime-stereotypes-2373077 (accessed on 6 February 2016).

8. Erinn Velez. "Breaking the Mold: *Puella Magi Madoka Magica* Flips the Magical Girl Genre On Its Ear." *PopCults.com*, 9 March 2013. Available online: http://www.popcults.com/puella-magi-madoka-magica- anime-review/ (accessed on 6 February 2016).

9. Tsuyoshi Hariyoshi. "Various Reactions to Mami's Death in Madoka." *YouTube*, 18 July 2011. Available online: https://www.youtube.com/watch?v=RJcJkstDReQ (accessed on 6 February 2016).

10. Panderarchive. "An Average Reaction to Madoka: Episode 3." *YouTube*, 12 February 2013. Available online: https://www.youtube.com/watch?v=E5Fliy0kEQ8 (accessed on 6 February 2016).

11. Time Keeper. "Madoka Magica—Episode 3 Reaction Compilation." *YouTube*, 26 July 2015. Available online: https://www.youtube.com/watch?v=AYIgv5OP9X0 (accessed on 6 February 2016).

12. *Pretty Soldier Sailor Moon*. Directed by Junichi Sato. Tokyo: Toei Animation, 1992–1993.

13. *Labyrinth*. Directed by Jim Henson. Dayton: Henson Associates, Inc. and Lucasfilm Ltd., 1986.

14. *Pan's Labyrinth*. Directed by Guillermo del Toro. Sherman Oaks: Esperanto Films, 2006.

15. Dorothy Noyes. *Fire in the Plaça: Catalan Festival Politics after Franco*. Philadelphia: University of Pennsylvania Press, 2003.

16. Michael Dylan Foster. *Pandemonium and Parade: Japanese Monsters and the Culture of Yokai*. Berkeley: University of California Press, 2008.

17. Vanessa Compton. "Labyrinths in the Landscape: A Primer." *Landscapes/Paysages* 16 (2014): 23–25.

18. Jeff Saward. *Magical Paths: Labyrinths and Mazes in the 21st Century*. London: Mitchell Beazley, 2002.

19. Maddy Cunningham. *Integrating Spirituality in Clinical Social Work Practice: Walking the Labyrinth*. New York: Pearson Press, 2011.

20. Lizzie Hopthrow. "Labyrinth: Reclaiming an ancient spiritual tool for a modern healthcare setting." *Journal of Holistic Healthcare* 10 (2013): 38–41.

21. Sally Welch. *Walking the Labyrinth: A Spiritual and Practical Guide*. London: Canterbury Press, 2010.

22. Stith Thompson. *The Folktale*. Berkeley: University of California Press, 1977.

23. Jennifer Schacker, and Christine Jones. "Introduction: How to read the critical essays." In *Marvelous Transformations: An Anthology of Fairy Tales and Contemporary Critical Perspectives*. Edited by Jennifer Schacker and Christine Jones. New York: Broadview Press, 2013, pp. 485–92.

24. John Ronald Reuel Tolkien. "On Fairy Stories." In *The Tolkien Reader*. New York: Ballantine Books, 1966, pp. 3–84.

25. Dani Cavallaro. *The Fairy Tale and Anime: Traditional Themes, Images and Symbols at Play on Screen*. London: McFarland & Company, Inc., 2011.

26. Claire Lauer. "What's in a name? The Anatomy of Defining New/Multi/Modal/Digital/Media Texts." *Kairos: A Journal of Rhetoric, Technology, and Pedagogy*, 2012. Available online: http://kairos.techn orhetoric.net/17.1/ (accessed on 20 February 2016).

27. Lev Manovich. *The Language of New Media*. Cambridge: Massachussetts Institute of Technology, 2001.

28. Jody Shipka. *Toward a Composition Made Whole*. Pittsburgh: University of Pittsburgh Press, 2011.

29. Anne Frances Wysocki. "Opening New Media to Writing: Openings and Justifications." In *Writing New Media: Theory and Applications for Expanding the Teaching of Composition*. Edited by Anne Frances Wysocki, Johndan Johnson-Eilola, Cynthia L. Selfe and Geoffrey Sirc. Logan: Utah State University Press, 2004, pp. 1–42.

30. Susan Delagrange. "*Wunderkammer*, Cornell, and the Visual Canon of Arrangement." *Kairos: A Journal of Rhetoric, Technology, and Pedagogy*, 2009. Available online: http://kairos.technorhetoric.net/13.2/topoi/ delagrange/ (accessed on 20 February 2016).

31. Susan Delagrange. "When Revision is Redesign: Key Questions for Digital Scholarship." *Kairos: A Journal of Rhetoric, Technology, and Pedagogy*, 2009. Available online: http://kairos.technorhetoric.net/ 14.1/inventio/delagrange/ (accessed on 20 February 2016).

32. Sherry Turkle. "Introduction: The Things That Matter." In *Evocative Objects: Things We Think With*. Edited by Sherry Turkle. Cambridge: Massachusetts Institute of Technology, 2007, pp. 3–10.

33. Stewart Whittemore. "Finding and learning: Exploring the information management practices of a technical communicator." Paper presented at IEEE International Professional Communication Conference, Waikiki, HI, USA, 19–22 July 2009, pp. 1–7. Available online: http://ieeexplore.ieee.org/xpl/articleDetails. jsp?arnumber=5208677 (accessed on 20 February 2016).

34. Jeana Jorgensen, and Brittany Warman. "Molding Messages: Analyzing the Reworking of 'Sleeping Beauty' in *Grimm's Fairy Tale Classics* and *Dollhouse*." In *Channeling Wonder: Fairy Tales on Television*. Edited by Pauline Greenhill and Jill Terry Rudy. Detroit: Wayne State University Press, 2014, pp. 144–62.

35. Antti Arne, Stith Thompson, and Hans-Jörg Uther. *The Types of International Folktales. A Classification and Bibliography*. Helsinki: Finnish Academy of Science and Letters, 2011.

36. Charles Perrault. *The Complete Fairy Tales in Verse and Prose*. Translated by Stanley Appelbaum Mineola. New York: Dover Publications, 2002.

37. Jakob Grimm, and Wilhelm Grimm. *Children's and Household Tales*. Edited by Ken Mondschein. San Diego: Canterbury Classics, 2011.

38. Hans Christian Andersen. *The Complete Fairy Tales and Stories*. Translated by Erik Christian Haugaard. New York: Random House, 1983.

39. *The Little Mermaid*. Directed by Ron Clements and John Musker. Burbank: Walt Disney Pictures, 1989.

40. *Ponyo*. Directed by Hayao Miyazaki. Tokyo: Studio Ghibli, 2008.

41. *Sleeping Beauty*. Directed by Clyde Geronimi. Burbank: Disney, 1959.

42. *Maleficent*. Directed by Robert Stromberg. Burbank: Disney, 2014.

43. Kristie Fleckenstein. "Affording New Media: Individuation, Imagination, and the Hope of Change." In *Composing (Media)=Composing (Embodiment): Bodies, Technologies, Writing, the Teaching of Writing*. Edited by Kristin L. Arola and Anne Frances Wysocki. Boulder: University of Boulder Press, 2012, pp. 239–58.

44. Donna Haraway. "A Manifesto for Cyborgs: Science, Technology, and Socialist Feminism in the 1980s." In *The Donna Haraway Reader*. New York: Routledge, 2004, pp. 7–46.

"I Am the Wolf: Queering 'Little Red Riding Hood' and 'Snow White and Rose Red' in the Television Show *Once Upon a Time*"

Brittany Warman

Abstract: In season one, episode 15 of the television show *Once Upon a Time*, viewers are given a glimpse into the history of Ruby/Red, the series' version of Red Riding Hood. The episode reveals that, contrary to most oral and written versions of the ATU 333 tale, Red herself *is* the wolf: a werewolf who must wear an enchanted red cloak in order to keep from turning into a monster. The episode also features the beginnings of the close friendship between Red and Snow White. The sisterly bond that quickly forms between the two women, combined with the striking images of their respective red and white cloaks, easily calls to mind a less familiar fairy tale not explicitly referenced in the series: "Snow White and Rose Red" (ATU 426). Taking queer readings of this text as starting points, I argue that this allusion complicates the bond between the two women, opening up space for a compelling reading of Red's werewolf nature as a coded depiction of her then latent but later confirmed bisexuality.

Reprinted from *Humanities*. Cite as: Warman, B. "I Am the Wolf: Queering 'Little Red Riding Hood' and 'Snow White and Rose Red' in the Television Show *Once Upon a Time*". *Humanities* **2016**, 5, 41.

1. Introduction

The first season of the television show *Once Upon a Time* (henceforth *OUAT*), currently in its fifth season on ABC, centers on the adventures of fairy tale characters transported via curse to our own, mundane world.[1] There they are given alternate memories that force them to forget who they really are. Key characters such as Snow White, Prince Charming, Rumpelstiltskin, Little Red Riding Hood, and Cinderella are trapped in a land without happy endings, frozen in time and doomed to suffer a vague discontent associated with being separated from their true identities. The first season of the series weaves its story largely through flashbacks to the

---

[1]   Claudia Schwabe describes this set up as a "rapprochement of the dichotomy between the familiar, visible, nonmagical, ordinary, and rational (the everyday) and the unfamiliar, invisible, magical, extraordinary, and nonrational (the magical)", arguing that the show "synthesize[s] quotidian reality with supernatural/magical reality, forming a new reality with magical influences" ([1], p. 295).

fairy-tale land that was, letting us see new imaginings of the "true" versions of these well-known tales.[2]

In season one, episode 15, viewers are shown scenes from the past life of Ruby/Red (Meghan Ory), the series' version of Red Riding Hood. The episode reveals that, contrary to most oral and written versions of the ATU 333 tale[3], Red herself *is* the wolf: a werewolf who must wear an enchanted red cloak in order to keep from turning into a monster [5].[4] The episode also features the beginnings of the close friendship between Red and Snow White (Ginnifer Goodwin). The sisterly bond that quickly forms between the two women, combined with the striking images of their respective red and white cloaks, easily calls to mind a less familiar fairy tale not explicitly referenced in the series: "Snow White and Rose Red" (ATU 426). Taking queer readings of this text as starting points (see, for example, [6]), I argue that this allusion complicates the bond between the two women, opening up space for a compelling reading of Red's werewolf nature as a coded depiction of her then latent but later confirmed bisexuality[5].

In this article, my use of the word "queer" to describe a possible reading of both a character and a television adaptation as a whole relates both to the established use of the term, that which "implicate[s] lives and theories relating to sexes and sexualities beyond the mainstream and deviating from the norm", and the broader definition that is becoming more and more prevalent in scholarship, that which addresses "concerns about marginalization, oddity, and not fitting into society generally" and "embraces more than sex/gender/sexuality to deal with the problematics of those who for various reasons find themselves outside conventional practices" ([8], p. 4). A queer reading, as I understand it here, "unpick[s] binaries and reread[s the] gaps, silences, and in-between spaces" of a text ([9], p. 5)—it is not, to call on Alexander

---

[2] This structure is very similar to another television show, *Lost* (2004–2010), for which *OUAT* series creators Adam Horowitz and Edward Kitsis worked as writers and producers. *OUAT* frequently features "Easter eggs" evoking *Lost* that are meant to serve as insider winks for fans of both series [2].

[3] While Red transforming into a wolf herself is not frequently seen in either oral or written versions of the traditional fairy tale, there are several other films and television programs that do make use of this idea. See the work of Pauline Greenhill and Steven Kohm, particularly "Criminal Beasts and Swan Girls: The *Red Riding Trilogy* and Little Red Riding Hood on Television" in *Channeling Wonder: Fairy Tales on Television* [3] and "*Hoodwinked!* and *Jin-Roh: The Wolf Brigade*: Animated "Little Red Riding Hood" Films and the Rashômon Effect" in the journal *Marvels & Tales*, for several key examples [4].

[4] All quotations and descriptions are from season one, episode 15 unless otherwise noted.

[5] I use the term "coded"/"coding" as a way of marking "covert expressions of disturbing or subversive ideas" ([7], p. vii)—and queerness is, at least to corporations like Disney, still quite subversive. My use of this term is indebted to the introduction to *Feminist Messages: Coding in Women's Folk Culture* by Joan N. Radner and Susan S. Lanser entitled "Strategies of Coding in Women's Cultures" [7]. Though Radner and Lanser's particular essay focuses on women exclusively, the strategies of coding discussed may be used by anyone facing oppression "to refuse, subvert, or transform conventional expectations" ([7], p. 23). In calling lycanthropy a code for queerness, I am suggesting the use of the coding strategy they identify as "indirection" ([7], pp. 16–19).

Doty's work, an alternative reading to a presumptively normative heterosexual analysis, but rather an equally valid reading that is not "any less there, or any less real, than straight readings" ([10], pp. 1–2). Depictions of queerness on mainstream television nonetheless remain controversial subjects in Western society. While significant positive "[s]hifts in public attitudes toward lesbian and gay stories [...] became apparent in the 1990s, especially on television" ([11], p. 2), programs that feature queer romance are still met with significant resistance, both from anti-queer viewers and from those who identify as queer themselves. Recurring criticism from within the queer community includes objections to tokenism, stereotypical depictions that "limit what it means to be lesbian, gay, or queer" ([11], p. 4), and portrayals seen as showing queer people to be ultimately "innocuous and inoffensive" to hegemonic interests. ([12], p. 4).[6]

2. "Little Red Riding Hood" (ATU 333)

As any close reading of any fairy-tale adaptation must, I will begin with a brief look at the primary source material. While all fairy tales exist in a myriad of forms and variations, my focus here will be on the Grimm version of "Little Red Riding Hood", called "Little Red Cap", and, later, the Grimm version of "Snow White and Rose Red". My reasoning for this is, simply, that they are by far the most popular to adapt and, I would argue, the chief source texts for fairy tales beyond Disney for *OUAT* in particular.[7]

The Grimm's fairy tale "Little Red Cap", (henceforth "Little Red Riding Hood" when speaking generally, as that is its most common name) (ATU 333) is a familiar one to most of Western civilization. It is popular to tell and retell in various ways. Its fame has made it frequently one of the first tales thought of when asked for an example of a fairy tale. The Grimm version of the story is relatively simple—a young girl who always wears a red cap is given a piece of cake and a bottle of wine to bring to her beloved grandmother, who is ill. To get to her, she must travel through a forest, where she encounters a wolf. The wolf is cunning, and schemes a way to be able to eat both the grandmother and the little girl—he tells her to slow down

---

6   There has been considerable and extensive scholarship examining queerness on television—examples include [12–15].

7   As ABC is owned by the Disney Corporation, the majority of the fairy tale stories adapted on *OUAT* at least begin with the version of the tale presented in a major Disney film. Neither ATU 333 nor ATU 426 have been adapted into full length Disney motion pictures, though the corporation has produced shorts based on ATU 333. *OUAT* does, however, incorporate fairy tales beyond those that have been made into major animated Disney films—aside from the two discussed in this article, *OUAT* also adapts, for example, the stories of "Rumpelstiltskin" (ATU 500) and "Hansel and Gretel" (ATU 327a). All of the non-Disney fairy-tale adaptations seem to have markers suggesting retellings that began with the Grimms' *Kinder- und Hausmärchen* as their starting point.

and pick some of the flowers that grow just off the path, and despite her mother's warning not to stray, she does so. He then rushes to the grandmother's home and eats her, puts on her clothes, and pretends to be her when Little Red Cap arrives at the house. After the famous "what big ears [*etc.*] you have" exchange, the wolf eats the girl as well. Luckily, a huntsman happens to overhear the wolf's snoring, finds him in the house, kills him, and opens up his belly, revealing a still alive Little Red Cap and grandmother. The story ends by saying that Little Red Cap learns from the experience and, when another wolf tries the same thing, she and her grandmother are able to foil him on their own [16].

Interpretations of this story have been wide-ranging, from psychoanalytic [17], to socio-historical/ cultural and feminist [18], to the most common conception that the story is simply a metaphor for the dangers young girls face from predatory men. Jack Zipes argues that the tale's status as "the most popular and certainly the most provocative fairy tale in the Western world" stems from the fact that it "raises issues about gender identity, sexuality, violence, and the civilizing process in a unique and succinct symbolic form that children and adults can understand on different levels" ([18], p. 343). As Rita Ghesquiere acknowledges, that dual appeal to both young and old has also "managed to inspire creators of various kinds who have transposed the story not only for a young but also for a grown-up audience" ([19], p. 87).

"Little Red Riding Hood" is, in many ways, ripe for contemporary adaptation. Particularly popular are feminist retellings in which the titular character emerges triumphant, often killing the wolf herself. Jennifer Orme locates a queer retelling in David Kaplan's film version of the tale as well [20] and, though *OUAT* is not the first adaptation of the story to make Red herself a werewolf, it is perhaps the most popular and wide-reaching one to do so.[8] Several reviewers of the fifteenth episode of season one admitted to being shocked by the twist, indicating that the idea was new to many of those watching (see, for example, [22,23]). Phillip A. Bernhardt-House acknowledges, however, that "[t]reatments of female sexuality and sexual initiation in relation to wolves have often focused on the tale" ([24], p. 169) and, further, that tales of female werewolves frequently seem to serve as representations of "the uncontrollable and dangerous nature of the female" ([24], p. 168).

3. Blending the Fairy Tale to Queer It

In the fifteenth episode of season one of *OUAT*, entitled "Red-Handed", the audience is given a look into the past life of Ruby, a young woman with rebellious

---

[8]   The other major contender is the 1984 film *The Company of Wolves* based on Angela Carter's short stories [21].

tendencies who works at her grandmother's diner in Storybrooke. She is, of course, an updated interpretation of Little Red Riding Hood. The show depicts a relatively familiar version of the character as she has been modernized in recent years—tough and unconventional, but also kind, vulnerable, slightly naive, and uncertain of her place in the world.[9] Ruby fights with her grandmother, called Granny (Beverley Elliott), frequently, often because she feels trapped in the small town (as she indeed is.) In this particular episode, when the scenes shift to contemporary Storybrooke, they quarrel over the necessity of the tedious paperwork associated with the diner and Ruby's increasing desire to see the world. The Storybrooke parts of the episode further feature Ruby quitting her job, attempting to leave the town but being stopped, getting a new job as an assistant at the sheriff's office with the show's main character Emma (Jennifer Morrison), helping Emma solve what they believe is a murder, and ultimately reconciling with Granny and coming back to work for her [5].

What I would like to focus on here, however, are the flashback scenes that take place in the Enchanted Forest many years before the scenes set in Storybrooke. There, Ruby is a lighthearted girl nicknamed Red who has a crush on a boy named Peter (Jesse Hutch).[10] She lives with her grandmother, who is quite strict and makes Red always wear a particular red cloak during what their village calls "Wolf's Time", the time each month that an enormous, ferocious wolf terrorizes the area. Red wants to go with the people who want to hunt the wolf, but her grandmother will not allow it, instead making her help secure their cottage. She also reminds Red to wear her cloak always, as red is supposed to repel wolves, but it seems as though Red has a history of not remembering to do this.

The next morning, Red finds a hiding Snow White in their chicken coop and agrees to help her, despite Snow admitting that she is a known fugitive. After the slaughter of the men who went to hunt the wolf is discovered, Red confesses to Snow that she wants to be with Peter, but knows that she can't while the wolf is free because Granny will never let her. She and Snow go to search for the wolf on their own and discover via footprints that the wolf can transform into a human. When they see that the prints lead to Red's window, they assume that Peter must be the wolf, as he was the only person Red can think of that had been there. That night, Red sneaks out to tie up Peter so that he won't hurt anyone, vowing to stay with him despite her revelation about him, while Snow pretends to be Red by wearing

---

[9]   Zipes would argue that Red has always been "individualistic and perhaps nonconformist", even having "certain potential qualities which could convert her into a witch or heretic" ([25], p. 122). He further states that Red "becomes at one with the wolf" when she is eaten, an act that realizes "her 'natural' potential to become a witch" ([25], p. 124). Though *OUAT* does not follow this reading exactly, Red's werewolf nature certainly qualifies her as both supernatural and "one" with the wolf.

[10] This, of course, additionally alludes to the 1936 Russian musical composition and story of "Peter and the Wolf" by Sergei Prokofiev.

her cloak and lying on her bed at home. When Granny discovers that Red is gone, without her cloak, she panics and rushes from the cottage with Snow close behind. When they get to the tree where Red had tied up Peter, however, it is too late—Peter is not the wolf, Red is, and she has devoured him in her wolf form. Snow and Granny throw the cloak over Red, which transforms her back into a human and thus reveals its magical properties and why Granny wanted Red to wear it all the time. Red is confused and horrified by what she has done but the group hears a hunting party coming and Granny forces her to escape with Snow into the woods.

What is perhaps most interesting about these Enchanted Forest scenes, aside from the twist reveal of Red herself being the wolf, is the fact that they clearly connect to another fairy tale completely separate from "Little Red Riding Hood"—"Snow White and Rose Red" (ATU 426).[11] Though a less familiar fairy tale, "Snow White and Rose Red" is still recognizable to many and is, for those who know it, a far more interesting and subversive tale than many of those that have gained considerably greater popularity.[12] This intertextual blurring of two fairy tales allows the texts to "mingle with one another, anticipating, evoking, interrupting, and supporting one another in unpredictable ways" ([26], p. 79).

To summarize, the Grimm version of "Snow White and Rose Red" is the story of a poor widow who has two daughters that resemble the rose bushes outside their home ([27], p. 475). The two sisters are very close but also very different—as Andrew J. Friedenthal notes, "Rose Red is [...] figured from the story's very outset, in comparison with her sister, as wilder and less domestic" ([6], p. 163)—she "prefer[s] to run around in the meadows and fields, look for flowers, and catch butterflies", while Snow White likes to "sta[y] at home with her mother [and] hel[p] her with housework, or read to her" ([27], pp. 475–76). The colors associated with each also emphasize this difference—"Snow White, associated with the color of cleanliness and innocence, of inexperience and childhood, is, literally, pure in essence. Rose Red, in contrast, is named for the color of blood and passion" ([6], p. 165). Regardless of these differences, however, the two sisters love each other dearly and often explore the forest together.

One day, during a cold winter, a bear asks for shelter in their home. Though they are all afraid at first, they soon come to love the bear. The two sisters care for

---

[11] The "Snow White" in "Snow White and Rose Red" is not traditionally the same "Snow White" of the other fairy tale with that title. The majority of the story of the Snow White depicted on *OUAT* is modeled after the other story (and, of course, the Disney version of that), but the show seems to have chosen to conflate the two characters into one in its particular fairy-tale universe.

[12] Friedenthal argues that the relative obscurity of the tale "may reflect centuries-old cultural taboos against both lesbianism and free expression of female sexuality" ([6], p. 163). It is also worth noting, as Friedenthal does later in his chapter, that the cultural taboo of incest is also in play in this story ([6], p. 166).

him and like to play with him by the fire. When the bear leaves the cottage in the summer, Snow White is particularly sad. Later, when the girls are in the forest, they come upon a dwarf twice with his beard stuck in various places and once almost being carried away by an eagle. Each time the sisters free him but he shows no gratitude. Eventually it is revealed that this is the dwarf who had cursed their friend the bear, who is really a prince transformed. Of course, the tale ends with the dwarf defeated and the return of the prince to his rightful human form. Snow White then, as is expected, marries him and Rose Red, in what seems almost like an afterthought, marries his brother [27].

When arguing for the queer reading of "Snow White and Rose Red", it is prudent to note that the tale was not originally included in the Grimms' *Kinder- und Hausmärchen*—indeed it did not make an appearance in the collected text until the abridged second edition in 1833, then subsequently appeared in the third edition of the full text in 1837. Part of the reason for this is that the tale is Wilhelm Grimm's retelling of a German literary fairy tale by Caroline Stahl and not an oral tale—there is even evidence to suggest that the Grimms took pains to retell the story in a way that would encourage readers to identify it as an oral folktale ([28], pp. 148–50). One can speculate, as Cristina Bacchilega and Heinz Rölleke do, that the tale appealed to the Grimm brothers because "the sisters' devotion to one another plays a key role in the tale and mirrors that of the two Grimms" themselves ([26], p. 85). This perhaps helps explain its inclusion, despite the fact that the lack of any clear evidence of an oral history for the tale should theoretically have excluded it from the Grimms' collection.

Though at first the two traditional tales drawn from for this episode of *OUAT* seem quite different, they do feature a few interesting similarities. For example, "Snow White and Rose Red", like "Little Red Riding Hood", centers its story on several women seemingly on their own. In *OUAT*, Granny, Red, and Snow function as a team of women against the men of the village who wish to kill the wolf, thus mirroring that female-centered focus. "One could argue that the Grimm tales [...] largely reference a female-centered world, where relationships between women–whether or not they are sexualized and/or eroticized–become the primary area of concern" ([8], p. 9), but these two tales in particular seem to be among those that do so most prominently. Both stories also feature the intrusion of a male figure into a previously female exclusive space (first the wolf and then the huntsman in "Little Red Cap" and the bear prince in "Snow White and Rose Red") and the idea of transformation—in "Little Red Cap", the wolf does not literally transform but does don the appearance of an old woman (a cross-dressing act that is perhaps queer in and of itself[13]) and, in "Snow White and Rose Red", the bear is of course a transformed prince. The *OUAT* episode uses this concept of transformation in their choice to make Red herself the wolf—she is a human girl who transforms into an animal, a werewolf. The idea of the deep forest is also crucial to both stories, though in quite different ways. In "Little Red Cap", the forest symbolizes an unfamiliar, potentially frightening world outside that which had been previously experienced. The "Snow White and Rose Red" story, in contrast, depicts the woods as the comforting, well-known space of the two sisters. In making the forest the domain of the wolf, *OUAT* associates it with danger a la "Little Red Riding Hood" tales. In making *Red* the wolf, however, *OUAT* also brings in elements of the familiar space where one truly belongs that is captured in "Snow White and Rose Red".

In the context of the "Red-Handed" *OUAT* episode, however, the inclusion of such clear "Snow White and Rose Red" allusions in a "Little Red Riding Hood" retelling most significantly suggests a queer reading of that retelling in line with the "subtle themes of lesbianism and female sexual empowerment in ATU 426" ([6], p. 161). As Friedenthal notes, "[t]hough the Grimms' "Snow White and Rose Red" may lack overt expression of incestuous lesbianism, the entire tale centers on a series of queer images and symbols"—he singles out, for example, the roses (particularly their thorns), the "fecundity and fertility" of the forest surrounding the sisters' home, and the repetitions of the color red throughout the tale ([6], pp. 166–67). Though "Red-Handed" does not feature roses, the forest, as previously noted, and the color red both play key roles in the narrative. Aside from the obvious fact that Red's cloak is a bright red brocade, the episode strongly relies on images of blood as a way of cementing the terror of the wolf. For example, when Red and Snow go out to a well to get water for the cottage, the bucket brings up only a dark red substance. Red puzzles over it while Snow notices that behind them are the bloody corpses of the entire hunting party who went out after the wolf the night before. Their blood had seeped through the ground and into the water of the well. This focus on blood hints at an idea that is later confirmed by Granny—Red only began transforming into a wolf once a month when she turned thirteen, connecting the transformation strongly with ideas of sexuality, puberty, and the beginning of menstruation.[14]

Lastly, and most importantly, the "Snow White and Rose Red" story is characterized by the closeness of the two sisters. *OUAT* mimics that closeness admirably in the short time it has for Red and Snow to get to know each other in the "Red-Handed" episode—an almost instant understanding forms between the two

---

[13] For an in-depth discussion of this idea, see the concluding chapter of Marjorie Garber's *Vested Interests: Cross-dressing and Cultural Anxiety* [29].

[14] Even the term used by Red's village for when the wolf prowls, "Wolf's Time", suggests "Moon Time", a phrase often used for the period when a woman is menstruating.

women, and intimate conversations and co-planned schemes soon follow. Indeed it is Snow who inspires Red to defy her grandmother and gives her the means with which to do so—Red could not have left the house during Wolf's Time if it were not for Snow agreeing to wear the cloak and pretending to be her. This co-transgression cements the strong tie connecting them. It is this same "intense intimacy [that] lends the [traditional] tale an air of homoeroticism" ([6], p. 171). Indeed, in the Grimm tale, this closeness "often finds physical expression: they "loved each other so much that they always held hands whenever they were out"; they swear never to leave each other as long as they live and they sometimes "would lie down next to each other on the moss and sleep until morning came" ([6], p. 166, quoting [27]). What's more, though the sisters do both marry princes in the tale, their respective marriages do not result in their separation. As Bacchilega argues, there is "no need [in the tale] for married life to replace sisterly bonds" and the sisters are not "dependent on males" ([26], pp. 86–87).[15] This small but unexpectedly powerful move is a direct challenge to a hegemonic, heteronormative, and patriarchal understanding of marriage and thus perhaps the queerest thing about the traditional story. While OUAT does not suggest any (non-incestuous) romantic relationship between their Snow and Red characters—Snow White is quite clearly heterosexual throughout the series—the intertextual presence of the "Snow White and Rose Red" tale allows for such a reading to shimmer on the edges of viewer consciousness even as Red's awakening to her bisexuality shimmers on the edges of her own.[16]

4. Reading the Werewolf as a Code for Queerness

Combining the evocative lesbian imagery of "Snow White and Rose Red" with the story about how Red discovers her true nature reveals a new way of conceptualizing the concept of the werewolf in the OUAT world. As Bernhardt-House notes, there has been "[s]ome discussion of vampirism in relation to queerness" but "little or no discussion of lycanthropy", with, of course, the exception of his own chapter on the subject ([24], p. 164). As he aptly points out, however, the werewolf's position as a "'hybrid' figure of sorts—part human and part wolf—and its hybridity and transgression of species boundaries in a unified figure is, at very least, unusual, thus the figure of the werewolf might be seen as a natural signifier for queerness in its

---

[15] Doty makes a similar argument in his bisexual analysis of the 1953 film *Gentleman Prefer Blondes* ([10], pp. 131–53).

[16] The depiction of Snow and Red in *OUAT* might also put viewers in mind of what is perhaps the most popular adaptation of "Snow White and Rose Red", the one featured in Bill Willingham's *Fables* series [30]. Willingham's story draws strongly on the differences between the two girls and even, as Friedenthal notes, hints at incestuous lesbianism between them ([6], pp. 175–76, 178, n. 7). Bacchilega adds that other adaptations also "underscore Snow White and Rose Red's intimate bond", such as Francesca Lia Block's short story "Rose" (2000) ([31]; [26], p. 90).

myriad forms" ([24], p. 159). Harry M. Benshoff adds the fact that "the figure of the monster throughout the history of the English-language horror film can in some way be understood as a metaphoric construct standing in for the figure of the homosexual" generally ([32], p. 4). Following this logic, Red's story can be understood as an "activist adaptation", to use Bacchilega's term ([26], p. 80). "Activist adaptations" are those that "take a questioning stance towards their pre-texts, and/or take an activist stance toward the fairy tale's hegemonic uses in popular culture, and/or instigate readers/viewers/listeners to engage with the genre as well as with the world with a transformed sense of possibility" ([26], p. 80). In making Little Red Riding Hood into a werewolf, and then coding that werewolf as queer in various ways, *OUAT* participates in an adaptation that questions traditional "Little Red Riding Hood" stories, particularly their emphasis on Red as a victim in need of rescue by a man, and encourages viewers to see new things in an old story.

In *OUAT*, Red's werewolf side is at first seen as a shameful, monstrous secret that must be kept at all costs. Her grandmother, tellingly, keeps it from her, believing her to be safer if she does not know the truth about herself. "Red-Handed" shows the consequences of that choice—as the wolf, Red unknowingly kills numerous townspeople and even her potential heterosexual love interest, Peter. This framing of the werewolf as a dangerous creature who terrorizes normative society and destroys the possibility of heterosexual love is in keeping with heterosexual fears regarding queer sexualities—particularly the idea that homosexuality is "a threat to the community and other components of culture—[that] homosexuals supposedly represent the destruction of the procreative nuclear family, traditional gender roles, and [...] 'family values'" ([32], p. 1). As Benshoff argues, "[i]n short, for many people in our shared English-language culture, homosexuality is a monstrous condition" ([32], p. 1) and one that must be suppressed. The connection between lycanthropy and homosexual desire in *OUAT* is further strengthened by the fact that Red does not find out she is the wolf until the appearance of Snow White, with whom she has an almost immediately close relationship (as discussed above.) When Red does discover the truth about herself, she and Snow must even flee together into the woods to avoid persecution by the nearing hunting party from the town. Though Snow is decidedly heterosexual, her appearance at this crucial moment in Red's life, combined with the instant bond between the two women that mirrors a tale with strong homosexual possibility, seems to clearly hint at the eventual confirmation of Red's bisexuality in season five [33]. It is not a far stretch of the imagination to presume that Red's first real feelings of same-sex attraction were for the girl who is, after all, the "fairest in the land" [34].

In a later episode of the series, "Child of the Moon" [35], the story of what happens to Red and Snow after they leave Red's hometown is revealed. On the run, the two girls happen upon a group of men who are after Snow White, and Red's cloak is ripped as they escape. Worried that the magic of the cloak will no longer work, Snow and Red agree to separate for the night, as it is a full moon. The next morning, Red meets a fellow werewolf about her age, Quinn (Ben Hollingsworth), who takes her back to the werewolf lair he shares with several others like himself. There she meets the leader of the group, Anita (Annabeth Gish), another werewolf who turns out to be her biological mother. Anita informs Red that Granny kidnapped her, telling her that "[Granny] didn't want you to find out the truth about who you really are. She believed the wolf is something to be ashamed of. I see things differently. Humans want us to believe we are the monsters. The moment you believe them... that's when you become one" (35). Anita believes that once a werewolf accepts the wolf as a part of him or herself, he or she can then control it and revel in it—in short, that the wolf to her represents both "natural urges and social noncomformity" ([18], p. 81).

However, as Red soon sees, that reveling comes with the price of abandoning one's humanity and the rest of society entirely. The group of werewolves her mother leads believes that humans are evil and that living among them necessitates the suppression of their superior wolf characteristics. They have thus completely removed themselves from the rest of the world and no longer seek any sort of acceptance or human connection. This ultimately false narrative of having to choose between living with deep shame and hiding *vs.* embracing one's true self but, in doing so, also choosing a profound separation from the rest of the world can easily extend the lycanthropy/homosexuality metaphor. These are not, however, the only choices possible for Red, who ultimately chooses to embrace both her human and her wolf side—she decides to stay with Snow, stating that "[m]y mother wanted me to choose between being a wolf and being a human. Granny did, too. You are the only person who ever thought it was okay for me to be both" (35). Again, viewers are seemingly given a clue to Red's bisexuality—Red believes, with the support of her closest friend, that she can embrace being *both* a human girl and a wolf[17]. While this reading does once again problematically conflate humanity with heterosexuality and the monstrous wolf with homosexuality, thus potentially furthering the stereotypical fears about queerness that Benshoff argues are always already present in mainstream media [32], the show seems to seek a more nuanced adaptation of this same idea. Red embraces her dual nature in a way that can be seen as a more progressive and positive depiction of these concepts. Snow's complete acceptance and unquestioning support of her friend is perhaps a further reflection of a changing Western society.[18]

---

[17] And, indeed, it is important to note that Ruby does show further sexual interest in men in Storybrooke in the first several seasons of the show. It is not until her same-sex relationship in season five that her sexuality is confirmed.

[18] One should also note that this reading is "working within conventional binaries" that "understand [bisexuality] as a movement between, or a combination of, heterosexuality and homosexuality and the

5. Conclusions

Queer understandings of *OUAT* have existed almost since the series' pilot aired in 2011. Indeed, as Rebecca Hay and Christa Baxter note, many fans have long hoped for the inclusion of a homosexual relationship on the show—the "Swan-Queen" advocates, those pushing for a romantic relationship between Emma, the daughter of Snow White and Prince Charming (Josh Dallas), and Regina (Lana Parilla), the evil queen, have been particularly vocal since the beginning ([36], p. 329). The possibility of an actual homosexual relationship on *OUAT* was first truly put forward, however, with the introduction of Mulan (Jamie Chung) from Disney's *Mulan* (1998 [37], based on a traditional Chinese ballad) and Aurora (Sarah Bolger) from the fairy tale "Sleeping Beauty" [38]. Fans zeroed in on a perceived sexual tension between the two women and heavily advocated for a relationship to form between them in earnest on the show. Though *OUAT* ultimately followed through with the marriage of Aurora to Prince Philip (Julian Morris) as the traditional fairy tale dictates, the show strongly hinted—particularly in episode three of season three, "Quite a Common Fairy", when Mulan appeared to be ready to confess her feelings for Aurora [39]—that Mulan was heartbroken by the realization that Aurora is in love with Philip, not her. Seemingly largely in response to the outpouring of support for that relationship, Adam Horowitz and Edward Kitsis confirmed soon after that season five would feature a romantic same-sex relationship [40].

There was reason to suspect that this relationship would be between Mulan and Red. At the end of the ninth episode of season five, "The Bear King" which aired in November of 2015 soon before the series took a break for a few months, Red and Mulan were seen deciding to team up together to search for other werewolves [41]. Given the potential queerness of both characters, it seemed a good guess that they would be the promised queer romantic relationship on *OUAT*. However, the show chose instead to have Red fall in love with Dorothy Gale (Teri Reeves) from *The Wizard of Oz*, a union that was confirmed by a magical "true love's kiss" in the April 2016 episode "Ruby Slippers" [33].[19] This confirmation of Ruby/Red's bisexuality

---

straight and lesbian or gay identities that are usually attached to these desires and practices"—other understandings of bisexuality include those who "find their bisexuality works itself out as a desire for both the same sex and the opposite sex in tandem with a social or political identification with either gayness, lesbianism, or straightness" and those who "see it as having desires for both the same sex and the opposite sex within bisexual identities that don't reference straight or lesbian or gay ones, but may reference less binarily defined queer or non-straight identities" ([10], p. 131).

[19] Melanie E. S. Kohnen argues that mainstream media tends to form a "limited and limiting conceptualization of a queer visibility structured around white gay and lesbian characters in committed relationships [that] has become the embodiment of progressive, LGBT media representations" ([15], p. i). In choosing to develop the show's first same-sex romance between two white characters (as opposed to a white character and an Asian character, a union that seemed almost inevitable), *OUAT* seems to be perpetuating—consciously or not—this significant issue, a fact

adds a level of complexity to *OUAT*'s adaptation of the fairy tale form and distances the show significantly from Disney's usual notoriously heteronormative politics. The queer reading of Red's lycanthropy—a tantalizing possibility from her very first focal episode—seems to suggest that, perhaps, the show has always strived to present a far more unconventional and progressive reimagining of the Disney fairy-tale world than many first imagined it could or would.

Conflicts of Interest: The author declares no conflict of interest.

Abbreviations

OUAT   Refers to the television show *Once Upon a Time*

References

1.   Schwabe, Claudia. "Getting Real with Fairy Tales: Magical Realism in *Grimm* and *Once Upon a Time*." In *Channeling Wonder: Fairy Tales on Television*. Edited by Pauline Greenhill and Jill Terry Rudy. Detroit: Wayne State University Press, 2014, pp. 294–315.
2.   Lambe, Stacy. "Why *Lost* Fans Should Watch *Once Upon a Time*." *VH1*. Available online: http://www.vh1.com/news/88358/once-upon-a-time-lost-similarities/ (accessed on 26 February 2016).
3.   Greenhill, Pauline, and Steven Kohm. "Criminal Beasts and Swan Girls: The *Red Riding Trilogy* and Little Red Riding Hood on Television." In *Channeling Wonder: Fairy Tales on Television*. Edited by Pauline Greenhill and Jill Terry Rudy. Detroit: Wayne State University Press, 2014, pp. 189–209.
4.   Greenhill, Pauline, and Steven Kohm. "*Hoodwinked!* and *Jin-Roh: The Wolf Brigade*: Animated 'Little Red Riding Hood' Films and the Rashômon Effect." *Marvels and Tales* 27 (2013): 89–108.
5.   "Red-Handed I, 15." *Once Upon a Time*. Directed by Ron Underwood. Written by Jane Espenson. Disney, ABC Television Group, 11 March 2012.
6.   Friedenthal, Andrew J. "The Lost Sister: Lesbian Eroticism and Female Empowerment in 'Snow White and Rose Red.'." In *Transgressive Tales: Queering the Grimms*. Edited by Kay Turner and Pauline Greenhill. Detroit: Wayne State University Press, 2012, pp. 161–78.

---

that problematically underscores the progressive move of featuring a same-sex romance in the first place. The relationship was met by other criticism from the queer community as well, including the fact that Dorothy and Red are not main characters (and thus only appear infrequently on the show) and that their "true love" was developed seemingly half-heartedly over the span of only one episode, lending it an air of tokenism—see [42–44] for more on these issues. Other fans were predictably not happy with the show depicting a queer relationship at all, as is evident from the string of angry comments on the show's Facebook page following the airing of the episode in question [45]. All of this said, the overall reaction to the relationship from fans seems to be largely positive.

7. Radner, Joan N., and Susan S. Lanser. "Strategies of Coding in Women's Cultures." In *Feminist Messages: Coding in Women's Folk Culture*. Edited by Joan N. Radner. Urbana: University of Illinois Press, 1993, pp. 1–29.

8. Turner, Kay, and Pauline Greenhill. "Once Upon a Queer Time." In *Transgressive Tales: Queering the Grimms*. Edited by Kay Turner and Pauline Greenhill. Detroit: Wayne State University Press, 2012, pp. 1–24.

9. Giffney, Noreen, and Myra J. Hird. "Introduction: Queering the Non/Human." In *Queering the Non/Human*. Edited by Noreen Giffney and Myra J. Hird. Hampshire: Ashgate, 2008, pp. 1–16.

10. Doty, Alexander. *Flaming Classics: Queering the Film Canon*. New York: Routledge, 2000.

11. Demory, Pamela, and Christopher Pullen. "Introduction." In *Queer Love in Film and Television: Critical Essays*. Edited by Pamela Demory and Christopher Pullen. New York: Palgrave Macmillan, 2013, pp. 1–9.

12. Keller, James R. *Queer (Un)Friendly Film and Television*. Jefferson: McFarland, 2002.

13. Demory, Pamela, and Christopher Pullen, eds. *Queer Love in Film and Television: Critical Essays*. New York: Palgrave Macmillan, 2013.

14. Beirne, Rebecca. *Televising Queer Women: A Reader*. New York: Palgrave Macmillan, 2008.

15. Kohnen, Melanie E. S. *Queer Representation, Visibility, and Race in American Film and Television: Screening the Closet*. New York: Routledge, 2016.

16. Zipes, Jack, trans. "Little Red Cap." In *The Complete Fairy Tales of the Brothers Grimm*, 3rd ed. Edited by Jack Zipes. New York: Bantam Books, 2002, pp. 93–96.

17. Dundes, Alan. "Interpreting 'Little Red Riding Hood' Psychoanalytically." In *Little Red Riding Hood: A Case Book*. Edited by Alan Dundes. Madison: University of Wisconsin Press, 1989, pp. 192–236.

18. Zipes, Jack, ed. *The Trials and Tribulations of Little Red Riding Hood*. New York: Routledge, 1993.

19. Ghesquiere, Rita. "Little Red Riding Hood Where Are You Going? " In *Toplore: Stories and Songs*. Edited by Paul Catteeuv, Marc Jacobs, Sigrid Rieuwerts, Eddy Tielemans and Katrien Van Effelterre. Trier: Wissenschaftlicher Verlag, 2006, pp. 84–99.

20. Orme, Jennifer. "A Wolf's Queer Invitation: David Kaplan's *Little Red Riding Hood* and Queer Possibility." *Marvels and Tales* 29 (2015): 87–109.

21. *The Company of Wolves*. Directed by Neil Jordan. Performed by Sarah Patterson, Angela Lansbury, Stephen Rea and David Warner. ITC, Cannon, 1984.

22. Phillips, Tracy. "*Once Upon a Time*'s Meghan Ory on Her 'Big Bad' Twist." *Xfinity*. Available online: http://my.xfinity.com/blogs/tv/2012/03/18/once-upon-a-times-meghan-ory-on-her-big-bad-twist/ (accessed on 26 February 2016).

23. Ratcliffe, Amy. "*Once Upon a Time*: 'Red-Handed' Review." *IGN*. Available online: http://www.ign.com/articles/2012/03/12/once-upon-a-time-red-handed-review (accessed on 26 February 2016).

24. Bernhardt-House, Phillip A. "The Werewolf as Queer, the Queer as Werewolf, and Queer Werewolves." In *Queering the Non/Human*. Edited by Noreen Giffney and Myra J. Hird. Hampshire: Ashgate, 2008, pp. 159–83.

25. Zipes, Jack. "'Little Red Riding Hood' as Male Creation and Projection." In *Little Red Riding Hood: A Case Book*. Edited by Alan Dundes. Madison: University of Wisconsin Press, 1989, pp. 121–27.

26. Bacchilega, Cristina. "Fairy-tale Adaptations and Economies of Desire." In *The Cambridge Companion to Fairy Tales*. Edited by Maria Tatar. Cambridge: Cambridge University Press, 2015, pp. 79–96.

27. Zipes, Jack, trans. "Snow White and Rose Red." In *The Complete Fairy Tales of the Brothers Grimm*, 3rd ed. Edited by Jack Zipes. New York: Bantam Books, 2002, pp. 475–80.

28. Hameršak, Marijana. "A Never Ending Story? Permutations of 'Snow White and Rose Red' Narrative and Its Research across Time and Space." *Narodna Umjetnost: Croatian Journal of Ethnology and Folklore Research* 48 (2011): 147–60.

29. Garber, Marjorie. *Vested Interests: Cross-Dressing and Cultural Anxiety*. New York: Routledge, 2011.

30. Willingham, Bill. *Fables*. Comic series. New York: DC Comics, 2002–2015.

31. Block, Francesca Lia. "Rose." In *The Rose and the Beast: Fairy Tales Retold*. New York: Harper Collins, 2001.

32. Benshoff, Harry M. *Monsters in the Closet: Homosexuality and the Horror Film*. Manchester: Manchester University Press, 1997.

33. "Ruby Slippers V, 18." *Once Upon a Time*. Directed by Eriq La Salle. Written by Bill Wolkoff and Andrew Chambliss. Disney, ABC Television Group, 17 April 2016.

34. Zipes, Jack, trans. "Snow White." In *The Complete Fairy Tales of the Brothers Grimm*, 3rd ed. Edited by Jack Zipes. New York: Bantam Books, 2002, pp. 181–88.

35. "Child of the Moon II, 7." *Once Upon a Time*. Directed by Anthony Hemingway. Written by Ian B. Goldberg and Andrew Chambliss. Disney, ABC Television Group, 11 November 2012.

36. Hay, Rebecca, and Christa Baxter. "Happily Never After: The Commodification and Critique of Fairy Tale in ABC's *Once Upon a Time*." In *Channeling Wonder: Fairy Tales on Television*. Edited by Pauline Greenhill and Jill Terry Rudy. Detroit: Wayne State University Press, 2014, pp. 316–35.

37. *Mulan*. Directed by Tony Bancroft, and Barry Cook. Performed by Ming-Na Wen, Eddie Murphy and B. D. Wong. Walt Disney Pictures, 1998.

38. "Broken II, 1." *Once Upon a Time*. Directed by Ralph Hemecker. Written by Edward Kitsis and Adam Horowitz. Disney, ABC Television Group, 30 September 2012.

39. "Quite a Common Fairy III, 3." *Once Upon a Time*. Directed by Alex Zakrzewksi. Written by Jane Espenson. Disney, ABC Television Group, 13 October 2013.

40. Gelman, Vlada. "*Once Upon a Time* EPs: Same-Sex Romance in the Works for Season 5." *TVLine*. Available online: http://tvline.com/2015/09/18/once-upon-a-time-lgbt-lesbian-storyline-season-5/ (accessed on 13 February 2016).

41. "The Bear King V, IX." *Once Upon a Time*. Directed by Geofrey Hildrew. Written by Andrew Chambliss. Disney, ABC Television Group, 15 November 2015.

42.   Stauf, Samantha. "The Problem with the Red and Dorothy Love Story on *Once Upon a Time*." *SheKnows*. Available online: http://www.sheknows.com/entertainment/articles/1120653/the-problem-with-the-red-and-dorothy-love-story (accessed on 3 June 2016).

43.   Still, Jennifer. "Why Ruby & Dorothy's Relationship on *Once Upon a Time* Missed the Mark." *Bustle*. Available online: http://www.bustle.com/articles/155329-why-ruby-dorothys-relationship-on-once-upon-a-time-missed-the-mark (accessed on 3 June 2016).

44.   Carbone, Gina. "*Once Upon a Time* Fans Have Strong Feelings About That LGBT Storyline." *Moviefone*. Available online: http://www.moviefone.com/2016/04/18/once-upon-a-time-fans-strong-feelings-lgbt-storyline/ (accessed on 3 June 2016).

45.   Facebook. "Once Upon a Time." Available online: https://www.facebook.com/OnceABC/ (accessed on 3 June 2016).

The Magic and Science of *Grimm*: A Television Fairy Tale for Modern Americans

Julianna Lindsay

Abstract: The National Broadcasting Company's (NBC) *Grimm* uses fairy tales and an altered history to explore modern issues in American society such as environmental concerns, individuality, and social and cultural change through magic and magic-tinged science. Worldwide chaos and strife are easily explained as part of the *Grimm* universe (Grimmverse) through Wesen (humanoid creatures who share characteristics with animals such as appearance and behavior), leading to a more united view of humanity and equality of human experience. Evil is often more scientifically explained, and what may appear random within our reality becomes part of a pattern in *Grimm*. *Grimm* gives its American audience a form of societal unity through historic folklore and a fictional explanation for the struggles Americans perceive to be happening within their own society as well as in other parts of the world.

Reprinted from *Humanities*. Cite as: Lindsay, J. The Magic and Science of *Grimm*: A Television Fairy Tale for Modern Americans. *Humanities* **2016**, 5, 34.

1. Introduction

Fairy tales evoke a variety of images in American culture, often associated with Disney, Shrek, the brothers Grimm, or even bedtime stories. These stories explore cultural themes such as good *versus* evil through magical, alternative worlds which mirror our own lives and physical space [1]. Marie-Catherine d'Aulnoy coined the term *fairy tale* in 1697 when she published her first volume of tales, leading to a new classification for these stories [2]. Although fairy tale origins are disputed [3,4], they are a tradition that dates back to at least three centuries with many scholars believing they extend even further back in European storytelling traditions [1,5].

Simon Bronner studied fairy tales in American culture and the influence the Brothers Grimm had on the American perceptions of these stories. Jacob and Wilhelm Grimm have one of the largest and most famous fairy tale legacies. The Grimms have two connections to Americans—through the popular culture view of their fairy stories as children's tales and the academic view of the Grimms linked to national theory. In American popular culture, the Grimm tales are believed to have a universal appeal. To Americans, the Grimm tales forge a connection to nature, solidify a national or group unity, and provide wish fulfillment. The peasants in

114

the stories became folk heroes akin to the American farmers, tying peasants to the Jeffersonian ideal of a small farm and living off the land that permeated American culture by the time these stories reached North American shores [6,7]. Bronner noted that although the Grimm stories are the paramount example of fairy tales in American culture, Hollywood's adaptations of stories into films such as *Snow White* or *Cinderella* rooted these stories more deeply into the nation's consciousness. In America, the Grimm fairy tales had gained popularity as children's morality tales and Americans postulated that they would excite the imaginations of children living in what they considered a dull, industrial age [6]. This emphasis on morality and imagination bled into the Disney films involving fairy tales, further influencing future generations. In turn, the values present of tolerance and diversity helped fuel the social and cultural revolutions of the 1960s further extending the influence the Grimm stories, or versions of these stories, had on Americans [8].

Each retelling of fairy tales carries with it the values of the culture in which the tale is reimagined and the time in which it is produced [8]. According to Tatiana Podolinská and Milan Kováč, there are two types of reasoning or ways to see reality—mythical or logical. Podolinská and Kováč note that belief, magic, logic, and causality intersect differently within each culture and person [9]. However, Barbara A. Strassberg posits that magic, religion, science, technology, and ethics are the four categories which coexist within every culture and society mixed together in varying amounts, evolving over time. Strassberg writes that magic and religion are based in faith, whereas science and technology rely on the observable and testable. These elements correspond to different individual, social, and cultural needs. None of the four elements are interchangeable according to Strassberg. She states that magic in our modern society is often found in lucky numbers, lucky charms, horoscopes, or paranormal beliefs. Religion is often viewed as personal within. Strassberg believes our public discourse has shifted away from private beliefs to instead an increasing interest in science, a movement often fueled by the belief in becoming an informed consumer. Technology has become pervasive in individual lives and society now expects it as part of everyday life. Ethics have become a mixture of universal rules and personal morals. She writes that the evolution of these components happens at varying rates within each culture and society. Individuals tend to initially resist change within any of these elements through a cognitive, emotional, or actionable response, but once acceptance happens, it can spread into other areas of the culture. These seemingly contradictory elements exist within each person's reality without conflict due to the internal perceptions of reality and the uniqueness of cultural and personal filters [10].

Fantasy genres such as fairy tales often engage in reinvented reality and history using varying amounts of magic, science, technology, and ethics. Claudia Schwabe theorizes that recent televisual adaptations of fairy tales create a magic realism

115

where the story is set in our current reality, but with the addition of a supernatural element which is not separate from, but rather intertwined with our world. The fantasy in fairy tales is used to explore questions such as the place of technology in society, individualism, or evil through the vehicles of magic coupled with modern science [11]. Recently, popular culture has seen an increase in science fiction, fantasy, and fairy tales in film and television. Movies such as *Snow White and the Huntsman* or television series such as *Once Upon a Time* have captivated new audiences by retelling old stories. One of these new stories is *Grimm*, a television series which premiered on NBC in 2011, and is described on NBC's website as a procedural drama inspired by the classic Brothers' Grimm fairy tales. The hero, Nick Burkhardt, discovers he is descended from a line of Grimms (people who can see and who fight *Wesen*: humanoid creatures who can look human or like anthropomorphic animals). Nick befriends a former suspect, Eddie Monroe, who is a reformed, now vegetarian, Blutbad (wolf-like Wesen). As the show progresses, a cast of Wesen such as Rosalie Calvert, a Fuchsbau (fox-like Wesen) are added to Nick's group of friends. Wesen usually look human to the majority of people, but they can *woge* (change into their animal-like state) at will. According to Monroe, Wesen can be seen as Wesen if they wish to be seen, but Grimms can see Wesen when they do not wish to be seen. Wesen can lose composure when emotional, and this lack of control allows Grimms to see their true form. In response, if a Wesen looks into the eyes of a Grimm when woged, they see reflected back to themselves their true form and bottomless darkness in the eyes of the Grimm [12–14]. These Wesen in the *Grimmverse* (*Grimm* universe) are the origin of monsters in fairy tales, according to the show [14]. In much the same way that Angel and Buffy in *Buffy the Vampire Slayer* became unlikely allies, *Grimm* pairs Nick and Monroe in the Grimmverse together as a vehicle of humor, social commentary, and interest. *Grimm* focuses on the current vogue for dark fairy tales, mixing gothic horror akin to *Frankenstein; or, The Modern Promethus* with an emphasis on science and pseudoscience employing the view that fairy tales cover the primal urges of humans, suppressed by society [15]. These urges are shaped into Wesen, whose natural, or pseudoscientifically defined behaviors within the writings of the Grimm books compiled by Grimm ancestry often belie a dark side of human nature. These behaviors are linked to the type of Wesen and the behavior of the corresponding animal they resemble, such as Blutbads liking to run in packs and hunt much like wolves. In *Grimm*, Wesen are the monsters hiding invisibly within humanity.

Americans have become increasingly concerned with sociocultural, political, economic, and environmental issues such as immigration, religious strife, the domains of religion and science, terrorism, economics, civil rights, religious freedom and boundaries, racial upheaval, societal evolution, and the place of the United States in the global order. American politics and culture is seemingly increasingly polarized in recent years, with little end in sight. With the recent rise in fairy tale related movies and television shows, this author questioned whether or not the retelling of fairy tales in NBC's *Grimm* could be a way for American audiences to regain emotional control in a modern and changing world amidst social and cultural anxieties through temporarily retreating into a safe space of making monsters into scientifically explained species and including just enough magic to retain wonder and interest in audiences. *Grimm* becomes a recast reality of magic realism [11] where magic only retains a small place in the present and science instead becomes the explanation for many of the world's myths and criminal problems. This retelling allows the story to remain enjoyable to the audience as a metaphor to everyday concerns [11].

2. Results and Discussion

The creators and writers of *Grimm* have mixed modern science with traditional fairy tale magic and magic realism [11] to create their Grimmverse. Science is most prominent in *Grimm* through genetics. Genetics are a prominent explanation for monsters and heroes in the stories and fighting monsters or being monsters becomes inherited. Grimm-ness is a trait which is not passed on to every descendent of a Grimm. Nick's ability to see Wesen is explained as an extra cone in his retina, referencing 2012 research on Tetrachromacy [14,16,17], a trait which may also explain the deep blackness of a Grimm's eyes as reflected to Wesen when they are transformed into their animal form. A Grimm's retinas might be interpreted to produce a magical version of the tapetum lucidum, the reflective surface on the back of the eyes of nocturnal animals. Wesen also have inherent behavioral and phenotypic characteristics. Only some Wesen behaviors can be changed through enormous self-discipline. Several Wesen traits are explained through the magnification of natural human biological processes or elements. Dämonfeuer (dragon type Wesen), for example, are able to metabolize their body fat through ketosis, mix the fat into an aerosol, and then spew the vapor into the air where it is ignited. In development, most Wesen are unable to transform until a version of Wesen puberty, making their woge biological in origin as opposed to a more magical metamorphosis such as a vampire bite. Hexenbiests (witch-like Wesen) are some of the most supernatural of Wesen, able to produce spells and engage in reality-defying actions. However, Hexenbiests all possess a certain amount of similarities with an attractive phenotype, inherited personality traits such as loyalty to those for whom they work, pathological deceit, and a mark under the tongue. Through a reliance on the biological origins of Wesen behavior, many nefarious events and personages become scientifically explained in the Grimmverse [14].

Through the use of science in combination with magic and magic realism [11], *Grimm* addresses several modern American sociocultural, environmental, historical, and occasionally economic concerns. Social change is explored in *Grimm* through a variety of means, including using the cultural and ancestral past in the present where fairy tales become informants on present of reality, and ancestors are protectors of the present. One way ancestors become protectors is through actions such as telling cautionary tales or writing the Grimm volumes, books written by Grimms from the Grimmverse, on Wesen. There is an acceptance of the ancestral Grimm tales as truth and the ancestor experience as an invaluable resource. Each tale is written and illustrated in the original Grimm's native language, and translations are often provided by Nick's Wesen friends Monroe or Rosalie, who often make comments about the language and a time they recall using or learning it. Monroe and Rosalie also often discuss the Wesen in the stories and their own ancestral ties to the accounts, rumors, or objects from the Grimm narrative. There is much emphasis throughout the show text of how Nick is different than past Grimms because unlike the Grimm stories, he does not kill every Wesen and instead judges each individual by moral character and actions. This is an emphasis on how Nick is a product of social change: his enlightened, modern, and accepting attitude as opposed to his ancestor's specist attitudes. However, when it suits the situation, Nick will bring up past Grimm reputation, titles, or stories to frighten or intimidate a Wesen he is questioning, interrogating, or fighting. Although his character attempts a more moral stance on killing Wesen, he still uses the fear his ancestors instilled in the Wesen community through terror and murder as a means of obtaining what he wants at the time if he deems it necessary. The reputation of his ancestors being a feared and terrible force against Wesen is a convenient truth Nick can accept or deny depending on the situation. Monroe often uses his ancestral past, connections, and family stories as a means to help Nick. Monroe waxes poetic at times while describing something from his lineage, engaging in strong nostalgia about the past, his ancestry, or Germany. Another means of ancestor protection is when Nick's mother appears in the story and saves his life. Nick had thought his mother was deceased, and he was raised by his Aunt Marie. In Season 1 Episode 22, his mother, Kelly Burkhardt, reappears in his life just as he is attempting to fight one of the men who caused the car crash in which he thought she had died. Although she is later killed in Season 4 Episode 21, he relies heavily on her for a time and her experience and protection are invaluable [14].

Class is another social issue which appears in *Grimm*. Wesen are often organized in a hierarchy of prey and predator. Wesen also have the overarching hierarchy of institutions like the Wesen Council which controls Wesen affairs. Globally across humans and Wesen are the ultimate authority: the Royals, seven royal families which control the world politics, society, and economics. The Wesen Council is reminiscent of the Watcher's Council in *Buffy the Vampire Slayer*, although not as directly involved in the storyline. The introduction of this particular hierarchical feature may be on the part of Greenwalt who was co-executive producer on *Buffy* prior to *Grimm* [14].

Prey and predator are arranged in relation with the faunal equivalent of the Wesen. For example, Lausenschlange (a snake-like Wesen) are often predators of Maushertz (mice-like Wesen). Blutbads who mirror wolves are traditional hunters and enemies of Bauerschwein (pig-type Wesen) in clear reference to the "Three Little Pigs". The Wesen hierarchy of prey and predator and Wesen's knowledge of the other types of Wesen is often based on their species' placement within the hierarchy influencing how that type of Wesen subjectively defines the positivity or negativity of the other Wesen and the type of relationship the types of Wesen may experience based on their perceived status. Humans who do not know about Wesen exist in a nearly separate realm from this Wesen hierarchy, while Kehrseite (those humans who cannot see Wesen but know they exist) become integrated into Wesen affairs as tangential to Wesen society. The royal families also have a part in the hierarchy, but as Kehrseite who are rulers of the world. Wesen are obligated to obey or at minimum respect Royals, no matter where the Wesen or Royals may live. Instead, Wesen are most directly affected by the Wesen Council, a group which determines most international Wesen affairs [14].

Grimm addresses environmental issues as well, especially those prominent in current American popular culture such as extinction. In *Grimm*, there are several instances of rare Wesen: Wesen which were often hunted to near extinction. Glühenvolk are one example of an endangered Wesen. Glühenvolk are a Wesen that have a glowing skin and alien features. This Wesen craves cow ovaries when pregnant, giving a *Grimm* explanation to alien sightings and the cattle mutilation found in American conspiracy theory and popular culture. The Glühenvolk skin is sold for high prices on the black market, making it a very secretive Wesen living in constant fear of discovery. When Nick encounters a man and his pregnant wife who are Glühenvolk, Monroe and Rosalie are shocked believing those Wesen no longer existed—hunted to extinction. Endangered species and extinction are a hot topic in many parts of the world, but especially dear in places like the Pacific Northwest where the spotted owl made such a strong impression upon American cultural awareness of deforestation and its effects [14].

There is also an emphasis on the forests surrounding Portland. The forest is the opposite of society, urbanity, and civilization. Forests are the natural world. Woodlands can also be seen as dangerous, unpredictable, magical, and challenging. *Grimm*, set in Portland, becomes a place of lush forests echoing the towering Black Forest of German legends. Periodically, this wood becomes the setting of stories which typically involve some of the wilder or often magical elements of the characters, where, for example, Wesen can roam freely and chase prey. However, the forest itself in *Grimm* is not presented as a place of constant fear or inherent danger. The forest is simply another setting. The majority of crimes and major occurrences of brutality through monsters are in cities, exposing a primal order to nature in *Grimm* in opposition to increased urban disorder in the Grimmverse. This is perhaps turning the traditional fairy tale forest on its head, where the home or village was the safe place and the wilderness was the wild space of danger. This may also be due to the popularity of the forest in American culture as a space that is inherent to American national and historic identity and locally important to the Pacific Northwest as an identifier of place and space [14,18].

Grimm lauds originality and individualism, important American values, through its storylines and character plots. Although Wesen have certain cultures in conjunction with biologically driven urges, they are also not victims of their nature entirely. Wesen are subject to their wills, emotions, and reason. Monroe, for example, chooses to not engage in hunting or eating meat since he does not approve of how he behaves when doing either. He also chooses to pursue a relationship with a Wesen of another type, Rosalie, despite inter-Wesen relationships being looked down upon by many within the community. The relationship between Nick and Monroe is also contrary to the established social order, and Nick's choosing to relate to Wesen as friends or even trusted confidants attests to his individuality and uniqueness, his individual agency being retained through his own decisions [14].

Individual choice and agency as well as inter-Wesen relationships all have strong correlations to American social issues of race, class, gender, and sexual orientation debates as well as strong traditional correlations to American beliefs in individualism and self-agency. Grimm unites human persons against a common nefarious element of Wesen as the enemy and shows that although there is violence and confusion in the world, even ordinary people can make a difference through personal choices. The explanation of evil Wesen as a source of woe in the world brings an order to chaos. Grimm consistently ties past events such as the Third Reich to present events in the Grimmverse with as the rise of the extremist group Black Claw, giving the present a thread of consistency with crime and terror in world history. Humans are faced with needing to unite to overcome Wesen problems, problems most do not even know about. This connection binds all Kehrseite with a heritage of fighting and suffering at the hands of Wesen perpetrated violence. In a present world where Americans view many religious, political, and ethnic groups as hopelessly fractured, Grimm's use of Wesen as an author of world troubles explains how the enemy is actually a fantastical element as opposed to human.

Wesen are also noted as responsible for several violent and non-violent crimes from reality. As Americans were recovering from the real estate crash in 2008, "Plumed Serpent" addressed the copper thefts from abandoned homes that rose throughout the country as potentially being related to Dämonfeuer who collected copper and other shiny metals they traditionally hid in caves. Rosalie and Monroe are victims of Wesen extremists, the Secundum Naturae Ordinem Wesen who are akin to the Ku Klux Klan—frowning upon inter-Wesen relationships and going to the extremes of murdering Wesen who engage in these relationships. Black Claw is another Extremist Wesen group that is seeking to put Wesen in charge of the world and to out Wesen to humanity. Adolf Hitler was a member of Black Claw in the Grimmverse, and Black Claw is blamed for many acts of mass murder, genocide, and terrorism. As Americans become increasingly fearful of global violence and religious extremism, Grimm puts a Wesen face on many crimes as opposed to the human face that adorns the perpetrators in reality, For a short time, an extremely contentious topic in American culture, politics, and media becomes othered in fantasy to become not an American problem or even a human problem, but instead a global conspiracy of non-human origin. Secundum Naturae Ordinem Wesen become Black Claw members, not simply home-grown human bigots. The Grimmverse allows Americans to retain more idealism, even if it is not utopic. The world suddenly becomes less haphazard and more patterned [14].

3. Conclusions

Through televisual media, Grimm allows audiences a chance to explore societal issues and fears within its stories. Fairy tales are shaped by the time and place they are retold [19], giving this retelling of the Grimm stories its own uniqueness. *Grimm* matters because it provides a window on the current American fears of world disorder and social upheaval giving viewers and researchers a small piece of the larger societal and cultural concerns. The storylines and Grimmverse can be seen as reactions to fears about the instability of the global or domestic economies, wars, and other worrisome events over which individuals have no control. Instead, control in the Grimmverse comes through personal action coupled with a scientific or primarily genetic relationship between problems and solutions. Control is gained through safely examining social issues through fantastical storylines emphasizing personal onus of action. In order to counteract the inexplicable, magic is drawn into the story to provide just enough wonder to keep events interesting and perhaps as an acknowledgement that not every event or behavior has a clear explanation. Past actions of Grimms bring current responsibility for solving problems to Nick based on cultural value systems present in the actions of ancestral individuals and within precursor movements. These heritage values [20] also comment on the deep concerns individuals in the present have. By drawing on the past values, the characters bring the perceived success of their ancestors to the crises of today. The larger success of *Grimm* demonstrates a modicum of cultural agreement or resonance with these fears and ways in which Americans either choose to engage in escapism from the anxieties or wishfulness at the simplicity of the Grimmverse blame and solution.

Conflicts of Interest: The author declares no conflict of interest.

References

1. Asma Ayob. "The Mixed Blessings of Disney's Classic Fairy Tales." *Mousaion* 28 (2010): 50–64.
2. Jack Zipes. "The Meaning of Fairy Tale within the Evolution of Culture." *Marvels & Tales: Journal of Fairy-Tale Studies* 25 (2011): 221–43.
3. Ruth B. Bottigheimer. "*Fairy Godfather*, Fairy-Tale History, and Fairy-Tale Scholarship: A Response to Dan Ben-Amos, Jan M. Ziolkowski, and Francisco Vaz da Silva." *Journal of American Folklore* 123 (2010): 447–96.
4. Dan Ben-Amos. "Introduction: The European Fairy-Tale Tradition between Orality and Literacy." *Journal of American Folklore* 123 (2010): 373–76.
5. Francisco Vaz Da Silva. "The Invention of Fairy Tales." *Journal of American Folklore* 123 (2010): 398–425.
6. Simon J. Bronner. *Following Tradition: Folklore in the Discourse of American Culture.* Logan: Utah State University Press, 1998.
7. Lucy R. Lippard. *The Lure of the Local: Sense of Place in a Multicentered Society.* New York: The New Press, 1998.
8. Tracey Mollet. "'With a smile and a song . . . ' Walt Disney and the Birth of the American Fairy Tale." *Marvels & Tales: Journal of Fairy-Tale Studies* 27 (2013): 109–24.
9. Tatiana Podolinská, and Milan Kováč. "'Mythos' Versus 'Logos': Strategies of Rationalization at the Boundaries of Two Worlds in the Conceptions of Supernatural Beings in Slovak Countryside." *Dialogue and Universalism* 12 (2002): 85–99.
10. Barbara A. Strassberg. "Magic, Religion, Science, Technology, and Ethics in the Postmodern World." *Zygon* 40 (2005): 307–22.
11. Claudia Schwabe. "Getting Real with Fairy Tales: Magic Realism in *Grimm* and *Once Upton a Time*." In *Channeling Wonder: Fairy Tales on Television*. Edited by Pauline Greenhill and Jill Terry Rudy. Detroit: Wayne State University Press, 2014, pp. 294–315.
12. NBC. "Grimm." Available online: http://www.nbc.com/grimm (accessed on 16 May 2016).
13. Wikipedia. "Grimm (TV Series)." Available online: https://en.wikipedia.org/wiki/Grimm_%28TV_series%29 (accessed on 16 May 2016).
14. *Grimm*. Directed by David Greenwalt, Jim Kouf, and Stephen Carpenter (Creators). BNC, 2011.
15. Kristiana Willsey. "New Fairy Tales are Old Again: Grimm and the Brothers Grimm." In *Channeling Wonder: Fairy Tales on Television*. Edited by Pauline Greenhill and Jill Terry Rudy. Detroit: Wayne State University Press, 2014, pp. 210–28.
16. Wikia. "The Grimm Wiki." Available online: http://grimm.wikia.com/wiki/Grimm (accessed on 29 February 2016).
17. Veronique Greenwood. "The Humans with Super Human Vision." *Discover Magazine*, 18 June 2012. Available online: http://discovermagazine.com/2012/jul-aug/06-humans-with-super-human-vision (accessed on 26 May 2016).
18. Marco R. S. Post. "Perilous Wanderings through the Enchanted Forest: The Influence of the Fairy-Tale Tradition on Mirkwood in Tolkien's *The Hobbit*." *Mythlore* 33 (2014): 67–84.

19. Laurence Talairach-Vielmas. "Beautiful Maidens, Hideous Suitors: Victorian Fairy Tales and the Process of Civilization." *Marvels & Tales: Journal of Fairy-Tale Studies* 24 (2010): 272–96.

20. George Smith, Phyllis Mauch Messenger, and Hillary Soderland. "Introduction." In *Heritage Values in Contemporary Society*. Edited by George Smith, Phyllis Mauch Messenger and Hillary Soderland. Walnut Creek: Left Coast Press, 2010, pp. 46–48.

"They All Lived Happily Ever After. Obviously.": Realism and Utopia in *Game of Thrones*-Based Alternate Universe Fairy Tale Fan Fiction

Anne Kustritz

Abstract: Fan fiction alternate universe stories (AUs) that combine *Game of Thrones* characters and settings with fairy tale elements construct a dialogue between realism and wonder. Realism performs a number of functions in various genres, but becomes a particularly tricky concept to tie down in fantasy. Deployments of realism in "quality TV" series like *Game of Thrones* often reinforce social stigmatization of feminine genres like the romance, melodrama, and fairy tale. The happily-ever-after ending receives significant feminist criticism partly because it falls within a larger framework of utopian politics and poetics, which are frequently accused of essentialism and authoritarianism. However, because fan fiction cultures place all stories in dialogue with numerous other equally plausible versions, the fairy tale happy ending can serve unexpected purposes. By examining several case studies in fairy tale AU fan fiction based on *Game of Thrones* characters, situations, and settings, this paper demonstrates the genre's ability to construct surprising critiques of real social and historical situations through strategic deployment of impossible wishes made manifest through the magic of fan creativity.

Reprinted from *Humanities*. Cite as: Kustritz, A. "They All Lived Happily Ever After. Obviously.": Realism and Utopia in *Game of Thrones*-Based Alternate Universe Fairy Tale Fan Fiction. *Humanities* **2016**, *5*, 43.

1. Introduction

Once Upon a Time and *Game of Thrones*, which both premiered in 2011, each portray themselves as, at least, partly realistic medieval-based fantasy worlds in contrast to "traditional" fairy tales [1,2]. Yet, while HBO's[1] *Game of Thrones* largely conveys realism through graphic sex, violence, and a dystopian refusal of anything approaching a "happy ending", *Once Upon a Time* uses a network-approved form of melodrama to muddy up familiar fairy tale characters' motivations. *Once Upon a Time* parodied this tonal dichotomy in the finale of its fourth season, when a magical

---

[1] HBO, or Home Box Office, is an American premium cable channel.

plume sent the characters into a dark alternate universe very much like *Game of Thrones* where, as one character explained to another, "It's cold, there's no running water, and things are always trying to kill you" [3]. Yet, despite its protests and pretensions, *Game of Thrones'* realist narrative contains numerous fairy tale tropes and references, which offer fans clear openings to enact their own genre displacement of the narrative and imagine different possible futures. By examining fan-written fairy tale versions of *Game of Thrones*, these continuities become increasingly clear. This project thus unravels the consequences of *Game of Thrones'* characteristically quality TV construction of realism through the normative principles of intelligibility and probability, separating that which may be culturally received as realistic from that which becomes unrealistic in contrast. The project then investigates feminist, queer, and historical criticism of one particularly "unrealistic" fairy tale trope: the "happily-ever-after" ending with its tendencies toward proscriptive normative closure, as it interacts with fan fiction distribution networks that enable narrative proliferation. Finally, the paper then examines five examples of *Game of Thrones*-based fairy tale AU (alternate universe) fan fiction, demonstrating the range of fan fiction authors' experimentation with fairy tale tropes. By juxtaposing *Game of Thrones* and fairy tales, modern fan authors reflect on the conditions of modern and historical life, expressing otherwise unrealistic political, sexual, and cultural possibilities through the language of magic and wonder.

2. Quality TV and the Riddle of Realism

As argued by Michael Newman and Elana Levine, contemporary "quality TV" like *Game of Thrones* legitimates itself through several strategies, including realism, to substantiate its claims to social, political, and artistic merit [4]. The fairy tale, on the contrary, often functions as cultural shorthand for unrealistic idealism, as discussed by Vanessa Joosen [5]. The clichéd phrase, "this isn't a fairy tale" generally indicates, in the vernacular, that things are about to "get real", typically meaning dark, complicated, and decidedly unhappy. Programs like *Game of Thrones* thus inhabit a place within a much longer conversation on the meaning and construction of realism and cultural value, and, as a result, these longstanding internal contradictions of realist representation play themselves out within *Game of Thrones'* narrative and reception, as well as in fan rewrites. The significance of fan writing that reframes *Game of Thrones* within a fairy tale narrative thus pivots upon the contested meaning of realist storytelling, especially within the context of gendered genres and the history of queer and feminist forms of fairy tale revision. Such tales, when placed within fan distribution networks, may recuperate both the pleasures and politics of stories beyond the bounds of what contemporary "quality TV" deems realistic, particularly when realism is defined through the normative criteria of the intelligible and the probable.

The question of realism in television has long been tangled up in intersecting hierarchies of taste, quality, gender, and the politics of the possible. While many classic scholars of television, such as Raymond Williams, preferred sociological over aesthetic study of the medium as part of a critical approach to the social violence inflicted by taste cultures, which often brands all TV as low culture trash, analysis of so-called "quality TV" and television's cultural value has become increasingly important to the field and the industry [4,6–14]. Scholars, including Cristine Geraghty, argued that value judgments are necessary to understand how most people think about TV, while others began mapping out specific criteria by which quality might be measured in a genre- and medium-specific manner, such as Jason Mittel's work on "complex TV" [7,11]. For Robert Thompson, quality TV most often, "creates a new genre by mixing old ones ... tends to be literary and writer-based...The subject matter...tends towards the controversial [and]...it aspires toward 'realism'" ([15], pp. 14–15). Although Thompson wrote in 1996 about network TV programs like *Hill Street Blues* and *ER*, his description maps closely onto *Game of Thrones* and the branding strategies of contemporary cable companies that market themselves as a quality alternative to network TV, most notably HBO whose catch phrase for over ten years was "It's not TV. It's HBO" [4,10]. Realism of some description thus functions as one of the key criteria by which the quality of television has come to be judged, and the definition of realism thereby also becomes a critical question in understanding the cultural position of modern television programs and their associated fan works.

Game of Thrones neatly sutures several of Thompson's criteria for defining realism, and its media reception begins to suggest the problematic excisions performed by quality TV's claims to represent realistic subject matter. Based on a genre-defying series of books known for appropriating and questioning aspects of fantasy, fairy tale, and historical fiction, *Game of Thrones* nicely meets Thompson's requirement that quality programs are literary and challenge genre conventions. Yet, most importantly for this inquiry, Thompson groups together the requirement that quality programs employ controversial subject matter and a realist aesthetic, what Kim Akass and Janet McCabe call the ironic nexus of "sex, swearing, and respectability" [6,15]. Known for its gritty quasi-mediaeval storyworld overflowing with graphic sex, graphic violence, and graphic sexual violence, subject matter allowed only on cable by American broadcast censors, *Game of Thrones* draws on both controversy and realist claims to secure its place within HBO's pantheon of quality dramas [16]. As a mark of its success, the series has become a critical darling, heralded in articles that emphasize its realism and applicability to actual political and social issues with titles like: "Why *Game of Thrones* is More than Fantasy," "How *Game of Thrones* Teaches Us About the Syrian Refugee Crisis," and "The Real Human History Behind *Game of Thrones*" [17–19]. Key to *Game of Thrones'* positioning in this respect is its frequently cited basis in real history, namely the War of the Roses in mediaeval England. These realist historical bonafides are frequently discussed in interviews with the author, George R. R. Martin, and form the basis of significant fan activity, including the website "History Behind *Game of Thrones*", dedicated to voluminous excavation of the historical basis for the series' characters and plots, as well as educational videos like TedTalk-sponsored "The Wars that Inspired *Game of Thrones*" [20–22]. Coupled with its reliance on graphic subject matter, *Game of Thrones* thus exemplifies the quality TV implication that reality is inherently too dark for network TV.

Yet, realism can also be a surprisingly difficult quality to pin down. Luc Herman's *Concepts of Realism* begins with the observation, "Realism in literature can mean a great many things" ([23], p. 9). The aesthetics and politics of realism have long been in dispute, and for nearly as long realism has been tied to claims about seriousness and quality. Take, for example, Andrew Higson writing in *Screen* in 1984 about British realist films: "The term 'realism' is used because it is the key term in that discourse mobilized by contemporary critics and film historians alike to validate these films as the most worthy aspects of British film making" ([24], p. 2). Yet, immediately another definition of "realism" surfaces in opposition to the association of realism with quality, as Higson's frames his paper with three quotations. The third, written in 1963 in the *Society of Film and TV Arts Journal* by an unnamed commenter, defines realism as follows: "Today most people talk about a New Realism—a realistic realism, and that would mostly seem to cover swearing, talking about contraceptives, two people just up to the moment of sexual intercourse and That Long Shot of Our Town from That Hill" ([24], p. 2). This quotation precipitously deflates the grand claims to the artistic and political merit of films validated through realism by pointing to the specific aesthetic, narrative, and cinematographic conventions that are used to convey "realism" to audiences, opening a space of critique between the magic and weight of realist effects and the actual contrivance of their production.

Higson's discussion of realism as an aesthetic contrivance highlights the gap that stubbornly remains in realist forms between the real and the representation of the real; yet it also points toward the relationship between realism and normative systems of social legibility. The corollary to his conclusion suggests that at the far other end of narrative forms that emphasize their status as fiction unfolding within highly constructed story worlds with very different rules and natural conditions from our own, that is, high fantasy, fairy tale, and science fiction storyworlds, including *Game of Thrones*, reality effects and truth claims may still function because realism is largely a matter of visual and narrative conventions, not access to actually unfolding reality. However, this also implies that the language, structures, and feeling of realism will be highly contextual and historically contingent. Thus, while in 1963 the mention of contraception may have felt shockingly realistic, audience expectations and genre structures have shifted, which says nothing about the actual state of contraceptive use, but quite a lot about the underlying structures of intelligibility within the mainstream media industry over time. Intelligibility thus emerges as a key underlying normative function of the realist mode. That which can be shown on screen and considered real in a given era structures a boundary between sense and nonsense, possibility and impossibility. The unintelligibility of sexual choices outside of heteronormative frameworks forms a central preoccupation of Judith Butler's *Gender Trouble*, wherein she writes, "The task here is...to redescribe those possibilities that *already* exist, but which exist within cultural domains designated as culturally unintelligible and impossible" ([25], p. 203). Likewise, realist quality TV like *Game of Thrones* marks a cultural boundary of controversial but intelligible images, beyond which less culturally valued forms, including fan fiction and the fairy tale, may excavate a collective archive of culturally unrealistic and impossible stories and lives.

As a result, the status of realism in *Game of Thrones* reveals important shifts in the cultural status of TV, the fairy tale, transmedia storytelling, and gendered pleasures within the modern media industry. Thus, in addition to legibility, probability functions as a second critical criterion for evaluating realist claims; in other words, whose pleasures are considered reasonable and probable, and whose pleasures are considered unrealistically improbable? Both fantasy and fairy tales carry strong associations with unreality. This may be partly because, as Maria Nikolajeva argues in "Fairy Tale and Fantasy", the fantasy genre emerged from fairy tales, and though fantasy translated fairy tales from archaic to modernist cosmologies, it still shares some of the fairy tale's underlying tropes and iconography [26]. Yet, in her study of realism in modern fairy tale rewrites, Joosen makes a distinction between theorists who define realism as excluding magic and the supernatural, which would immediately disqualify both fairy tales and fantasy, and those like Jack Zipes who see realism in narratives that utilize metaphor and allegory to reveal historical or contemporary social truths [5,27,28]. She thus quotes Bernd Wollenweber's assertion that "fairy tales are not fantastic or unrealistic, on the contrary, they are highly realistic. They represent experiences, they show actual conflicts, they describe private and social relationships" ([5], p. 229). Yet, fairy tales still struggle to attain cultural status as realist, while HBO's *Game of Thrones* utilizes several specific strategies to distance itself from fantasy's "unrealistic" and feminized fairy tale roots, and align itself with serious realist drama, primary among which is the refusal of "improbable" "happily ever after" narrative closure. The realist mode is repeatedly, though not always, associated with dystopian and cynical portrayals of history, society, and everyday life, often in opposition to genres like romanticism, utopianism, the pastoral, and the hero's journey. Yet the association between realism, quality, graphic content, and negative outcomes also reinforces a gendered binary with narratives like the melodrama and the fairy tale, which are deemed unrealistic, partly because of what Nikolajeva calls "morally fixed" happy or tragic outcomes [26]; she argues that such outcomes lack complexity, the defining characteristic of quality narration highlighted by Mittell [8,9,29,30]. The opening contrast between *Game of Thrones* and *Once Upon a Time* exemplifies this divergence in value between the quality cable drama, whose dominant register is fantasy, and the unrealistic network melodrama, whose dominant narrative element is the fairy tale. Differences in these programs, therefore, map onto gendered underpinnings of taste culture hierarchies, which theorists Michael Newman and Elana Levine argue mark quality TV as a masculine realm of distinction and regular TV as a feminized space of consumption [4]. In their co-written book, *Legitimating Television*, they explain that the ascent of quality TV comes with a cost, namely the further intensification of cultural shame and disparagement directed toward populations still associated with "non-quality TV", like *Once Upon a Time*, namely "children and women", whose desires and media objects remain at the bottom of taste hierarchies ([4], p. 16). Even Geraghty, who championed the study of TV quality, cautioned that the uncritical embrace of quality TV discourse would merely "end[ed] up with a version of the 'difficult', male-orientated, naturalist drama of an earlier television studies" ([7], p. 32).

Fairy tales, especially in the happily-ever-after mode, thus function as the unreasonable feminine other, in contrast to reasonable realist masculine drama. It is no mistake, therefore, that Nikolajeva proposes a gendered narrative of progress from the fairy tale, which she characterizes as overly simplistic, to the more sophisticated fantasy genre [26]. Debra Ferreday underlines this gendered cultural association when she explains that, despite the voluminous and productive history of feminist and queer fantasy literature, most commentators still assume there are no female fantasy writers or fans, and react with amazement when confronted by *Game of Thrones'* large female fan following ([16], p. 24). Joosen discusses this hidden, gendered criteria of reasonableness or probability within the construction of realism, writing, "When critics use the term 'realism' on the level of content, it can mean both what is 'possible' or what is 'probable'" ([5], p. 229). Both fairy tales and fantasy violate the criterion of the possible, as both contain magical and/or supernatural elements; yet it is the criterion of the probable that fairy tale happy outcomes appear to violate with their unreasonable feminine optimism.

Thus, realism functions within *Game of Thrones* as part of a branding strategy to maintain separation from regular television on the grounds of quality [10,13]. While scholars like Thompson and Mittell have discussed a number of characteristics associated with the construction of quality TV, Newman and Levine emphasize that gendered hierarchies and elitism centrally structure judgments about the taste value of television [4,11]. As a signatory of quality, realism, particularly as defined by the characteristics of the probable and legible combined with a focus on gruesome subject matter and concomitant repudiation of fairy tale happy endings, thereby adds to the problematic gendered hierarchies that construct quality on contemporary TV. *Game of Thrones'* claims to quality via realism thus connect to a rejection of feminized "unrealistic" modes of storytelling, and for the fantasy genre that particularly means rejection of its seed-genre the fairy tale, with its "improbable" embrace of positive possible outcomes. Therefore, fan fiction stories that recombine *Game of Thrones* with fairy tale elements offer fan audiences a glimpse of stories and lives made improbable and unintelligible by the framework of value that underpins quality on contemporary TV.

3. Feminists, Fans, and Dreams of a Transmedia Utopia

Although fairy tales have often been associated with women, they have frequently also been characterized as bad for women, especially the "happily-ever-after ending" as popularized by Disney [31]. Although children form the dominant expected modern fairy tale audience, critics like Deborah Ross and Marcia Lieberman argue that romantic fairy tales experienced in childhood continue to affect adult women's expectations about their gender role and their future heterosexual relationships [32–34]. Thus, in particular, the happily-ever-after ending receives criticism as both too dangerously oppressive and too unrealistically positive both for women and for politics [34–38]. Yet, such criticisms needlessly foreclose possibilities for both the personal and political imagination of different futures made possible through utopian storytelling. As a practice of the possible, which structurally undermines any authoritative version of fictional events, fan fiction provides space for unexpected encounters between *Game of Thrones'* realist-dystopian fantasyscape, and the utopian possibilities for change and alternate futures found within fairy tale conventions. *Game of Thrones* AUs featuring happily-ever-after endings thus explore productive political and aesthetic hybridities unavailable to either genre form in isolation, facilitated by the non-profit distribution infrastructure of the fan community.

Feminist critiques of the happily-ever-after ending often emphasize either its oppressive tendency toward normativity and closure or its wholehearted embrace of heterosexual bliss. Thus, it is a curious problem that the lives of female fairy tale protagonists seem to always end with marriage, especially in Disney versions, as argued by Stone [31]. Not only does marriage mark the end of the plot, but also quite literally the end of the characters' lives, because the phrase "happily ever after" indicates an unchanging stasis. As a result, a great many feminist reinterpretations of fairy tales attempt to break the narrative closure sealing fairy tale heroines into the forever-stasis of happiness, to allow them to continue growing, changing, and living interesting lives [27,39,40]. Theorist Jack/Judith Halberstam argued that this narrative structure reinforces larger cultural systems of heteronormativity and patriarchy by normalizing one single life path that ends in heterosexual marriage and children, making the many other potential life paths seem abnormal, improbable, and unintelligible [41]. In contrast, he offers the concept of "queer time" to describe all the many alternate ways a lifetime might be structured when the normative ways of organizing time, and narrating it into coherence, are abandoned. Combined with the momentum that propels readers toward the resolution of fictional conflicts and makes those resolutions feel satisfying, feminist critiques of the ever-after ending conclude that such fairy tales are not only powerful because they remove alternate options and storylines, but because they make women's disempowerment feel like pleasure [42].

On the contrary, another source of happily-ever-after criticism decries such endings as unrealistically happy. Fairy tales, so one is told, give women unrealistically high expectations of men. They lead women to believe that their inevitable, or compulsory, in Adrienne Rich's terms, future husbands will be loving and kind, and that marital relationships are fulfilling and, above all, happy [43]. This is, apparently, far too much to expect from life, or more specifically, from men who, in this evaluation, are much more likely to be cruel or indifferent. Similar critiques surface in Tania Modleski and Janice Radway's discussions of the romance genre, another offspring of the fairy tale for scholars, including Linda Lee, who argue that the genre primarily functions to transform what they describe as the normative female experience of male cruelty into a sign of love capable of producing happiness [32,44,45]. It is also an idea that *Game of Thrones'* version of realism nearly specializes in disrupting. This pattern is perhaps most apparent in Sansa Stark's storyline, which begins with a nearly fairy tale structure, as a beautiful and naive young princess arrives in a distant land to marry the prince and live happily ever after. Yet *Game of Thrones* quickly quashes Sansa's and the audience's expectations with a sharp dose of "realism," as the prince turns out to be a psychopath, incapable of redemption via the storied love of a good woman, and Sansa ends up beaten, humiliated, and rejected. Sansa, perhaps unsurprisingly, becomes a popular heroine of fan fiction fairy tale AUs, since her story directly evokes and then rejects the fairy tale form.

In political terms, the happily-ever-after ending is a form of utopianism, and comes with the same foibles and potentials as many forms of utopian storytelling. Many post-structuralists critique political projects aimed at utopian dreams of a better future largely because, in Michel Foucault's conception, they do not actually do away with power, and for Lee Edelman, they require expensive and cruel sacrifices in symbolic exchange for a more perfect tomorrow, which never arrives [46–49]. As historian and theorist James C. Scott explains, utopian thinking has strong costs because it proposes an unfeasible "end to history" when everything will be perfect, no other challenges or problems will emerge, and further change will be unnecessary—in fairy tale terms, the happy couple fades into the sunset [36–38]. In addition, Scott continues, utopian political projects also tend toward authoritarianism, as individual desires and local circumstances are subsumed within a larger collective agenda—thus the happily-ever-after ending's coercive suppression of alternate life paths.

Yet, at the same time, Scott cautions that some form of utopian thinking may always be necessary for political action, and in the case of fiction, Scott's work could suggest that coercive closure may be necessary for narrative pleasure [36–38]. Without imagining a better, different future, how might people be motivated to act collectively to improve their circumstances? In her book, *Cruel Optimism*, Lauren Berlant explores this crossroads in her consideration of the same political critique that is often leveled against fairy tale happy endings: when placed within a utopian genre form, oppression can feel like pleasure, and many of our most culturally cherished stories about liberation and happiness actually trap us in a situation that, like patriarchy and capitalism, is actively cruel, exploitative, and limiting [50]. Berlant's attempts to imagine an anti-neo-liberal politics leading to a "better good life" without the promise of a single static definition of political good places her in dialogue with Scott's description of the ultimate political challenge left by the dissolution of many utopian political projects of the 20th century into authoritarianism: how might we imagine and collectively act upon dreams of a better future without instantiating an oppressive and smothering end of history? In other words, is there such a thing as a happy life after happily ever after?

Fairy tale traditions and fan fiction cultures offer key critical alternatives to mass-mediated storytelling in their ability to undermine the coercive inevitability of any one ending; as such, they also open alternative political and narrative uses of utopian storytelling, including "happily ever after." The singularity of utopian endings, which make all other endings illegitimate, only becomes feasible because of the monopoly on storytelling granted to authors via copyright law and cultural authority, from the print era onward [51–53]. There is, indeed, life after happily ever after when the author does not automatically have the last say, and anyone can reopen closed narratives to tell their own version of past and future events. In his landmark article "The Death of the Author", Roland Barthes unpacks the cultural and linguistic influences that place texts, not so much as individual works of genius, but as part of a collective history of meaning creation and storytelling [54]. Fairy tales represent an extreme version of this principle, since many derive from a long legacy of oral culture and communal storytelling practice wherein the notion of a "correct" version makes little sense. Yet, Foucault cautions that, even when authors do not or cannot exist, within the present cultural paradigm someone or something must still serve the author-function [55]. For fairy tales, collectors like the brothers Grimm have often served the author-function, but, within the modern mass media, Disney

Corporation frequently takes this position and the associated authority through its ability to reach an enormous global audience, and through strategic use of copyright law [56]. Although Stone is suspicious of some oral storytelling versions as well, she and many other theorists often reserve their greatest vitriol for the particular way in which Disney versions of fairy tales dominate the cultural conversation and appear to take characters and stories that were once part of a living tradition and freeze them in time, never to be modified again [31]. Copyright and mass distribution are the tools through which the Disney version of fairy tales becomes inescapable and inevitable—or essential and authoritarian—because it makes all other versions and alternatives illegitimate and unspeakable in public media space (or at least makes a strong attempt) [56,57].

In this sense, the folk history of fairy tales and the rise of modern transmedia storytelling, convergence culture, and fan cultures provide an important alternative to mass media and an important democratizing context for mass-mediated stories. In her examination of the diffuse, multi-authored, and multi-media networks through which fairy tales have always proliferated, Cristina Bacchilega coins the term, "fairy tale web", to describe the vast complexity of interconnected meanings that underlie fairy tales [58]. She argues that although Disney certainly has an outsized affect on public awareness and interpretation of fairy tales, at this point in history it is difficult to remain unaware of at least some of the other parts of the fairy tale web, which include transnational, critical, and amateur retellings. Bacchilega makes the case that audiences can and do have an unpredictable series of encounters with fairy tale media, and they bring all of those experiences to bear on future interaction with and interpretation of fairy tale narrative elements. In other words, every happy ending can only be the beginning of a new story, because within the fairy tale web, no individual story can maintain ultimate authority. Henry Jenkins and Carlos Scolari extend a similar argument to all sorts of transmedia storytelling, which forms an increasingly central part of the modern media industry [59–62]. Because media corporations more and more often disperse story elements across a variety of media, and a variety of media spaces, while inviting fans to participate and add to the story themselves, transmedia storytelling undermines clear distinctions between legitimate and illegitimate authors, or between a canon or core narrative and peripheral fan works [63,64]. Judith Fathallah documents *Game of Thrones'* transmedia deployment of its narrative elements, including explicit calls for fan-created transmedia extensions despite the author's stated disapproval of fan works, a move which thus destabilizes the author's intentions as the chief determinant of narrative cohesion [65]. As a result, Jenkins, Scolari, and Marie-Laure Ryan argue that, for audiences, amateur or fan additions to a transmedia storyworld may be received as equally legitimate to those produced by professionals [60–62,66].

Jenkins has also argued that modern fan cultures who produce transformative works act in continuity to oral, communal storytelling cultures like those that first produced fairy tales [67]. In this way, fan communities and fan fiction are the modern inheritors of a storytelling tradition that predates copyright, in which all people had the authority to add their own version of events to the ongoing story of shared culture. Thus, Mafalda Stasi has argued that fan fiction is a form of "palimpsestic literature", wherein each story is heavily intertextual and its full depth cannot be understood by analyzing the text itself, but necessitates consideration of all the many layers of texts and intertexts which underlie it [68]. *Game of Thrones* fairy tale AUs perfectly exemplify this principle, as these fan works reconceptualize the HBO show, the books the show is based on, and the fairy tale genre, as well as other fan-specific genre conventions, while the books themselves also draw heavily on numerous layers of fairy tale, alternate history, and fantasy novels, films, and stories as intertexts. Such complexity emphasizes the status of authors as communal actors who reorder an existing discursive field; as discussed by scholars like Julie Levin Russo, the politics and aesthetics of fan works must not, therefore, be considered in terms of the qualities of the text alone, but in contrast to the entire amateur and professional cultural milieu, as fan authors' and artists' expressions are frequently only made implicitly via their subtle departures from other versions and narrative norms [69–72].

Fan fiction also maintains a strong element of utopian thinking, since, especially in the internet era, it allows audiences space to circulate their most expansive dreams with no editorial controls [73]. As I have argued elsewhere, the free or at-cost circulation of internet fan fiction ensures that, although trends and taste communities form, fan production of transformative works, including fan fiction, may continue far in excess of demand, meaning that neither the legal nor economic realities of the media industry limit how much fan material can be published, and how much cultural and narrative experimentation can occur [70]. As a result, fan authors have the freedom to write and circulate material that professionals shy away from, a phenomena described by fan author Ellen Fremedon as the "Id vortex", wherein fans may more openly embrace material considered naive, utopian, and taboo than the industry [74]. Similarly, Elizabeth Woledge especially calls sexual fan fiction an "intimatopia", wherein unrealistic perfection and seamless intimacy often become the norm [75]. While her discussion does not take into account the many genres of fan writing dedicated to dystopia, gruesome subject matter, and unhappiness, the utopian urge certainly still forms a strong tradition in fan writing communities, and the open space of fan fiction distribution provides for dialogue between all these possible versions of characters' lives [71,76–78]. This allows, to some extent, for fan utopias to enjoy the best of both worlds—they benefit from utopian storytelling's ability to point toward a better future, which can motivate the desire for change, while not foreclosing the possibility for critique and revision, since no one utopia ever maintains authority. As a result, *Game of Thrones* fairy tale AUs offer a unique form of cultural and narrative experimentation made possible by combining utopian, fairy tale, and fantasy genres within the context of amateur, fan distribution networks.

4. Game of Thrones Meets a Fairy Tale Ending: the Fairy Tale AU

Fan fiction stories that combine fairy tale narratives, storyworlds, and tropes with *Game of Thrones* characters, situations, and settings make that which is impossible on *Games of Thrones* possible: namely, the happily-ever-after ending. In particular, the fairy tale AU, or alternate universe, genre can allow for a subtle form of critique by constructing beautiful images of future happiness and implicating *Game of Thrones*, and dominant structures of representation more broadly, in their refusal to allow the realization of this pleasurable and desirable end. In this manner, it is sometimes the very unrealisticness of the happily-ever-after ending that makes it political, questioning the institutions and systems that prevent certain kinds of relationships from being represented, and certain lives from being lived, marking them as improbable and consigning them to illegibility. Thus, despite their perhaps unrealistic utopian urge, some fairy tale AUs based on *Game of Thrones* may have more in common with Halberstam's concept of queer time than expected, because they detail all the potential paths to good lives that *Game of Thrones*, quality TV tropes, and the constraints of the dominant mass media suppress as frivolous, illegible, and impossible. A series of case studies will be examined, based on "The Princess and the Frog", "Cinderella", "Beauty and the Beast", and "Bluebeard", published on the "Archive of Our Own" non-profit fan fiction repository [79–81]. Although these stories represent only a drop of the flood of available fan works taken from only one central archive, they still begin to suggest the range of thought experiments possible when the *Game of Thrones* storyworld collides with the fairy tale, and the way in which fan spaces set all these visions of the better good life into dialogue.

First, "The Princess and the Direwolf" by WelshCakes68 borrows from the tale of "The Princess and the Frog", as well as "Little Red Riding Hood", to make impossible lesbian desires between *Game of Thrones* characters manifest via magic [82]. The story breaks with realism, both in terms of possibility and plausibility, and yet still addresses real feelings and politics on a metaphorical register. At the opening of the story, Margaery Tyrell slips out of a stuffy ball, away from the scrutiny of her grandmother, to sit alone in a garden, near a pond. There she is approached by an enormous wolf, but her initial fear quickly gives way to tenderness when the wolf nuzzles her hand, asking for affection. After snuggling with and feeding the wolf, Margaery tells it that despite her family's pressure, she does not want a husband, and then recounts the legend of the princess who kissed a frog, next to the very pond where they sit; the frog turned into a handsome prince, Margaery says, and they

135

lived happily ever after. Margaery finishes the story with an impossible wish: "If I kiss a wolf instead of a frog, what are my chances that you might turn into a beautiful princess instead?" Setting aside doubt, she leans in to kiss the wolf's snout, and luckily magic intervenes; the wolf does indeed become a princess, transforming into Sansa Stark.

The grandmother reference and the wolf connect to "Little Red Riding Hood", while the story-within-a-story connects to "The Princess and the Frog", both of which fall under the larger category of fairy tales featuring animal transformations. Such "transbiology" stories carry latent queer possibilities, according to Pauline Greenhill, as they construct potential animal–human relationships and subjectivities that push the boundaries of normative sexual imagination, and offer fertile ground for building LGBTQIA[2] narratives [83]. However, this rich symbolic source of alternate sexual storytelling is foreclosed in the *Game of Thrones* version of realism, not because of the impossible feat of a human transforming into a wolf, but because of the implausible possibility of lesbian desire and relationships in even a fantastic version of the Middle Ages. In the historically-inflected storyworld of *Game of Thrones*, patriarchy severely limits the mobility and social power of women, to the extent that they often have little choice but to marry men for survival. Princesses, in particular, have little control over their romantic destiny, as they must marry to forge political alliances. Margaery's and Sansa's character paths are both foreclosed by these principles, as Margaery becomes the serial widow of three (would be) kings and princes, and after her rejection by her betrothed psychopathic prince, Sansa is ruthlessly pursued by others who would like to solidify their claim to the throne or family alliances by marrying into her royal line and the territory her husband inherits. Erotic relationships between men exist in *Game of Thrones*, but erotic relationships between women are limited to two female prostitutes performing together for the pleasure of their paying male customers [16].

Without access to their own funds, space, and legal status, it is indeed logically difficult for women in *Game of Thrones* and in actual medieval Europe to form same-sex relationships, as noted by historian of gay identity John D'Emilio in his landmark work on the emancipatory effect of capitalist wage labor for many gay and lesbian people [84]. However, difficult and impossible are not the same, as attested by the work of historians who excavate early lesbian history like Carol Smith Rosenberg, Valerie Traub, Judith Bennett, and Ann Cvetkovich [85–88]. Forgetting that such women existed reinforces a violently heteronormative erasure of real history. Public articulation of the wish for a same-sex partner still remains contentious in modern media, making this story not only relevant to the past, but also the lived reality of contemporary audiences [89]. The impossible wish that comes true in

---

[2] Lesbian, Gay, Bisexual, Trans, Queer/Questioning, Intersex, and Allies.

"The Princess and the Direwolf" is a kind of utopian storytelling that both names the injustice and limitations that constrain action and imagination, and seeks to imagine a possible future beyond them. It attempts to make impossible desires possible, first by articulating them into legibility, then by making them manifest. The unrealistic and unrealizable space between the wish and the appearance of the princess is the space of desire, and the engine of change.

Secondly, several retellings drawn from "Cinderella" and "Beauty and the Beast" utilize the fairy tale framework's nearly irresistible momentum toward a happy ending in order to make their culturally unrealistic couples seem inevitable and right for each other [90]. The Cinderella-based story, "A waltz among the cinders", by Empress Irony pairs Sansa Stark with Stannis Baratheon, a relationship made improbable by the couple's large age gap, disparate personalities, and lack of meaningful interaction in the source text [91].[3] Interestingly, the authors' notes state that "A waltz among the cinders" draws primarily from the Moacube graphic novel game version of the Cinderella story, titled "Cinders" [93]. This underscores its unique situatedness within Bacchilega's fairy tale web as an intertext, not primarily with the Disney Cinderella, but between a transmedia feminist revision and *Game of Thrones* [58]. Empress Irony's inspiration by Moacube's version, which gives the player a trophy whenever their choices open a non-normative story path, becomes apparent in Sansa's representation as a sexually aggressive, active, and self-possessed heroine; she rejects the narcissistic prince once she arrives at the ball and instead dances the last dance with her kind but stoic fairy protector, as Stannis takes the place of the fairy godmother in this retelling [91]. However, unlike the computer graphic novel, which offers over 300 different possible endings, "A waltz among the cinders" can only end in happily-ever-after for Sansa and Stannis, a narrative structure whose built-in satisfactions may to some extent displace audiences' surprise and potential resistance to their romance. In a way, the very strangeness of Stannis as an unlikely prince charming underscores Sansa's agency as a feminist revision of Cinderella. Whether the audience understands her motivations or not, Sansa actively and eagerly chooses Stannis, and the narrative structure legitimates her as a choosing agent. The last line of the story, reproduced in the title of this article, reinforces the inevitability of this improbable couple's happiness: "And they all lived happily ever after. Obviously" [91]. That "obviously" performs a tricky function of simultaneous

---

[3] For comparison, of the couples discussed here, there are currently 131 stories featuring Sansa and Stannis on the *Archive of Our Own*, while there are 626 stories about a relationship between Sansa and Margaery, and 1747 stories about Brienne and Jaime. Thus, even in fan circles, the Stannis/Sansa relationship seems relatively unlikely. Critically, the *Archive of Our Own* is only one among many archives and social networks where fan fiction is published and distributed, so these numbers are only suggestive, not definitive [92].

closure and disruption as this outcome for Sansa and Stannis is anything but obvious, and at the same time that line, the fairy tale structure, and readers' willingness to believe, can make it so.

Also based on Cinderella, "cedar + gold" by Atlantisairlock again utilizes the near certainty that this tale must end with a happily-ever-after romance to position the union of its same-sex pair as good, right, and inevitable [94]. Sansa again plays Cinderella, and Margaery plays the princess she falls in love with at the ball. Unlike "The Princess and the Direwolf" which makes lesbian desire and relationships a utopian dream within the frame of the narrative, "cedar + gold" takes the opposite tack, making princesses who marry each other just as much part of the fabric of the fairy tale universe as mice who turn into horses, or direwolves who turn into horses, in this case. Yet, the story functions similarly because of the gap between its utopian storyworld and the world portrayed on the TV series. Class difference still functions as a damaging form of social hierarchy in "cedar + gold", but the author sets aside the patriarchal and heteronormative conditions of the source text to imagine a Margaery completely unburdened from the necessity of securing a royal husband, allowed to take on her own political authority, roam the city unchaperoned, and seek the hand of anyone she loves, including a lady. The author explicitly states the utopian wish, which remains utopian to this day, that motivates the storyworld in the author's notes, writing, "In this AU, nobody really cares that Margaery's lover is female" [94]. The ability to articulate a vision of a world in which desire between women goes completely unremarked may seem as unrealistic as fairy godmothers with excellent fashion sense; yet that very comparison provides the story its underlying real political and emotional resonance.

In addition, "Beauty and the Beast" provides the framework within which another unlikely couple, by modern media and cultural standards, comes to appear perfectly suited for a happily ever after. The "Beauty and the Beast" storyline offers not only the happily-ever-after ending but also a curse as tools to reinforce the couple's status as legitimate; if only true love can break the story's curse, then breaking it magically reinforces the strength of the couple's bond. Imagineagreatadventure's "Beauty and the Beast" pairs *Game of Thrones* characters Brienne of Tarth and Jaime Lannister [95].[4] While Jaime's character slides almost seamlessly into the role of Beast, since both begin their tales as vain, wealthy, and beautiful men whose arrogance brings about a devastating change in their appearance and the beginning of a redemption arc. On the contrary, while

---

[4] "Heartsick" by Lady Blade WarAngel offers a similar story structure wherein the breaking of a curse reinforces the rightness of the Brienne/Jamie relationship. However, while clearly inspired by fairy tale tropes, Lady Blade WarAngel constructs an original storyline that does not strictly reproduce any single fairy tale [96].

Imagineagreatadventure still calls Brienne "Beauty" within the story, she makes clear that the nickname is a cruel joke, as Brienne maintains her appearance from the series, wherein she is explicitly called ugly. Brienne's masculine appearance and behavior lend themselves to interpretation as signifiers of lesbianism, but perhaps the more challenging characterization for dominant beauty standards is to propose a union between an enormously tall, broad-shouldered, muscle-bound women seen as ugly by her contemporaries, and an attractive, high-status man.

This is the problematic also exposed in the runaway success of transnational adaptations of *Yo Soy Betty la Fea/Ugly Betty*, which proposed to break the mold of beauty culture by following the life of an ugly woman working in the fashion industry. Yet most versions of the show notoriously cast very beautiful actresses, only made "ugly" with makeup and accessories, which the makeover-inspired narrative required must be removed before her happily-ever-after romance with her boss could come to its culmination [97,98]. Imagineagreatadventure constructs an opposing utopian fantasy by proposing that Brienne can find her happy ending without a makeover, and without giving up her masculine behaviors or self-presentation; this conclusion may seem all the more improbable with a male rather than a female partner, wherein Brienne may be read as straightforwardly butch within a butch–femme dynamic. Thus, once again, like the Cinderella-based stories, Imagineagreatadventure utilizes "Beauty and the Beast's" built-in momentum toward utopian plentitude and closure to set up the union between Brienne and Jamie as acceptable and satisfying. In this manner, the happily-ever-after ending and its utopian storytelling structure can perform a perhaps surprisingly progressive political function.

Finally, "The Chamber Below the Dreadfort" by Phoenixflame88 places *Game of Thrones* characters within Angela Carter's "The Bloody Chamber", a feminist rewrite of the Bluebeard tale, in order to draw a parallel feminist critique [40,99]. Phoenixflame88 closely follows Carter's version, placing Sansa Stark as the protagonist, who, like Carter's heroine, tells the story from her point of view, although in a third-person rather than first-person perspective. Ramsay Bolton, a serial murderer and torturer, easily takes on the role of Bluebeard, and his captive Theon Greyjoy/Reek becomes Carter's blind piano tuner. "The Chamber Below the Dreadfort" utilizes Carter's feminist fairy tale revision to similarly critique *Game of Thrones* for the way it presents Sansa as a weak, innocent victim, unable to control or express her own sexuality. Both stories follow the life of a young woman who has agreed to marry an older man with a dark reputation, largely for social and financial stability for herself and her family. This also neatly describes the season five *Game of Thrones* storyline about Sansa's marriage to Ramsey. Carter and Phoenixflame88 depart from other tellings, including *Game of Thrones*, when their heroine begins to fantasize about the sexual aspects of her coming marriage, and later enjoys her sexual encounters with her husband, a theme that Phoenixflame88 especially develops.

However, following from Bluebeard, the heroine soon discovers a hidden room containing the dead bodies of her new husband's previous wives, and in both the TV series and "The Chamber Below the Dreadfort" Theon's/Reek's restrained, mutilated body serves this purpose, as well as the dead bodies of Ramsay's other victims. However, in the TV series, these events are reversed, with Sansa encountering the tortured Theon/Reek before the consummation of her marriage, which then does not lead to the discovery of her own sexual self, but instead culminates in a grotesque rape that Theon/Reek witnesses as a further form of torture. Finally all versions then end in the heroine's escape, although in most traditional retellings and the TV series, it is men, the brothers of Bluebeard's victims in one case and an army in the other, who free the heroine, while in the Carter and Phoenixflame88 version it is the heroine's mother who performs the role of hero and protector, killing Bluebeard/Ramsay to save her daughter. In all versions, perhaps except the TV show, the heroine goes on to live happily ever after, although the nature of that happiness varies; as for the traditional version she remarries, while in Carter's version the heroine, piano tuner, and mother form an intergenerational household, and in Phoenixflame88's story Sansa takes authority over her family seat in Winterfell alone, only later to be joined by Theon.

"The Chamber Below the Dreadfort" expresses utopian critiques of *Game of Thrones* in at least three ways. First, simply by so easily transposing the TV characters and plots into the Bluebeard myth and applying Carter's rewrite in so straightforward a fashion, Phoenixflame88's version indicts the source text on the same grounds, as a narrative that disempowers and victimizes women, robbing them of mature sexual agency ([100], pp. 10–12). The fact demonstrated by Phoenixflame88 that *Game of Thrones* basically repeats the Bluebeard myth speaks for itself, in a sense. Secondly, Phoenixflame88's repetition from Carter of Sansa's sexual awakening and growing maturity, culminating in her utopian achievement of full independent adulthood responsibilities as the sole ruler of Winterfell at the story's happily-ever-after ending, also implicitly criticizes the character's limited and disempowering storylines in the official show, in which she is passed between three successive sadistic or unwanted husbands. Finally, while Sansa's mother Catelyn Stark rescues her at the end of Phoenixflame88's story, like the mother figure in Carter's rewrite, in the *Game of Thrones* TV series Catelyn is long dead by the time Sansa marries Ramsey, leaving her alone and specifically without connections to other women. Although Brienne maintains loyalty to Catelyn even after her death and tries to protect Sansa, this is not possible within the *Game of Thrones* storyworld. Few women in *Game of Thrones* maintain significant emotional ties to other women or have the resources or status to protect other women, and the powerful bond between Catelyn and Sansa in "The Chamber Below the Dreadfort" offers another utopian vision of an alternate future wherein female characters do not become isolated victims, but instead act collectively in mutual solidarity.

In sum, while fan fiction stories come in numerous genres, ideologies, and formats, these examples demonstrated that combining *Game of Thrones* with fairy tale elements can produce culturally potent utopian visions. In "The Princess and the Direwolf", a utopian wish reveals the painful constraints of the *Game of Thrones* story world and questions our ability to imagine the possibility of pre-modern (and post-modern) lesbian lives. By situating culturally unlikely couples as inevitably bound for a happily-ever-after ending, fairy tale AUs can question sex and gender hierarchies, and imagine a world in which women are agents of their own desires, princesses can marry each other, and a butch woman may love a beautiful beast of a man. Positioning these couples' happiness at the resolution of a stereotypical fairy tale romance challenges the cultural standards that made them seem like unlikely pairs, and structurally primes the audience to experience their union as pleasurable and meant to be. While the content of "The Chamber Below the Dreadfort" may at first appear rather dark, it nonetheless culminates in a happily-ever-after ending that questions the character's fate in the TV series, while constructing an alternate future in which women are able to exert political power, reach sexual maturity, and maintain bonds of solidarity with each other. All of these utopian dreams strongly critique the world of the series, the boundaries of quality TV realism, and, to a certain extent, contemporary reality as well, by the injustice of their unattainability, and for the institutional conditions that make these visions still seem unrealistic.

5. Conclusions

To conclude, fan fiction AUs that combine *Game of Thrones* characters and settings with fairy tale elements construct a dialogue between realism and wonder. In so doing, they may uncover poetic and political possibilities unavailable to either genre in isolation. While realism functions within HBO's branding strategy as a signatory of "quality TV", often at the expense of deriding feminine genres, including melodrama and the fairy tale, reinserting these feminine pleasures and plots into *Game of Thrones* opens new horizons of representation, and points out stifling erasures within the series' realist storyworld. As such, *Game of Thrones*-based fairy tale AU fan fiction demonstrates some surprisingly radical uses for the frequently criticized happily-ever-after ending, namely, for its ability to point out the media and social institutions that still make some couples' success and some people's life course seem painfully unrealistic. Thus while "happily ever after" may become a cloying form of constraint, in the hands of fan fiction writers, circulating their works within a communal storytelling culture that normalizes dialogue between multiple versions, fairy tale endings may magically transform the limitations of utopian thought, and construct political and erotic dreams worth believing in.

Acknowledgments: This article results in part from support provided by the Social Sciences and Humanities Research Council of Canada Partnership Development Grant #890-2013-17, "Fairy Tale Cultures and Media Today". Thanks to my partnership colleagues Pauline Greenhill, Jill Rudy, Sadhana Naithani, Martin Lovelace, Steven Kohm, Catherine Tosenberger, Cristina Bacchilega, Jack Zipes, Naomi Hamer, Kendra Magnus-Johnston, and Lauren Bosc, as well as my research assistant Nina Köll, who have taught me a great deal about enchantment and wonder. Thanks also to the many fans who dedicate their time and passion to reimagining the characters of *Game of Thrones* through a fairy tale lens. Your work is inspiring and I thoroughly enjoyed spending many pleasant afternoons in your literary company.

Conflicts of Interest: The author declares no conflict of interest.

References

1. *Game of Thrones*. Directed by David Benioff, Alan Taylor and Daniel Brett Weiss. Written by David Benioff, George R. R. Martin and Daniel Brett Weiss. Home Box Office (HBO), 17 April 2011.
2. *Once Upon a Time*. Directed by Romeo Tirone and Ralph Hemecker. Written by Edward Kitsis and Adam Horowitz. ABC Studios, 23 October 2011.
3. "'Operation Mongoose.' 421/422." *Once Upon a Time*. Directed by Romeo Tirone and Ralph Hemecker. Written by Edward Kitsis and Adam Horowitz. ABC Studios, 10 May 2015.
4. Michael Newman, and Elana Levine. *Legitimating Television: Media Convergence and Cultural Status*. New York: Routledge, 2011.
5. Vanessa Joosen. "Disenchanting the fairy tale: Retellings of 'Snow White' between magic and realism." *Marvels & Tales* 21 (2007): 228–39.
6. Kim Akass, and Janet McCabe. "Sex, swearing and respectability: Courting controversy, HBO's original programming and producing quality TV." In *Contemporary Quality TV: American Television and Beyond (Reading Contemporary Television)*. London: I. B. Tauris, 2007, pp. 62–76.
7. Christine Geraghty. "Aesthetics and quality in popular television drama." *International Journal of Cultural Studies* 6 (2003): 25–45.
8. Anikó Imre. "Gender and quality television: A transcultural feminist project." *Feminist Media Studies* 9 (2009): 391–407.
9. Michael Kackman. "Quality Television, Melodrama, and Cultural Complexity." *Flow*, 31 October 2008. Available online: http://flowtv.org/?p\protect$\relax\ protect{\begingroup1\endgroup\@@over4}$2101#printview (accessed on 15 May 2009).
10. Marc Leverette, Brian L. Ott, and Cara Louise Buckley, eds. *It's Not TV: Watching HBO in the Post-Television Era*. New York: Routledge, 2008.
11. Jason Mittell. "Narrative complexity in contemporary American television." *The Velvet Light Trap* 58 (2006): 29–40.
12. Robin Nelson. "'Quality Television': '*The Sopranos* is the best television drama ever … in my humble opinion … '." *Critical Studies in Television: The International Journal of Television Studies* 1 (2006): 58–71.

13. Tobias Steiner. "Steering the author discourse: The construction of authorship in quality TV, and the case of *Game of Thrones*." *Series—International Journal of TV Serial Narratives* 1 (2015): 181–92.

14. Raymond Williams. *Television: Technology and Cultural Form*. London: Fontana, 1974.

15. Robert J. Thompson. *Television's Second Golden Age: From Hill Street Blues to ER*. New York: Continuum, 1996.

16. Debra Ferreday. "*Game of Thrones*, rape culture and feminist fandom." *Australian Feminist Studies* 30 (2015): 21–36.

17. Stefan Morrone. "How *Game of Thrones* Teaches Us about the Syrian Refugee Crisis." *Institute for Ethics and Emerging Technologies*, 3 December 2015. Available online: http://ieet.org/index.php/IEET/more/Morrone20151203 (accessed on 28 March 2016).

18. Jamie Seidel. "The Real Human History behind *Game of Thrones*." *News Corp Australia*, 9 April 2014. Available online: http://www.news.com.au/world/the-real-human-history-behind-game-of-thrones/story-fndir2ev-1226879236503 (accessed on 28 March 2016).

19. Matthew Taunton. "Why *Game of Thrones* is More than Fantasy." *New Humanist*, 3 June 2015. Available online: https://newhumanist.org.uk/articles/4883/why-game-of-thrones-is-more-than-fantasy (accessed on 28 March 2016).

20. Jamie Adair. "History behind *Game of Thrones*." Available online: http://history-behind-game-of-thrones.com/george-rr-martin/grrm-rolling-stone (accessed on 28 March 2016).

21. Alex Gendler. "The Wars that Inspired *Game of Thrones*." *TedEd*, 11 May 2015. Available online: https://www.youtube.com/watch?v=VjO55pKuBo4 (accessed on 28 March 2016).

22. Mikal Gilmore. "George R.R. Martin: The Rolling Stone Interview." *Rolling Stone Magazine*, 23 April 2014. Available online: http://www.rollingstone.com/tv/news/george-r-r-martin-the-rolling-stone-interview-20140423 (accessed on 28 March 2016).

23. Luc Herman. *Concepts of Realism*. St. Marys: Camden House, 1997.

24. Andrew Higson. "Space, place, spectacle." *Screen* 25 (1984): 2–21.

25. Judith Butler. *Gender Trouble: Feminism and the Subversion of Identity*. New York: Routledge, 2006.

26. Maria Nikolajeva. "Fairy tale and fantasy: From archaic to postmodern." *Marvels & Tales* 17 (2003): 138–56.

27. Jack Zipes. *Don't Bet on the Prince: Contemporary Feminist Fairy Tales in North America and England*. New York: Methuen, 1986.

28. Jack Zipes. *Why Fairy Tales Stick: The Evolution and Relevance of a Genre*. New York: Routledge, 2006.

29. Lynne Joyrich. "All that television allows: TV melodrama, postmodernism and consumer culture." *Camera Obscura* 6 (1988): 128–53.

30. Lynne Joyrich. *Re-Viewing Reception: Television, Gender, and Postmodern Culture*. Bloomington: Indiana University Press, 1996.

31. Kay Stone. "Things Walt Disney never told us." *The Journal of American Folklore* 88 (1975): 42–50.
32. Linda J. Lee. "Guilty pleasures: Reading romance novels as reworked fairy tales." *Marvels & Tales* 22 (2008): 52–66.
33. Marcia R. Lieberman. "'Some day my prince will come': Female acculturation through the fairy tale." *College English* 34 (1972): 383–95.
34. Deborah Ross. "Escape from wonderland: Disney and the female imagination." *Marvels & Tales* 18 (2004): 53–66.
35. Karlyn Crowley, and John Pennington. "Feminist frauds on the fairies?: Didacticism and liberation in recent retellings of 'Cinderella'." *Marvels & Tales* 24 (2010): 297–313.
36. James C. Scott. *Domination and the Arts of Resistance: Hidden Transcripts*. New Haven: Yale University Press, 1990.
37. James C. Scott. *Seeing Like a State: How Certain Schemes to Improve the Human Condition Have Failed*. New Haven: Yale University Press, 1998.
38. James C. Scott. *Weapons of the Weak: Everyday Forms of Peasant Resistance*. New Haven: Yale University Press, 1985.
39. Cristina Bacchilega. *Postmodern Fairy Tales: Gender and Narrative Strategies*. Philadelphia: University of Pennsylvania Press, 2010.
40. Angela Carter. "The bloody chamber." In *The Bloody Chamber and Other Stories*. New York: Penguin Books, 1990, pp. 7–40.
41. Jack/Judith Halberstam. *In a Queer Time and Place: Transgender Bodies, Subcultural Lives*. New York: NYU Press, 2005.
42. Deborah O'Keefe. *Good Girl Messages: How Young Women Were Misled by Their Favorite Books*. New York: Bloomsbury Academic, 2001.
43. Adrienne Rich. "Compulsory heterosexuality and lesbian existence." *Signs* 5 (1980): 631–60.
44. Tania Modleski. *Loving With a Vengeance: Mass Produced Fantasies for Women*, 2nd ed. New York: Routledge, 2007.
45. Janice Radway. *Reading the Romance: Women, Patriarchy, and Popular Literature*. Chapel Hill: The University of North Carolina Press, 1991.
46. Judith Butler. *Frames of War: When Is Life Grievable?* Brooklyn: Verso, 2016.
47. Lee Edelman. *No Future: Queer Theory and the Death Drive*. Durham: Duke University Press, 2004.
48. Michel Foucault. *The History of Sexuality, Vol. 1: An Introduction*. New York: Vintage, 1990.
49. Jack/Judith Halberstam. *The Queer Art of Failure*. Durham: Duke University Press Books, 2011.
50. Lauren Berlant. *Cruel Optimism*. Durham: Duke University Press Books, 2011.
51. Michele Boldrin, and David K. Levine. *Against Intellectual Monopoly*. Cambridge: Cambridge University Press, 2008.
52. Rebecca Tushnet. "Copyright as a model for free speech law: What copyright has in common with anti-pornography laws, campaign finance reform, and telecommunications regulation." *Boston College Law Review* 42 (2000): 1–79.

53. Rebecca Tushnet. "Legal fictions: Copyright, fan fiction, and a new common law." *Loyola of Los Angeles Entertainment Law Journal* 17 (1996): 651–86.

54. Roland Barthes. "The death of the author." In *Image/Music/Text*. New York: Hill and Wang, 1977, pp. 142–47.

55. Michel Foucault. "What is an author? " In *Aesthetics, Method, and Epistemology*. Edited by James Faubion. New York: The New Press, 1998.

56. Lawrence Lessig. "The creative commons." *Montana Law Review* 65 (2004): 1–14.

57. Jessica Litman. "Mickey Mouse emeritus: Character protection and the public domain." *University of Miami Entertainment & Sports Law Review* 11 (1993): 429–35.

58. Cristina Bacchilega. "Introduction: The fairy-tale web." In *Fairy Tales Transformed?: Twenty-First Century Adaptations and the Politics of Wonder*. Detroit: Wayne State University Press, 2013, pp. 1–30.

59. Henry Jenkins. *Convergence Culture: Where Old and New Media Collide*. New York: NYU Press, 2008.

60. Henry Jenkins. "Transmedia Storytelling 101." 2007. Available online: http://henryjenkins.org/2007/03/transmedia_storytelling_101.html (accessed on 10 January 2016).

61. Henry Jenkins. "Transmedia 202: Further Reflections." 2011. Available online: http://henryjenkins.org/2011/08/defining_transmedia_further_re.html (accessed on 10 January 2016).

62. Carlos Scolari. "Lostology: Transmedia storytelling and expansion/compression strategies." *Semiotica* 195 (2013): 45–68.

63. Anne Kustritz. "Seriality and transmediality in the fan multiverse: Flexible and multiple narrative structures in fan fiction, art, and vids." *TV/Series* 6 (2014): 225–61.

64. Maria Lindgren Leavenworth. "Transmedial Texts and Serialized Narratives." *Transformative Works and Cultures*, 2011.

65. Judith Fathallah. "Statements and silence: Fanfic paratexts for *ASOIF/Game of Thrones*." *Continuum: Journal of Media & Cultural Studies* 30 (2016): 75–88.

66. Marie-Laure Ryan. "Transmedial storytelling and transfictionality." *Poetics Today* 34 (2013): 361–88.

67. Henry Jenkins. *Textual Poachers: Television Fans and Participatory Culture*. New York: Routledge, 1992.

68. Mafalda Stasi. "The toy soldiers from leeds: The slash palimpsest." In *Fan Fiction and Fan Communities in the Age of the Internet: New Essays*. Edited by Karen Hellekson and Kristina Busse. Jefferson: McFarland and Company, 2006, pp. 115–33.

69. Karen Hellekson, and Kristina Busse. "Introduction: Work in progress." In *Fan Fiction and Fan Communities in the Age of the Internet: New Essays*. Edited by Karen Hellekson and Kristina Busse. Jefferson: McFarland and Company, 2006, pp. 5–32.

70. Anne Kustritz. "Slashing the romance narrative." *The Journal of American Culture* 6 (2003): 371–84.

71. Louisa Stein, and Kristina Busse. "Limit play: Fan authorship between source text, intertext, and context." *Popular Communication* 7 (2009): 192–207.

72. Julie Levin Russo. "User-Penetrated content: Fan video in the age of convergence." *Cinema Journal* 48 (2009): 125–30.

73. Amalia Ziv. *Explicit Utopias: Rewriting the Sexual in Women's Pornography.* Albany: SUNY Press, 2015.

74. Ellen Fremedon. "Id Vortex." Available online: http://fanlore.org/wiki/Id_Vortex (accessed on 6 May 2016).

75. Elizabeth Woledge. "Intimatopia: Genre intersections between slash and the mainstream." In *Fan Fiction and Fan Communities in the Age of the Internet: New Essays.* Edited by Karen Hellekson and Kristina Busse. Jefferson: McFarland and Company, 2006, pp. 97–114.

76. Jenny Alexander. "Tortured heroes: The story of ouch! Fan fiction and sadomasochism." In *Sex, Violence and the Body.* London: Palgrave Macmillan, 2008, pp. 119–36.

77. Anne Kustritz. "Painful pleasures: Sacrifice, consent, and the resignification of BDSM symbolism in *The Story of O* and *The Story of Obi.*" *Transformative Works and Cultures,* 2008.

78. Sarah Fiona Winters. "Vidding and the perversity of critical pleasure: Sex, violence, and voyeurism in 'Closer' and 'On the Prowl'." *Transformative Works and Cultures,* 2012.

79. Francesca Coppa. "An archive of our own: Fan fiction writers unite! " In *Fic: Why Fanfiction Is Taking Over the World.* Edited by Anne Jameson. Dallas: Smart Pop, 2013, pp. 274–80.

80. Alexis Lothian. "An archive of one's own: Subcultural creativity and the politics of conservation." *Transformative Works and Cultures,* 2011.

81. Alexis Lothian. "Archival anarchies: Online fandom, subcultural conservation, and the transformative work of digital ephemera." *International Journal of Cultural Studies* 16 (2013): 541–56.

82. WelshCakes68. "Femslash February 2015 Challenge: Chapter 27: Fairy Tale." 28 February 2015. Available online: http://archiveofourown.org/works/3273269/chapters/7550171 (accessed on 25 March 2016).

83. Pauline Greenhill. "Wanting (to be) animal: Fairy-Tale transbiology in the story-teller." *Feral Feminisms* 2 (2014): 29–45.

84. John D'Emilio. "Capitalism and gay identity." In *Powers of Desire: The Politics of Sexuality.* Edited by Ann Snitow, Christine Stansell and Sharan Thompson. New York: Monthly Review Press, 1983.

85. Judith Bennett. "'Lesbian-Like' and the social history of lesbianisms." *Journal of the History of Sexuality* 9 (2000): 1–24.

86. Ann Cvetkovich. *An Archive of Feelings: Trauma, Sexuality, and Lesbian Public Cultures.* Durham: Duke University Press Books, 2003.

87. Carroll Smith-Rosenberg. "The female world of love and ritual: Relations between women in nineteenth-century america." *Signs* 1 (1975): 1–29.

88. Valerie Traub. *The Renaissance of Lesbianism in Early Modern England.* Cambridge: Cambridge University Press, 2002.

89. Gay & Lesbian Alliance against Defamation. "GLAAD—Where We Are on TV Report—2015." Available online: http://www.glaad.org/whereweareontv15 (accessed on 1 April 2016).

90. Anne Kustritz. "Fan fiction." In *Routledge Companion to Fairy Tale Cultures and Media*. Edited by Pauline Greenhill, Jill Terry Rudy and Naomi Hamer. New York: Routledge, 2016, forthcoming.

91. Empress_Irony. "A Waltz among the Cinders." 7 March 2016. Available online: http://archiveofourown.org/works/6186253 (accessed on 25 March 2016).

92. "Achieve of Our Own." Available online: http://archiveofourown.org (accessed on 30 March 2016).

93. MoaCube. "Cinders." 2012. Available online: http://moacube.com/games/cinders (accessed on 20 March 2016).

94. Atlantisairlock. "Cedar + Gold." 16 September 2014. Available online: http://archiveofourown.org/works/2314460 (accessed on 25 March 2016).

95. Imagineagreatadventure. "Beauty and the Beast." 12 August 2015. Available online: http://archiveofourown.org/works/4077127?view_full_work=true (accessed on 25 March 2016).

96. Lady_Blade_WarAngel. "Heartsick." 6 June 2014. Available online: http://archiveofourown.org/works/1747424 (accessed on 25 March 2016).

97. Madeleine Shufeldt Esch. "Rearticulating ugliness, Repurposing content: Ugly betty finds the beauty in ugly." *Journal of Communication Inquiry* 34 (2009): 168–83.

98. Yeidy M. Rivero. "The performance and reception of televisual 'Ugliness' in *Yo Soy Betty la Fea*." *Feminist Media Studies* 3 (2003): 65–81.

99. Phoenixflame88. "The Chamber below the Dreadfort." 21 May 2013. Available online: http://archiveofourown.org/works/812308?view_full_work=true (accessed on 25 March 2016).

100. Patricia Duncker. "Re-Imagining the fairy tales: Angela Carter's bloody chambers." *Literature and History* 10 (1984): 3–14.

Don Draper Thinks Your Ad Is Cliché: Fairy Tale Iconography in TV Commercials

Preston Wittwer

Abstract: When examining the history of fairy tale iconography in advertising, folklore scholar Donald Haase's fairy tale encyclopedia compared the Pied Piper of Hamelin to a symbol of advertising who could "play his pipe ever so sweetly and the consumers following him without resisting his charming and manipulative music." In contrast, a 2012 episode of *Mad Men*, advertising luminary Don Draper shoots down a shoe commercial pitch featuring Cinderella, calling the idea "cliché". The temptation for advertisers to rely on fairy tale figures and iconography continues today and many ignore Don's aversion for cliché because it still gets the job done. However, there are some ads featuring fairy tales which avoid cliché and are truly innovative for their time. I'll examine how, and for whom, these fairy tale figures have been adapted decade by decade in order to examine popular culture's commercialized and hypnotic relationship with fairy tales in the most direct format available: television commercials.

Reprinted from *Humanities*. Cite as: Wittwer, P. Don Draper Thinks Your Ad Is Cliché: Fairy Tale Iconography in TV Commercials. *Humanities* **2016**, *5*, 29.

1. Introduction

For as long as television has been around commercials and sponsorships have operated as the stealth lifeblood pumping cash and life into the medium. In recent decades, additional revenue streams like syndication deals, DVD sales, and streaming rights have buoyed up the television industry, but there is no more important or influential facilitator of the TV industry than commercials.

The goals, restrictions, and lengths of commercials have varied dramatically over the years, but the premise has remained unchanged: a finite and small amount of time to sell a product, good, or service. Advertisers have precious little time to say what they want to say and to connect with their audience. Because of their limited time they've learned the shortcuts to attract attention and gain sympathies: peppy music, pretty people, cute animals, and a memorable tagline. The shortcut I'll be examining in this paper, however, is the strategic use of fairy tale iconography in commercials.

For many of us fairy tales play significant roles in the first stories we hear, the first movies we see, and the first television shows we watch. Our first brushes with heroes and villains, right and wrong, and the very concept of wonder often originate with fairy tales in one form or another. It didn't take long for advertisers to discover the tremendous relatability, love of, and staying power of fairy tales for the vast majority of the general public. Decade after decade advertisers have capitalized on this public awareness and love of fairy tales figures to sell us toothpaste, insurance, produce, and everything in between.

In this post-modern and increasingly media literate age, this reliance on fairy tale iconography in ads has not gone unnoticed by consumers and other creative professionals. In an episode of *Mad Men*, Madison Avenue 1960s-era advertising superstar Don Draper shoots down a shoe commercial idea featuring Cinderella, calling the idea "cliché" [1]. You can probably think of, and even remember, similar on-the-nose uses of fairy tale figures yourself.

The temptation for advertisers to rely on fairy tale figures and iconography continues today and many ignore Don Draper's aversion for cliché. With ads getting both louder and shorter due to rapid changes in the television industry is it even possible for contemporary advertisers to find fresh ways to feature fairy tales in advertising campaigns? In my research I'll be examining the intersection between fairy tales and TV commercials to answer these and other related questions.

2. Introducing America to Commercials

Let's start by looking at some of the earliest ads and promotions to feature familiar fairy tale iconography. On the first day of July in 1941 a few lucky New Yorkers with televisions tuned in to the WNBT station to see their Brooklyn Dodgers take on the visiting Phillies. The handful of baseball fans who got to their television sets early for this broadcast were about the experience history: they were about to see the first ever paid television advertisement.

Instead of the usual test pattern clock that was displayed between programs, viewers saw a modified test pattern clock modeled after Bulova brand watches, complete with the company logo and the tagline "America Runs On Bulova Watch Time". What lacks in the unimaginative tagline is made up for with the clever, almost too obvious, use of product placement in a familiar way. American television viewers saw a test pattern clock daily on their TV screens and it wouldn't come as too much a shock to any of them to see the same clock in a new context. Perhaps the advertisers for Bulova knew they would have to slowly teach American viewers what a TV advertisement was and how the viewers should respond.

Commercials as a medium were heavily influenced by the media that came before them, especially the cartoon short. Long before cartoon characters showed up on televisions in the family room they were appearing in movie theaters across the country. In this era before home television, feature films were shown with newsreels, movie trailers, and cartoon shorts. Animators like Chuck Jones, Ub Iwerks, Pat Sullivan, and Walt Disney made their bones early with specifically this kind of media.

When television entered the scene it didn't take long for these cartoon shorts to migrate, both as featured content and mimicked in the commercials.

When this migration of cartoons to TV finally occurred during the 1950s, a taxonomy of commercials was established. Commercials had an average length of 1 min and were typically animated. They featured jingles (usually full, original songs) and a steady stream of declarative information about the products and the stories used to tell them. And so we come to the first few commercials that quickly turned to familiar fairy tale iconography. (See Figure 1)

Figure 1. 1950s Bab-O Sink Smog Commercial.

This Bab-O Cleaner commercial is a textbook example of the 1950s television commercial. But even more interesting (for the purposes of this paper, anyway) is that this commercial acted as a primer for the series of Bab-O spots that would follow it—a series that featured figures from history and fairy tales interacting with the product. Below we see how Cinderella meshes with the 50s-era TV commercial style. (See Figure 2)

Integrating fairy tale motifs was handled without much elegance in the 50s. The figures of Cinderella's world use the same language and style as the declarative copy used in the first ad in the campaign. The fairy tale figures are secondary (by a long shot) to the goal of explaining what a product is and what it can do for the American shopper. Cinderella is inserted into a commercial and is nothing more than a familiar name. The same is essentially true of Pocahontas and John Smith's inclusion in a later Bab-O commercial.

Figure 2. 1950s Cinderella Bab-O Commercial.

This sloppy combination of ads and fairy tales wasn't a localized problem for Bab-O. Submitted for your viewing is a 1952 commercial for Halo Shampoo featuring Goldilocks and the 3 Bears. (See Figure 3)

Figure 3. 1950s Goldilocks Halo Shampoo Commercial.

Again, the idea of a folklore or fairy tale figure was repeated for this campaign, including other inelegant uses of mermaids, elves, and (again) Cinderella.

In her 1997 article "Fairy Tale Motifs in Advertising", Patricia Baubeta attempts to answer the question of why advertisers so quickly turned to fairy tale iconography and why they continue to decade after decade. She points out fairy tale figures are familiar, cute, and feel-good, but there is a factor even more important: "If we ask why advertisers use fairy tale motifs, the answer is obvious. Because they work" ([2], p. 37). And in the sixties the commercials had a lot more going for them in addition to the simple inclusion of fairy tale figures.

3. The Artistic Revolution of the 1960s

In Donald Haase's "The Greenwood Encyclopedia of Folktales and Fairy Tales: A-F" Wolfgang Mieder uses the tale of the pied piper of Hamelin to explain the practicality and efficiency of using folklore and fairy tale iconography in advertising. He likens the pied piper to a "symbol of the world of advertising" who would "play his pipe ever so sweetly and the consumers following him without resisting his charming and manipulative music" ([3], p. 5). While this is certainly true categorically of fairy tale-themed commercials, the tunes played and pipers playing them went through some drastic and experimental changes in the 1960s.

There are three key figures in the 60s advertising world that shaped the creative revolution: Doyle Dane Bernbach, David Ogilvy, and William Bernbach. Doyle Bernbach was the mind behind the infamous lemon Volkswagen ad campaign that cleverly presented all the criticisms of VW's cars as benefits. In his book "Confessions of an Advertising Man", David Ogilvy began to establish a taxonomy for modern advertising—a taxonomy founded on ethics and honesty [4]. And William Bernbach was one of the first advertisers to embrace the youth culture that was changing just about every other aspect of society in the 60s. Advertisers were getting to their audience in new ways through humor, honesty, and attempts at a genuine connection. The industry shifted from proclamations and lecturing consumers about their products to the idea of relationships and artistry.

In print media and on television there was a focus for increased visuals and less copy, fewer words. There was a desire to find new ideas, new characters, and new ways of selling products. Both the programing and advertising on television followed suit. Let's take a look at this TV spot for Ajax laundry detergent soap featuring a fabled White Knight of European lore that straddles the line between the showing of the 60s and the telling of the 50s: (See Figure 4)

The middle section betrays the energy and finesse of the start and end of the commercial. The TV spot ran in 1965, right when audiences were growing accustomed to the new, fast paced editing techniques while still familiar with the stilted delivery of 50s ad copy. In the 50s, the White Knight would have been named, would have directly addressed the audience, or simply would have been more explicitly involved. Instead, the knight streaks across the screen and the audience is supposed to connect the dots themselves between the majesty of the hero and the cleaning power of Ajax.

Figure 4. 1960s Ajax Soap Commercial.

Next, let's take a look at an advertisement that attempts to blend humor with a fairy tale figure. This time it's the Fairy Godmother, breaking the fourth wall to publicize a prize giveaway from Crest in connection with the 1965 television broadcast of Rodgers and Hammerstein's *Cinderella* (See Figure 5).

Figure 5. 1960s Crest Cinderella Sweepstakes Commercial.

What works about this commercial is that the fairy tale connection is played only for laughs. The visible wires, the malfunctioning wand, and the Fairy Godmother speaking directly to the stagehands controlling the pulley system keeping her up undercut any sense of majesty, wonder, or actual magic typically used to push products via fairy tale figures. Sure, she speaks directly to the viewer, but she does so with energy and personality.

It would be misleading to say that all or even most commercials of the 60s strove for artistry over clarity or suggestion over description. Take for example this ad for Hidden Magic hair spray starring Wanda the Wonderful Witch (See Figure 6).

Figure 6. 1960s Wanda the Witch Hidden Magic Hair Spray Commercial.

This commercial operates like a 50s commercial in many ways (abundance of ad copy, directly addressing viewers, catchy jingles, *etc.*), but it does show some signs of its decade. For one, the spot is live action as opposed to a cartoon. But for our purposes the most interesting and timely aspect of this ad is the character herself: Wanda the Witch. She was a character created whole cloth and not some existing figure shoehorned into a shoe commercial. She is undoubtedly modeled after *Bewitched*'s Samantha (and even relies on some of the same trick photography commonly used on Samantha's show), but there was at least some attempt to make her original. The same is true for Ajax's White Knight (again, it's not much, but it is there).

Where the 50s relied on and named known fairy tale figures in TV spots, the 60s borrowed more iconography than characters. This was mostly due to the artistic revolution sweeping creative fields. Following the late 50s debuts of Tony the Tiger, Mr. Clean, and the Trix Rabbit, demand was high for more original commercial mascots. The 60s delivered with still-popular figures like Ronald McDonald and The

154

Pillsbury Doughboy. In general, the trend in the 60s was to rely on new, or at the very least more recently created, pop culture icons.

For the 1960s that meant instead of Red Riding Hood and Cinderella hawking wares, TV audiences saw Alvin and the Chipmunks repping Post Cereal, The Muppets selling Dog Chow, Rocky and Bullwinkle pushing Cheerios, and Bugs Bunny as a mascot for baseball cards.

4. The Many Pivots of the 1970s

The 1970s is a decade characterized by many historians as a "pivot of change" for America politically, economically, and socially. There are few places that better show this drastic change in U.S. values and societal attitudes than the television programing of the 70s. At the beginning of the decade once powerhouse shows like *The Ed Sullivan Show* (the show famous for introducing The Beatles to American audiences) and *Gunsmoke* were canceled, effectively ending the reign of the Western as a TV genre. These shows were first replaced in popularity with family-focused shows including *Happy Days* and *The Brady Bunch*, then by more sexed up shows like *Charlie's Angels* and *Three's Company* all leading up to a wave of "social consciousness programming" like the female-centric and empowering *The Mary Tyler Moore Show* and *Sanford and Son*, one of the first shows about an African American family.

American culture in the 70s as a whole was moving away from the strong societal pull of community that blossomed in the 60s towards a reframing of the individual as the basic unity of society. Again, we can turn to television programs to see this change, but this time in the advertisements airing between the original programming.

In fact, television advertising has rarely worked as memorably or effectively as it did in the 70s. Advertisers doubled down on the value of the individual to unprecedented success. Take for example the now famous "I'm A Pepper" and "I'd Like to Buy the World a Coke", campaigns for Dr. Pepper and Coke respectively. Both emotionally promote feelings of self-esteem and individualism (look no further than the word "I" that starts and anchors both campaign ideas).

With these movements and shifts in mind we can turn our focus at last to the fairy tale figures still being heavily incorporated the ads of this era of self-consciousness. Let's begin with a spot for grocery store Safeway (See Figure 7).

In this ad Snow White is positioned as the head of a household who takes grocery shopping very seriously. The ad copy spoken by Snow White alternates back and forth from playful winking at the familiar story to speaking directly about her needs as an individual. Her line, "I serve my family with confidence" effective positions Snow White as an avatar for atomized individualism.

For the all the progress advertisements can capture in the moment with ads like Snow White's Safeway spot, media is too often painfully behind societal movements like feminism. A renewed push to secure social equality for women was well underway in the 70s and this movement helped women join the workforce in droves (including women like Mary Tyler Moore). Let's look at this series of anti-smoking Public service announcements (PSAs) featuring Rapunzel, the Frog Prince, and Sleeping Beauty that illustrates the reductive ways the media has depicted women via fairy tales (See Figure 8).

Figure 7. 1970s Safeway Snow White Commercial.

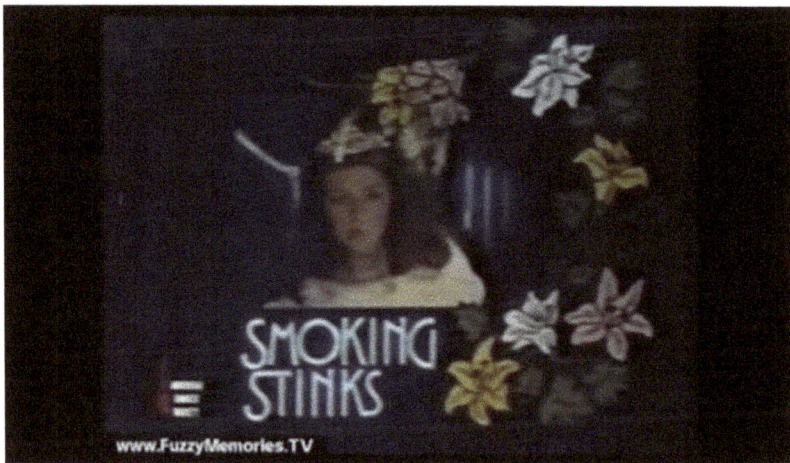

Figure 8. 1970s Rapunzel/Frog Prince/Sleeping Beauty Smoking PSA.

"Give it up, because it stinks" is an effectively simple focus for an important campaign like this, but ultimately what these commercials are really telling their audience is that women need to give up smoking to please men. This campaign touches on a troublesome nerve of the antiquated gender roles in fairy tales that has only become increasingly problematic since second wave feminism of the 1970s.

This practice of going broad and conservative in commercials is well-explained by Linda Dégh in her chapter of fairy tales in advertising from "American Folklore and the Mass Media". Speaking of the over-reliance on cliché and old-fashioned values, Dégh explains that "the advertising industry knows what dosage of primitiveness, awkwardness, and bad taste is called for to satisfy public demand. The results of penetrating market and laboratory research vouch for the efficacy of these commercials among the majority of consumers" ([5], p. 48).

There are plenty 70s commercials that skew heavily towards the awkward and primitive. In one commercial two children infiltrate a giant's castle and rely on the strengthening power of Cheerios to escape. In another ad, a weeping Cinderella deals with a Fairy Godmother who grants wishes in as literal a way as possible. The spots are cute and mostly harmless, but they do little more than use familiar settings and characters to get in and get out with their pitches—and that's exactly how the advertisers designed them.

5. Back to Basics in the 1980s

In 1984 Jack Zipes published "Folklore Research and Western Marxism: A Critical Replay" in which he summarized the research of several folklore scholars and ran it through a Marxist lens. In that article he concluded that fairy tales in television and film "exploit folklore to evoke images of the attainment of happiness through consumption" ([6], p. 334). And while Zipes doesn't specifically include television commercials in that article, the TV commercial is a perfect encapsulation and culmination of the exploitation of folklore iconography. Fairy tales and commercials mashup to show, through familiar faces, just how easily happiness can be bought. While happiness wasn't necessarily a defining theme of the 1980s, the decade was certainly livelier than the one it preceded. Earned or not, the 80s brought a renewed sense of enthusiasm through economic and technological advancements, reflected in media as what can only be described as an aggressive amount of energy. This was the decade MTV launched, the decade cable television became more accessible and popular, and the decade that saw video games go mainstream.

Apple's iconic 1.5 million dollar Super Bowl ad announcing the arrival of the Macintosh computer is the most famous television commercial from the 1980s. The ad was successful for many reasons, chief among them that it was such an outlier in the advertising conventions of the time. The trends Apple avoided include a hard resurgence of the jingle extended to commercial-length original songs, the co-opting of rock music heavy with synths, and a manic pace. Look no further than the Kool-Aid campaign from the 80s for evidence of these tendencies. The reason for these trends is understandable given the success of "I'm A Pepper" and "I'd Like to Buy the World a Coke" from the 70s, but in turning these concepts up to 11 the originality was lost. Let's look at a Sugar Free Dr. Pepper campaign from the 80s that dates itself in the first few frames with headbands and spandex (See Figure 9).

Figure 9. 1980s Little Red Riding Hood Sugar Free Dr. Pepper Commercial.

This first spot uses the story of Little Red Riding Hood with just small bits of originality. Red's optics are certainly modernized and she capably stands up for herself to the wolf, but these ideas are put on the back burner and eventually give way completely to romance once the product shows up. Another TV spot from this campaign uses a genie character with even less imagination, but features more blown-out hair.

Next let's examine a 1980s multimedia Huggies campaign built around the tagline "happily ever after" with a commercial starring Sleeping Beauty (See Figure 10).

The fairy tale angle ends up being nothing more than bookends to a by-the-numbers diaper commercial. Sleeping Beauty is introduced as sleeping for 100 years and dreaming of leak-free diapers, an inelegant combination of fairy tale jargon with straight ad copy. Some credit can be given, I guess, to the fact that no Disney-inspired design is used, but that might be more for copyright reasons than innovative ambition. Things just get more arduous with this Lucky Charms ad (See Figure 11).

Figure 10. 1980s Sleeping Beauty Huggies Commercial.

Figure 11. 1980s Three Bears Lucky Charms Commercial.

The bears, from Goldilocks' story though she is absent here, don't show up till the commercial is halfway done and they are never even named. And saddest of all they are summoned into existence by the magic of the cereal pitchman and only speak to talk about everything they love about Lucky Charms. Their entire role in the commercial is to exist only to sell happiness through products. Again, fairy tale figures aren't the only ones being mistreated and achingly marginalized in their own commercials. Just check out the way Roger Rabbit is used in this commercial for Diet Coke and how Slimmer, of *Ghostbusters* fame, became the face of a new Hi-C flavor. This isn't the first time this instance of slim traces of originality gave way to decades-old pat strategies has shown itself in television commercials. From previous research it is becoming clear this is the disappointing pattern and 80s was no time for exception and maybe even had the worst showing. At the very least, one can hope the coming decades won't bring commercials as tired as Fairy Tails, the unsuccessful My Little Pony spin off.

6. The 1990s Corporate Takeover

In Marina Warner's short history of the fairy tale, "Once Upon a Time", she posits that one of the primary functions of the fairy tale is the sharing of familiar stories with an audience. She goes on to explain "the stories' interest isn't exhausted by repetition, reformulation, or retelling, but their pleasure gains from the endless permutations performed on the nucleus of the tale, the DNA as it were" ([7], p. 45). While fairy tales have a long history of corporate usage, it is during the 1990s that the very DNA and nuclei of fairy tales became increasingly co-opted by media companies, by Disney in particular. Disney wasn't just using the Little Mermaid to sell shampoo, they were attempting to establish their version of the Little Mermaid to the public as the definitive take on the tale. Again, Disney had commercialized popular fairy tale figures before to great success, but the 1990s was a unique decade of interrupted commercial and critical success. This decade has been described as the Disney Renaissance, a span of years where the studio released 10 animated films, including *The Little Mermaid* (1989), *Beauty and the Beast* (1991), *Aladdin* (1992), *The Lion King* (1994), and others. During this decade, advertisers relying on fairy tale figures had to differentiate themselves stylistically from the Disney versions of the tales, both to establish their own unique place to sell products and presumably to avoid any legal action from the House of Mouse. So, while Disney's fairy tale figures were showing up unceremoniously in McDonald's Happy Meal commercials, other brands had to find new ways to exploit fairy tale iconography. In the Oxford Companion to Fairy Tales, Jack Zipes explains, "fairy tales are well suited to television commercials because they are popular and easily recognized. Their familiar motifs can be truncated and adapted for brief commercials while still remaining meaningful" ([8], p. 610). A perfect example of this truncated style of storytelling can be seen in a 1999 Ford commercial featuring the Three Little Pigs (See Figure 12).

This story is told without narration or dialogue, instead relying entirely on familiar iconography and recognizable animation styles. The only narration comes at the end: simple ad copy naming the product and connecting it to the tale with a quick pun. In a sense, Ford responded to the Disney takeover by featuring Looney Tunes and Sesame Street characters in their commercials for their latest Windstar minivans, a halfhearted attempt to set themselves apart. A 1997 Honey Nut Cheerios commercial uses a truncated version of the Little Red Riding Hood story, starting right in the middle of the familiar story without explanation, assuming audience familiarity with the tale. The story is quickly and literally interrupted by a corporate mascot (See Figure 13).

Figure 12. 1990s Three Little Pigs Ford Commercial.

Figure 13. 1990s Little Red Riding Hood Cheerios Commercial.

It is notable that even in this ad featuring lighthearted music, that also presents the wolf as an amusing if not comedic character, it still ends with an ominous reminder that the wolf ate Red's grandmother. The dark nucleus of Red's story survives, even as BuzzBee's rattles off the superlative qualities of Honey Nut Cheerios. One of the more interesting fairy tale-adjacent commercials of this decade comes from Levi's. The commercial opens with an image of a clock striking midnight and cuts next to the image of a woman running down stairs, leaving behind a shoe. The iconography is unmistakable and immediately recognizable as a Cinderella story (See Figure 14).

Figure 14. 1990s Cinderella Levi's Commercial.

After 7 or 8 s of these kinds of traditional establishing shots, the story starts to take unfamiliar turns. The prince charming figure chasing after Cinderella is scared away by another man on a motorcycle. The motorcycle man leaves behind an article of clothing himself as he quickly exits, leaving Cinderella to pick up the pair of jeans and begin her search for this illusive man. The commercial digs into this subversive gender-swapped narrative, empowering Cinderella with active agency as she looks for her perfect match. The men in the commercial are increasingly objectified to the point where when we finally see the motorcycle man again he is shirtless, sweaty, and shot in slow motion. This Levi's ad succeeds where so many other commercials featuring fairy tale iconography have stopped short. It knowingly comments on the tropes of fairy tale and updates them with modern sensibilities all while artfully remaining true to the DNA of Cinderella's story. And if that wasn't enough, it does all of this with artistic and imaginative shots and edits while additionally relying on depictions completely separate from the corporate-owned versions permeating the culture of the time. Would that all fairy tale commercials were this innovative.

7. The Digital Age of the 2000s

In the new millennium the buzzwords of the first decade were globalization and technology. Across the globe the internet, computers, and cell phones were bringing people together and changing the way people lived their lives. A pair of studies at the start and the end of the decade showed a jump from 6% to 62% of Americans having in-home internet access [9,10]. Cell phone popularity surged as well, fueled by advances in text messaging and mobile internet accessibility. In a very real way the world was changing. These sudden changes didn't come out of thin air—they had to be sold. And once again advertisers turned to fairy tale iconography to sell these new technologies. Using fairy tale stories to sell these innovative products was a natural fit, as Jack Zipes describes in his Oxford Companion, "basic fairy-tale elements like magic, transformation, and happy endings lend themselves perfectly to the advertiser's pitch that the feature product will miraculously change the viewer's life for the better. Products act as magic helpers who assist the heroes and heroines of the mini-fairy tale overcome whatever dilemma they face" ([8], p. 610). Cell phone commercials flooded the airwaves and haven't left since. Fairy tale types like Hansel & Gretel and Cinderella were inserted into commercials for AT&T and Cingular Wireless to explain their miraculous features and to humanize the gadgets. And one particular commercial from Nokia went long by comparing their phones to all the different kinds of magic in the fairy tale realm (See Figure 15).

Figure 15. 2000s General Fairy Tale Nokia Commercial.

In the commercial Nokia's cell phones are described as magic wands, shining stars, and hidden treasures promising to reveal secret worlds. Cell phones are perhaps the best modern example of the product-as-magic pitch described by Zipes. Even if the products advertisers were pitching weren't as easily marketed as life-changing, they still combined this message with fairy tales. For example, this Mercedes-Benz commercial featuring Peter Pan (See Figure 16).

In the ad, Peter returns to a grown-up Michael and invites him come fly again. Smash cut to Peter riding shotgun while Michael drives a new Mercedes across the English countryside by moonlight. "It's never too late to fly", says Peter in the ad. In other words, it's never too late to transform your life back to the happiness of youth through spending money. Other clichés from previous decades like sexualizing fairy tale figures continued, as seen in this Pepsi One commercial featuring Kim Cattrall as Goldilocks with the Chicago Bears. On the flip side, commercials like this 7 Up Red Riding Hood spot pushed back on those genre expectations by having Red head-butt the wolf stand-in at the end of the commercial. And other commercials, like this one from Adidas, went for an artistically bold modernization with a stripped-down narrative (See Figure 17).

Figure 16. 2000s Peter Pan Mercedes Benz Commercial.

Figure 17. 2000s Little Red Riding Hood Adidas Commercial.

The wordless and almost monochromatic ad (only the shoes and the wolf's eyes are shown in color), focuses on style and tone instead of product or story. The commercial is selling a personality and not a product. Product descriptions had been slowly become obsolete, as a result of branding becoming the main focus of commercials decade by decade. Meanwhile, Disney was successfully branding their fairy tale heroines as a collected franchise targeted at young girls and other companies were looking to share in the profits. Playmobil marketed a fairytale kingdom Sleeping Beauty play set, but the advertising goes out of its way to avoid the phrase "Sleeping Beauty". Barbie relaunched their direct-to-video film series with adaptations of the then-Disney free stories Rapunzel, Swan Lake, and Thumbelina, always releasing a new line of dolls to go along with the DVDs. Fairy tales figures in popular media were becoming increasingly gendered while fairy tale stories were leaned on heavily to sell everyone on joining the new digital world. The 2000s was a brave new world, but it still had room for fairies.

8. Fairy Tales in the 2010's Remix Culture

Harvard law professor Lawrence Lessig published a book in 2008 titled "Remix: Making Art and Commerce Thrive in the Hybrid Economy", which hypothesized about the societal effect of the internet, specifically for the way in which it gave rise to the remix culture [11]. Lessig recognized a trend in the rising popularity of derivative works that combine or edit together existing materials to produce something new. (One quick example is Pogo's "Alice", a song spliced together from images and sounds from Disney's *Alice in Wonderland* film.) What was a hypothesis in 2008 became a reality in the 2010s—remix culture was everywhere. Sampling became an inescapable trend in music, Wikipedia became a de facto source of knowledge, and Hollywood was continually attempting to reboot old intellectual properties into new franchises. At the same time originality was still very much present. In the opening months of 2010, Old Spice released a commercial that is still being adapted and repeated six years later. "The Man Your Man Could Smell Like" shot the advertising world with a bolt of manic energy, resulting in a privileging of the weird and the funny. Originality was still present, but it's copied and run into the ground with increasing speed. While Old Spice has doubled down on weird and funny ad campaigns, within a few years the tone-stealing derivatives have shown up less and less. Other brands like Geico settled back into controllable and innocuous humor, like this recent ad featuring Peter Pan (See Figure 18).

There were, of course, still unimaginative campaigns that featured individual variations on fairy tales with specific products (for example Red Bull featured Aladdin, Rapunzel, and the Frog Prince; Security Service Federal Credit Union relied on Snow White, Cinderella, and Red Riding Hood; and Sky Link used Aladdin, Frog Prince, and Princess & the Pea stories). But remix culture would manifest itself in television commercials with ads that featured half a dozen fairy tale types all at once, like this one from PNC Bank (See Figure 19).

Figure 18. 2010s Peter Pan Geico Commercial.

Figure 19. 2010s Fairy Tale Mashup PNC Bank Commercial.

The ad depicts a wedding attended by unicorns, teddy bears, ballerinas, soldiers, hummingbirds, and magically blooming flowers. The father, who walks his beautiful princess down the aisle, watches as his daughter marries prince charming. In the end it turns out the commercial takes place in the mind of a father watching his young daughter while she reads a book of fairy tales. Commercials like these are complicated by Marina Warner in "Once Upon a Time", where she comments on the fairy tale's spotty history with gender representation. "Current fairy tales on stage and screen reveal an acute malaise about sexual, rather than social, programming of the female, and the genre continues ever more intensively to wrestle with the notorious question Freud put long ago, 'What do women want?'" ([7], p. 173). The PNC Bank spot is perhaps a bit too Freudian as the father imagines what his grown daughter wants most as a fairy tale wedding, prompting him to open a new savings account to prepare for that eventuality. With this question of gender representation in mind, this Christmas commercial from Marks & Spencer (M&S) becomes almost painful to watch (See Figure 20).

Figure 20. 2010s Fairy Tale Mashup Marks & Spencer (M&S) Commercial.

This commercial is a paragon of remix culture, as the main character morphs into Alice, Red Riding Hood, Gretel, a carpet-riding beauty, and Dorothy from *The Wizard of Oz*. In the first minute alone the main character has five costume changes and two of them manage to present her slow-motion in just underwear. Marks & Spencer posits that what women want is purses, clothes, and (above all) shoes. When women are unmistakably in charge of using fairy tale imagery to tell stories the gender representation issues tend to be much less problematic. For example, an-all female college-prep academy created an ad campaign with the tagline, "Life's Not a Fairytale", which featured ad copy like "Don't wait for a prince", "Mirror, Mirror on the Wall. Be more than just the fairest of them all", and "You are not a princess". Another playfully perverse challenging of these dubious genre tropes came from comedian Amy Schumer. In the sketch "Princess Amy" from her television show Inside Amy Schumer, the realities of being a princess are explored: you have to marry a first cousin at age 14 to preserve the purity of the royal bloodline and are threatened with death if you can't produce a male heir. More than halfway into the 2010s, it is clear we aren't free from the same questions and concerns that have been raised by fairy tales for centuries. And for every innovative and subversive fairy tale-themed commercial produced, three (or more) cliché-ridden ads appear at the same time.

9. Conclusions

In his 1979 book, "Breaking the Magic Spell", Jack Zipes shared the story of Priscilla Denby, a researcher who spent an entire day watching TV in 1969 logging all the traditional folklore and fairy tale items featured in shows and commercials. In 1969 Denby logged 101 themes in one day of television ([12], p. 119). In 2016 we live in a time described (sometime jokingly, other times seriously) as Peak TV. As more channels and online content providers attempt to stake out ground and cement their place in the media landscape, more and more television shows are being produced. According to research done in 2015 from the television network FX, there has been an unprecedented rise in programming from all television networks and content producers in the last few years [13]. In 2009 there 211 original scripted series, 217 in 2010, 267 in 2011, 288 in 2012, 343 in 2013, 376 in 2014, and 409 in 2015 (See Figure 21).

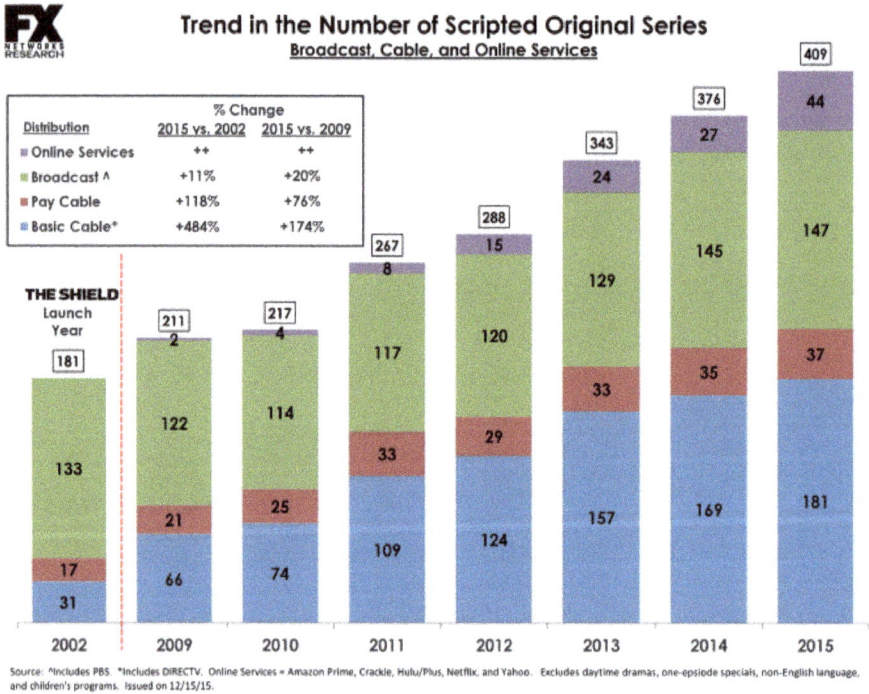

Figure 21. FX Peak TV Chart.

One can only imagine what a study like Priscilla Denby's would look like in 2016. In 1969 there were only a handful of channels and now there are hundreds. With more commercials and shows than ever before fairy tales have more opportunities than ever to show up on the small screen. In the introduction to "Channeling Wonder", a book exploring the fairy tale's role in the age of Peak TV, Pauline Greenhill and Jill Rudy explain, "television seriality works especially well for establishing the horizon of expectation while keying on a fluid relationship of fantasy and reality. Wonder invokes and responds to this fluid relationship, helping to illuminate fairy tale's persistence in, and even conscription of, new media." ([14], pp. 13–14). Television advertisements are by nature temporary and ethereal; it is impossible to quantify this genre collectively as a whole or even viewing most of them, however, it is still beneficial to examine and catalogue the wonder and storytelling operating within these artifacts when possible. The digital age and the new media it's brought have created an ideal environment for the fairy tale to adapt. The call Jack Zipes made in "Breaking the Magic Spell" is more relevant than ever as fairy tales find new places in commercials and television programs. According to Zipes, to counter the "corporate inundation of our imagination, the familiar fairy tales must be made strange to us again if we are to respond to the unique images of our own imagination and the possible utopian elements they may contain" ([12], p. 118). While Zipes was speaking specifically against mind-warping TV advertisements featuring fairy tales, there are still those rare commercials that genuinely make the tales strange to us again by commenting on the genre or showing us their place in the modern world. To close out this series let's examine one last commercial that manages to comment on online journalism, social media mobs, police brutality and militarization, privacy rights, conspiracy theories, insurance fraud, and the financial crisis. And the framing mechanism for all of this? The familiar tale of the Three Little Pigs (See Figure 22).

Figure 22. 2010s Three Little Pigs The Guardian Commercial.

Conflicts of Interest: The author declares no conflict of interest.

Abbreviations

BYU   Brigham Young University

References

1. Levin, Victor, and Matthew Weiner. "Mystery Date." In *Mad Men: Season 5*. Directed by Matt Shakman. Los Angeles: Lionsgate, 2012, Blu-ray.
2. De Baubeta, Odber, and Patricia Anne. "Fairy Tale Motifs in Advertising." *Estudosde Literatura Oral* 3 (1997): 35–60.
3. Mieder, Wolfgang. "Advertising." In *The Greenwood Encyclopedia of Folktales and Fairy Tales: A–F*. Edited by Donald Haase. Santa Barbara: Greenwood Publishing Group, 2007, p. 5.
4. Ogilvy, David, and Ray Atherton. *Confessions of an Advertising Man*. New York: Antheneum, 1963.
5. Dégh, Linda. *American Folklore and the Mass Media*. Bloomington: Indiana University Press, 1994, p. 48.
6. Zipes, Jack. "Folklore Research and Western Marxism: A Critical Replay." *The Journal of American Folklore* 97 (1984): 329–37.
7. Warner, Marina. *Once Upon a Time: A Short History of Fairy Tale*. Oxford: OUP Oxford, 2014.
8. Zipes, Jack, ed. *The Oxford Companion to Fairy Tales*. Oxford: OUP Oxford, 2015.
9. Bethea, Neil, Jacob Williams, and Yiwen Yu. "Broadband services in the United States: An analysis of demand." Available online: https://web.archive.org/web/20060904211822/http://www.nrri.ohio-state.edu/dspace/bitstream/2068/814/3/Article+1-Bethea+_Broadband_.pdf (accessed on 10 March 2016).
10. "Study: Broadband Penetration to Surge by 2010." Available online: http://www.cnet.com/news/study-broadband-penetration-to-surge-by-2010/ (accessed on 10 March 2016).
11. Lessig, Lawrence. *Remix: Making Art and Commerce Thrive in the Hybrid Economy*. New York: Penguin, 2008.
12. Zipes, Jack. *Breaking the Magic Spell: Radical Theories of Folk and Fairy Tales*. Lexington: University Press of Kentucky, 2002.
13. "Peak TV: Surge From Streaming Services, Cable Pushes 2015 Scripted Series Tally to 409." Available online: http://variety.com/2015/tv/news/peak-tv-409-original-series-streaming-cable-1201663212/ (accessed on 10 March 2016).
14. Greenhill, Pauline, and Jill Terry Rudy. *Channeling Wonder: Fairy Tales on Television*. Detroit: Wayne State University Press, 2014, pp. 13–14.

Between Earth and Sky: Transcendence, Reality, and the Fairy Tale in *Pan's Labyrinth*

Savannah Blitch

Abstract: Though it is now a decade since its release, Guillermo del Toro's *Pan's Labyrinth* (2006) remains a work of filmic art which plays upon our deep-rooted and mercurial relationship with fairy tales and folklore. By turns beautiful and grotesque, *Pan's Labyrinth* is a complex portrait of the clash between Ofelia's fairy tale world and that of the brutal adults around her. This article will provide an analysis of the juxtaposition of the film's imagery of closed/open circles, their respective realms, and how Ofelia moves between the two. I will argue that these aspects create an unusual relationship between the fairy tale universe and the physical one, characterized by simultaneous displacement and interdependency. Ofelia acts as a mediatrix of these spheres, conforming to neither the imposed rules of her historical reality nor the expected structural rules of fairy tales, and this refusal ultimately allows her transcendence from the circumscribed realm of the liminal into Victor Turner's "liminoid" space, escaping the trap of binarism.

Reprinted from *Humanities*. Cite as: Blitch, S. Between Earth and Sky: Transcendence, Reality, and the Fairy Tale in *Pan's Labyrinth*. *Humanities* **2016**, *5*, 33.

1. Introduction

Upon the release of *Pan's Labyrinth* in 2006, the film immediately caught and held international attention. Its premiere at the Cannes Film Festival was swiftly followed by swathes of praise as critics, used to overlooking 'popular' creators, were pleasantly surprised to find that "[t]he Mexican is not only a skilled director mining a rich vein in fantasy/horror; he is an artist full stop" [1]. In 2007, the year of its wide release, the movie became a much-announced title in worldwide awards, among its many wins were three Academy Awards, the Mexican Golden Ariel (the highest film award) and eight Silver Ariels, another eight Spanish Goyas, and three British Academey of Film and Television Arts Awards [2]. Guillermo del Toro's labor of love—"I gave back my entire salary in order to get the film made the way I wanted it."—had clearly struck a ringing chord [3].

By turns hopeful and brutal, fantastical and realistic, gruesome and beautiful, del Toro's story is fixated on the dualities inherent in humanity. In this paper, I will first establish the symbolism of reality *versus* that of the fairy tale, guided by Curtiss Hoffman's analogy of the line and circle in *The Seven Story Tower*. Then, by analyzing the juxtaposition of these symbols, their respective realms in the film, and further, how the child protagonist Ofelia moves between the two, I demonstrate that the film creates an unusual relationship between them characterized by simultaneous displacement and interdependency. Ofelia acts as a mediatrix of these spheres, conforming to neither the imposed rules of her historical reality nor the expected, structural rules of fairy tales. This refusal ultimately allows her transcendence from the circumscribed realm of the liminal into Victor Turner's "liminoid" space, thus escaping the trap of binarism.

2. The Dialectic of Fairy Tale and Reality: Closed and Open Circles

In the course of this paper, the closed (alternatively referred to as full) circle and the open (alternatively referred to as broken) circle will serve as representative of the real world and the world of fairy tales, respectively. The dichotomy of these symbols and their meanings is most easily described with the aid of Curtiss Hoffman, who covers symbolism in mythic narratives extensively in *The Seven Story Tower*. Although his interpretations of the seven designated "key" myths are not always the most convincing, heavily colored by Freudian readings and a rather mystical take on the Collective Unconsciousness, Hoffman does identify a number of interesting recurrent themes. His most useful ideas appear in the first chapter of the book ([4], pp. 1–21) where he introduces the model of an overarching "dialectic of science and myth" ([4], p. 8) that shapes human cultural practice. He identifies the former as linear and the latter as circular, and assigns the two fields their defining attributes accordingly. Science is "analytic", "progressive", "rational", and "masculine" where myth is "synthetic", "traditional", "transcendent", and "feminine". They act as complementary opposites of each other. While the relationship between the full *vs.* the broken circle is more subtle, the general principle remains the same. The closed circle describes reality, and, much like Hoffman's linear depiction of science, represents logic and stability. However, as informed by *Pan's Labyrinth* it additionally symbolizes repetition and masculine tendencies. The motion and fluidity often linked with the full circle is perverted into a locked holding pattern, where movement is only permitted in the sanctioned direction and the structure as a whole is constant and static. The broken circle, on the other hand, signifies emotion, volatility, liminality, and femininity.

In del Toro's characteristically ornate style, the film tells the story of Ofelia, a young, fanciful girl in the Spain of 1944, five years after the bloody Civil War. She is daughter to a sickly, pregnant mother and a wicked stepfather, one of the top-ranking generals of the fascist army. General Vidal moves them to the country to improve his wife's health, anxious for his unborn son. Their new residence shares the forest with an ancient labyrinth, home to an equally ancient faun who reveals that Ofelia is the reincarnation of Princess Moana of the Underworld. He presents her three tasks which she must complete before the moon becomes full if she ever hopes to escape the mortal world and reclaim her birthright [5]. Del Toro is a master of symbolism and subtext, a skill that takes center stage in a film such as *Pan's Labyrinth*, which is steeped in ambiguity and multiple meanings. However, some clarity can be gleaned from investigating how certain images such as the closed and open circles appear in the narrative, how they impact it, and thus how the overall meaning is affected.

First, the closed circle: it appears most prominently as the full moon, the cycle of reincarnation, and the clock imagery surrounding Captain Vidal. In the first case, initially the importance of the full moon to Ofelia's tasks would seem to align it more closely with the fairy tale world, but in fact the faun very clearly stipulates that she must complete the three trials *before* the full moon, when its circle is still incomplete. Only up until when the edges meet can she hope to counteract the pull of the second prominent full circle, her own pattern of reincarnation. While this is a fantastical device, its placement within the mortal world and its closed nature establish it as firmly representative of reality. According to the faun, her soul is being recycled between bodies and across centuries; she is stuck in a feedback loop, reinforcing her human existence the same way reality strengthens itself through constant directional movement. The third and most powerful of reality's symbolic strongholds is the imagery of the clock. Vidal's pocket watch accompanies him in almost every scene, and his quarters in the mill are dominated by huge ridged wheels which mimic clock gears. The strictly regimented turning of both very deliberately reinforces the relentless press of reality. Vidal maintains the watch meticulously to ensure its movement, just as he continues (and simultaneously overwrites) his father's legacy. "Time is linked to order, and order to oppression," Jack Zipes notes, and indeed, as the captain is consumed by the flow of time and his place in it, he excels at oppression ([6], p. 238).

The broken circle often appears in close connection to the full circle, notably as Ofelia's birthmark, the labyrinth, and the shattered clock face. Much like Vidal carries his pocket watch, Ofelia carries on her body the perpetually open symbol of the crescent moon, planting her firmly on the side of fairy tales. The structure of the labyrinth itself is an open circle, and intentionally situated right across from the full, turning wheels of the millhouse. The labyrinth's dilapidated condition speaks to one of the shortcomings of the structure of the broken circle, which is that although its openings allow for more flexibility and dynamism than the full circle, they are also points of weakness. Without the closed circle's benefit of feeding into itself, the open circle easily becomes brittle in the absence of attention and slips into dormancy. One of the most interesting appearances of the open circle is in Vidal's broken clock face. Overlaid on the strong realist symbol of the clock itself, the shattered circle is vehemently denied by Vidal, though he can never quite escape it. Paul Julian Smith remarks in a review for *Film Quarterly* that "Captain Vidal . . . embodies a masculinity . . . so exclusive it barely acknowledges the existence of the feminine," and just as he presumes to greet Ofelia and the pregnant Carmen with the masculine plural because he refuses to accept anything but a son, he refuses to allow the broken circle any foothold of emotion or feminizing influence by facing its presence ([7], p. 6).

3. A Series of Interlockings: the Dance of the Two Realms

As these worlds edge closer together throughout the film, Ofelia slowly bridging the gap between them, it becomes increasingly apparent that their interactions toe a delicate line between coexistence and separation. Tracie Lukasiewicz classifies this balance as "neomagical realism", which she uses in the sense of having neither a "conventional fairy tale's acceptance of magic within its fantasy world" nor "magical realism's incorporation of magic into the real world" ([8], pp. 61–62). Continuing my analogy of the closed and open circles, their relationship is what can best be described as a series of interlockings in which the mouth of the open circle hooks around the edge of its unbroken counterpart and for certain moments occupies not exactly the same space but nearly so, closely enough that their movements affect each other. From the moment that Ofelia makes contact with the fairy in the forest, the realms begin to converge upon and affect each other. Her initial meeting with the faun and the first task takes place deep in the labyrinth and the forest, completely immersed in the fairy world, and the object of power she receives, a magic book, allows her to access the fantastic while maintaining distance. Afterwards, the situation escalates as the faun appears in the midst of the real world, in her bedroom, and presents her with a talisman to further link them together: the mandrake root. Unlike the passive book, this object requires blood sacrifice that creates a concrete bond, the strength of which is demonstrated as Carmen throws the creature into the fire and immediately doubles over in agony, forfeiting the health it provides. The second task occurs at an even lower degree of separation, beginning and ending right in Ofelia's room. It cannot be chance, either, that the night that Ofelia is sent to bed without dinner in the real world, she is confronted with a supernatural feast in the other; at this point they are too closely linked for coincidence. Smith describes it thus: though the "plot is placed quite precisely in a historical moment ... the material effects of that desperate moment ... are juxtaposed with, are indeed inextricable from, the fantastic realms" ([4], p. 5). On the night of the final battle, when the realms are at their closest, Ofelia travels into the labyrinth and achieves immortality at its center, while in a direct inversion Vidal walks out of it and at its gate is condemned to death and, worse, obscurity.

Still, though the fantasy world deeply impacts Vidal, the film clearly illustrates the limited scope of the two worlds' connection when he confronts his stepdaughter in the labyrinth and, through a moment of changed camera perspective, there is only empty air where Ofelia sees the faun. At this instant, what has been suggested throughout the film—as when Mercedes, the housekeeper who becomes close to

Ofelia, admits that she does not believe in magic anymore, or when a distraught Carmen insists, "Magic does not exist. Not for you, me, or anyone else."— becomes cemented: Ofelia is the only one who possesses what Zipes calls "*real* double vision, unique powers that enable her to see two worlds at the same time" ([6], p. 237). By the nature of their interlocking, these worlds can coincide temporally and thematically without actually touching or otherwise mixing. As Lukasiewicz comments, "[t]here is no incorporation of one space into another, nor is there a point when they completely converge" ([8], p. 66). Del Toro constructs a universe where the worlds do not need to be melded in order to affect each other, and more importantly, where it becomes a conscious choice to cross into or even acknowledge the fairy tale realm. Among the cast of disillusioned adults, Ofelia is a unique figure: she makes the choice to believe, and it is this faith that allows her to stand on the rim of the full circle, look across the void, and see the rings of the open circle hovering beyond.

4. "One Can Only Get Lost in a Maze": The Symbolic Significance of the Labyrinth

The common questions of whether Ofelia's fantastic journey actually happened lose their urgency in this light. If the worlds were completely incorporated, there would be no reason to doubt the validity of our sojourns into Ofelia's "double vision"; if the worlds were never shown to overlap, then the easiest assumption would be that the events were nothing but fabrication. As it is, the tenuous almost-blurring of the boundaries fails to make a solid impression one way or another. While this ambiguity might be frustrating in other genres, in the case of the fairy tale film—and especially considering the reality-fantasy relationship established in *Pan's Labyrinth*—it is completely natural. The fantastic thrives upon in-betweens and suspension of disbelief. To fixate then on what "really" happened distracts from the actual focus of the narrative, which has little to do with any binary-driven interpretation of reality. Del Toro's film is driven by the *becoming* of its two main characters, Ofelia and Mercedes, which means that what is of most interest to the story is that they end beyond where they began, not necessarily where that point specifically is. What matters is the change, and that the audience experiences it with them, and it is for this reason that the labyrinth is so central to the film.

The Dictionary of Literary Symbols notes as an afterthought in its entry on labyrinths that "[t]here is a technical distinction between a labyrinth and a maze, the labyrinth being "unicursal" (with one path), and the maze "multicursal" (with branching paths)," meaning that "one can only get lost in a maze" ([9], p. 107). Accordingly, the movie—rather than presenting winding alternate routes and possibilities—follows a singular spiral path, one that may curve in on itself and challenge perceptions, but ultimately remains steady. Del Toro himself confirms the sentiment in an interview, commenting that "A maze is a place where you get lost, but a labyrinth is essentially . . . an ethical, moral transit to one inevitable center" [6]. Ofelia, by the end of the movie, has fully realized herself along the course of this transit, which positions her in a unique place to jump ship, as it were, into the waiting folds of the open-circle world of faerie. Characteristic of the non-linear, fantastical realm, this truth is actually given away within the opening minutes of the movie, the very first time we see Ofelia: she lies on the ground, breathing shallowly, the plaintive lullaby humming over her, and the blood on her face runs *backwards* into her nose. "The first scene reveals that she is alive after her death," Zipes notes, "and the rest of film . . . explain[s] why her blood returns to her and fills her with life" ([6], p. 238). Even this commentary, however, I feel places undue emphasis on categorizing her as alternatively "alive" or "dead", when the point is that she made it out of the sphere of restriction and dichotomies.

5. Memory and Forgetting: The Influence of the Spanish Civil War and its After-Effects

This is an especially remarkable achievement given that the movie takes place in a historical setting which was defined by those very two things. Ofelia is the child of a country which has just suffered the agony of a nation-wide ideological divide and continues to be plagued by the mentality of 'us *versus* them', as the conflict between the resistance fighters and Vidal's forces demonstrates. The northern Spain in *Pan's Labyrinth* is still a fictional version, however, and it is more shaped by the after-effects rather than the actual events of the time period in which it is supposed to take place. One of the strongest influences is the tension between the Pact of Forgetting and the Law of Historical Memory, as the debate leading up to the eventual passing of the latter was contemporary to the filming ([10], p. 26). Their vague, grand titles almost sound like they belong to fairy tales themselves, which perhaps communicates how profoundly the Civil War transformed Spanish identity. The first was not an official law but an informal agreement put in place shortly after Franco's death in 1973. Under the Pact, political scientist Omar Encarnación describes how

> the conflict came to be understood as a *guerra de locos* (war of collective madness) that produced no winners and losers, only victims. In this problematic formulation, both sides bore equal responsibility for the Civil War, which made it redundant to ascribe blame to any particular group in society. The important thing was to ensure that a similar conflict would never happen again, and the best way to achieve that result was to forget and look to the future ([11], pp. 28–29).

The 2007 Law of Historical Memory overturned this through an unequivocal condemnation of fascism and a number of policies intended to heal and reverse the damage of the Franco dictatorship, such as increased pensions for veterans, reparation payments, and, significantly, a set of injunctions for "the exhumation and reburial of unmarked Civil War graves" ([11], p. 166). These opposing policies not only represent changing forms of government but radically different perceptions of time as well. The Pact of Forgetting, although intended to smooth the state's transition into democracy, is characteristically fascist in tone, articulating the same single-minded focus on progress that motivates Captain Vidal. Thus, Ofelia implicitly becomes aligned with the redemptive Law of Historical Memory, which moves forward by turning to the past and redeems the living by bringing the dead back to the surface.

6. A Search for the Lost Self: Fairy Tale Tropes Re-imagined and Re-purposed by Ofelia

In a way, the Pact of Forgetting embodied the same sort of erasure inherent in the typical "and they lived happily ever after"; fairy tales often act as vehicles for the reinforcement of such cultural constructs. Characters enter and traverse a liminal space and come out the other end confirming or having learned those values. For example, Cinderella's ability to move between her identities and the social strata lasts only three nights, and the youngest daughter in "East of the Sun and West of the Moon" eventually leaves the magical land to settle into life with her now-permanently-human husband. *Pan's Labyrinth* incorporates several fairy tale tropes and narratives, but because Ofelia is the center of them, she de-stabilizes their traditional structure and undermines their sanctioned subtextual messages. Her general narrative fits neatly into the Aarne-Thompson-Uther tale type 425A, The Search for the Lost Husband: it begins with an enchanted bargain which goes wrong, followed by tasks of mounting difficulty and the helpers which aid her advancement [12]. The vital divergence is that rather than chasing after a vanished husband, Ofelia is laboring towards the recovery of her former self. The union at the end of the film is entirely internal and individual, and thus deeply subversive of the original type, which revolves around the repentance of the disobedient wife, demonstrating herself to be worthy of the union with her prince. The associated tasks reflect this by focusing on domestic skills, such as the washing of the shirt in "East of the Sun and West of the Moon" [13]. Ofelia's trials are not nearly so gender role–specific, and have her slaying monsters and traveling into the underworld; since her quest is to prove her worth to herself, her trials are about physical and moral courage, the things which are important to *her*, not a husband or society. She is that rare protagonist that possesses acute knowledge of the genre she inhabits, and when her "real" life intrudes (such as with the birth of her brother and death of her mother) she questions the rules and morality which govern that genre. *Pan's Labyrinth* becomes a film about a girl who amalgamates a new fairy tale out of those given to her; rather than conforming herself to their often strict rules, she creates her own narrative.

7. A World of Her Devising: The Liminoid in *Pan's Labyrinth*

In "A Review of 'Ethnopoetics'," Victor Turner introduces his conception of the *liminoid*, a state of being tangential to the liminal but "more flexible and multifarious than the liminal, which is bounded more firmly by ritual constraints … It is a world of as if, may be, might have been, sometimes should be" ([14], p. 341). It is a land of uncertainty and possibility, without the cultural demand to pass through and continue on. "Liminal phenomena" such as rites of passage are, he says, "integrated into the total social process," because they follow a script which must be seen through to its completion ([14], p. 85). On the other hand, "liminoid phenomena" spring up outside of the social system, in the realm of the experimental ([14], pp. 85–86). The liminoid is the liminal, uncaged, its mysteries kept unto itself and not submitted to maintenance of the societal structure.

Ofelia, in her Icarian escape from the labyrinth and the narrative, elects to be part of the undefined, liminoid territory. She takes her identity into her own hands instead of allowing society to stipulate when, where, and how she should make the many societal and cultural transitions expected of her. The most basic of these is her prematurely induced movement from childhood to adulthood, which in turn is triggered by the intrusion of the fascist, modernized present on the rural, mythic past. This latter frictive encounter is symbolized by the presence of the mill in the forest. Ofelia, though not the only character to move between the two, is the only one shown equally in both environments because of her liminal existence. However, rather than choose either one she instead moves outside the traditional dichotomy into the liminoid, where she is both ancient and ageless, the distant past and infinite present, a story and a real presence. Either/or does not exist in the intermingled space where the closed circle meets the open one. Her intimate connection with the world of fairy tales allows her to transcend such definitive labeling and binary thought, rising above all of the adult figures who abused or talked down to her, in a way that Smith proposes "perhaps [suggests] … that fantasy is somehow proportionate to or compensatory for the horrors of the real" ([7], p. 8). The small, delicate flower that del Toro chooses to close the film on seems a woefully inadequate reparation compared to the graphic and self-satisfied violence portrayed in the rest of the movie, but the possibility of the blossom, like the fairy tale world it springs from, is much bigger than itself. It opens to the sunlight the way the open circle turns towards the full one, less constant and more breakable than its counterpart but ready to receive whatever the other has to offer and return it better than it was given.

In the same interview where del Toro acknowledges the distinction between mazes and labyrinths, he also makes an equally important and infinitely more moving remark, that *"Pan's Labyrinth* is a movie about a girl who gives birth to herself into the world she believes in" [3]. Robbed of her father, her home, her mother, and finally her mortal life, the one thing Ofelia refuses to have taken from her is her childhood and the impenetrable faith that comes with it. At the close of the film, standing her ground in the center of her chosen world, Ofelia not only defends her brother but her own innocence and her right to keep something sacred to herself, outside of destructive binaries. She is a labyrinth—pure of direction and purpose—where the others are mazes, and having walked both the closed and open paths, combined she becomes better than them both, like her symbol the flower, with her feet in the earth but her face to the sky.

Conflicts of Interest: The author declares no conflict of interest.

References

1. José Arroyo. "Pan's Labyrinth." *Sight & Sound* 16 (2006): 66–68.
2. "Pan's Labyrinth: Awards." *IMDb.* Available online: http://www.imdb.com/title/tt0457430/awards (accessed on 12 May 2016).
3. BFI Film Forever. "Girl Interrupted." Available online: http://old.bfi.org.uk/sightandsound/feature/49337 (accessed on 12 May 2016).
4. Curtiss Hoffman. *The Seven Story Tower.* Cambridge: Perseus Publishing, 1999.
5. *Pan's Labyrinth.* Directed by Guillermo del Toro. New York: Picturehouse, 2006.
6. Jack Zipes. "Pan's Labyrinth." *Journal of American Folklore* 121 (2008): 236–40.
7. Paul Julian Smith. "Pan's Labyrinth (El Laberinto Del Fauno)." *Film Quarterly* 60 (2007): 4–9.
8. Tracie D. Lukasiewicz. "The Parellelism of the Fantastic and the Real: Guillermo Del Toro's *Pan's Labyrinth/El Laberinto Del Fauno* and Neomagical Realism." In *Fairy Tale Films: Visions of Ambiguity.* Edited by Pauline Greenhill and Sidney Eve Matrix. Logan: Utah State University Press, 2010, pp. 60–78.
9. Michael Ferber. *A Dictionary of Literary Symbols*, 2nd ed. New York: Cambridge University Press, 1999, p. 231.
10. Mar Diestro-Dópido. *Pan's Labyrinth.* London: Palgrave Macmillan, 2013.
11. Omar Guillermo Encarnación. *Democracy without Justice in Spain: The Politics of Forgetting,* 1st ed. Philadelphia: University of Pennsylvania Press, 2014.
12. Antti Aarne, Stith Thompson, and Hans-Jörg Uther. "Aarne-Thompson-Uther Classification of Folk Tales." *Multilingual Folk Tale Database.* Available online: http://www.mftd.org/index.php?action=atu (accessed on 10 February 2016).
13. Peter Christen Asbjørnsen, and Jørgen Moe. "East O' the Sun and West O' the Moon." *Multilingual Folk Tale Database.* Available online: http://www.mftd.org/index.php?action=story&act=select&id=3246 (accessed on 10 February 2016).
14. Victor Turner. "A Review of 'Ethnopoetics'." In *Symposium of the Whole: A Range of Discourse toward an Ethnopoetics.* Edited by Jerome Rothenberg and Diane Rothenberg. Berkeley: University of California Press, 1983.

We All Live in Fabletown: Bill Willingham's Fables—A Fairy-Tale Epic for the 21st Century

Jason Marc Harris

Abstract: Bill Willingham's *Fables* comic book series and its spin-offs have spanned fourteen years and reinforce that fairy-tale characters are culturally meaningful, adaptable, subversive, and pervasive. Willingham uses fairy-tale pastiche and syncreticism based on the ethos of comic book crossovers in his redeployment of previous approaches to fairy-tale characters. *Fables* characters are richer for every perspective that Willingham deploys, from the Brothers Grimm to Disneyesque aesthetics and more erotic, violent, and horrific incarnations. Willingham's approach to these fairy-tale narratives is synthetic, idiosyncratic, and libertarian. This tension between Willingham's subordination of fairy-tale characters to his overarching libertarian ideological narrative and the traditional folkloric identities drives the storytelling momentum of the Fables universe. Willingham's portrayal of Bigby (the Big Bad Wolf turned private eye), Snow White ("Fairest of Them All", Director of Operations of Fabletown, and avenger against pedophilic dwarves), Rose Red (Snow's divergent, wild, and jealous sister), and Jack (narcissistic trickster) challenges contemporary assumptions about gender, heroism, narrative genres, and the very conception of a fairy tale. Emerging from negotiations with tradition and innovation are fairy-tale characters who defy constraints of folk and storybook narrative, mythology, and metafiction.

Reprinted from *Humanities*. Cite as: Harris, J.M. We All Live in Fabletown: Bill Willingham's Fables—A Fairy-Tale Epic for the 21st Century. *Humanities* **2016**, 5, 32.

1. Introduction

Bill Willingham's contributions to fairy-tales in popular culture have spanned fourteen years: from twenty-two collected volumes of his completed *Fables* (2002–2015) comic book series and multiple spin-offs such as *Jack of Fables* (2006–2011) and *Fairest* (2012–2015), as well as the five episodes of the *Fables* video game *The Wolf Among Us* (2013), and the novel *Peter and Max* (2009).[1] *Fables* exemplifies how

---

[1] Fans of *Fables* also credit *Once Upon a Time* with being deeply influenced by Willingham's fairy-tale universe, although Willingham himself dismisses the idea. He offered a "call to disarm" to his fans and reminded readers and viewers that folklore is characterized by continuous development and adaptation to match contemporary tastes: "The Brothers Grimm didn't collect one version of every

fairy-tale characters continue to be meaningful in contemporary media. As Adam Zolkover identifies in "Corporalizing Fairy Tales", Willingham's work stands out from previous comic books that have engaged folklore: "[Neil] Gaiman [in *Sandman*] and [Alan] Moore [in *Promethea*] seem interested in using folklore to explore issues of imagination spirituality, and [...] [Walter] Simonson is interested in using myth to enrich a preexisting fictional landscape [*Thor*], Willingham's *Fables* works in the opposite direction, using the comic book medium [...] to comment on the fairy tales themselves" ([2], p. 40). What distinguishes *Fables* is not only the subtle and vivid framing with beautiful, intense, and varied illustrations, such as those by lead-artist Mark Buckingham, but the ways that Willingham deepens fairy-tale characters through innovative narrative techniques. *Fables* both respects and subverts tradition, revisiting and defying old tales by exploring new possibilities of fairy-tale characters' personal autonomy. *Fables* integrates comic book aesthetics, metafiction, folklore, satire, and synthesis with Willingham's libertarian ideology.

2. Innovative Imitations: The Use of Fairy-Tale Pastiche in *Fables*

The last couple decades have revealed alignments among narrative features of comic books, folklore, and post-modern literary techniques. As Gail de Voss explains, there is much in the reading experience of a comic book that relates to the audience participation with oral performance of folklore: "In the comic book format, the reader must speculate on what happens in the gutters (the space between the panels) as well as read the visual cues to interpret the story and, as in the oral tale, the experience and background of the reader not only enrich the story read but also individualize it" ([3], p. 152). Beyond de Voss's recognition of this folkloric dynamic of reading comic books, the comic book medium often veers towards a self-conscious mixture of narrative elements where a degree of imitation is inevitable—and especially fundamental in the case of fairy-tale comic books, which by story and design involve a vivid commentary on the preceding tradition. This use of pastiche is common with post-modern literary fiction, and it is no surprise that Willingham utilizes pastiche in his redeployment of previous approaches to the fairy-tale characters of *Fables*, but the use of this technique is far from the "dead language" of Fredric Jameson's conception of degraded literary parody.[2] Following Linda Hutchinson's emphasis that "postmodern parody does not disregard the context of the past" and her citation of Angela Carter as one of the examples of

---

folktale; they discovered dozens of versions of each one, because it's the nature of folklore to be altered to suit every different folk who wants to make use of it. Why should today be any different?" [1].

[2] "Pastiche is, like parody, the imitation of a peculiar or unique, idiosyncratic style, the wearing of a linguistic mask, speech in a dead language. But it is a neutral practice of such mimicry, without any of parody's ulterior motives, amputated of the satiric impulse, devoid of laughter ([4], p. 17).

"novelty and individuality" in the use of pastiche, I would argue that Willingham, like Carter, is successful in his parodic challenges of past fairy-tale narratives ([5], p. 90). Furthermore, Willingham's use of fairy-tale pastiche recalls much earlier authorial innovators with the fairy-tale tradition who had also underscored the adult themes of fairy-tales. Fairy-tale parodies in eighteenth-century France, for example, as Jack Zipes explains in *Why Fairy Tales Stick* "bordered on the burlesque and even on the macabre and grotesque. [...] Sentimental love was parodied. Numerous tales abandoned morality for pornography and eroticism" ([6], p. 76). Zolkover defines Willingham's "fairy-tale pastiche" as "a postmodernist blending of elements from a variety of loci within fairy-tale discourse that serves at once as commentary, play, and a fairy tale in its own right" ([2], p. 41). *Fables* is also a broad cultural text that engages aspects of contemporary America, with regard to media, sexuality, and politics. The *Fables* fairy-tale characters are richer for every perspective that Willingham explores, from classic literary renderings of famous collections to Disneyesque aesthetics and more violent, ribald, and horrific treatments.

Willingham's approach to fairy-tale narrative is syncretic but also idiosyncratic. Referring to his titular protagonist of *Jack of Fables* Willingham explains, "Jack can be Jack Horner, Jack of the Beanstalk, Jack in the Green, and Jack the Giant Killer, but absolutely not Jack Spratt. I needed Spratt to be his own fellow and so he was, by absolute writer's fiat" [7]. It is this very tension between Willingham's subordination of fairy-tale characters to his overarching narrative and the traditional folkloric identities that drives the storytelling momentum of the *Fables* universe. We see this narrative engine, building friction between invention and tradition, following comic book crossover precedents, folktales and booktales, national mythology and personal imagination—especially with such characters and stories as the Big Bad Wolf's redemption and romance with Snow White, the elaborate rivalry between Snow White and Rose Red, the bitterness of Pinocchio, the solipsistic deification of Jack, and the moral complexity of Frau TotenKinder, the fabled witch and cannibal of the Brothers Grimm' "Hansel and Gretel". Willingham's *Fables* reconfigures fairy tale characters as comic book demigods whose power depends upon both popular and traditional culture but whose choices can transcend the cultural constraints of previous narratives. The *Fables* universe values tradition but celebrates innovation.

3. Fabletown: Neverland in the Big Apple—Material Mapping of Magic for the Mundies

In the opening volume of *Fables* (issues 1–5) readers encounter some of the fundamental elements of the *Fables* universe ([8], p. 5–11). Fabletown is concealed in New York City. This secret stronghold is where a host of characters from folklore, myth, and legend have fled their homelands and learn to live near ordinary people, known as the "mundies". As Andrea Miller observes in her 2002 review of the opening issues of *Fables*, this retreat in New York City is "the most striking reference to ethnicity" with "conditions [similar to] the Jewish Diaspora" ([9], p. 253). Some conservatives have applauded while some liberals have decried *Fables* for what they perceive as a Pro-Israel stance.[3] Behind the invasion of the homelands is the Adversary, a shadowy figure whose mystique is at first reminiscent of Satan or the Dark Lord or Mordor, though his identity is eventually revealed as Geppetto. Yes, the same character who constructed Pinocchio. Speaking of the doll who had wanted to be a boy, Pinocchio is an example of Willingham choosing to include fantasy literature that is not strictly folkloric but resonates with traditional fabulism in its use of magic and impact on literary culture.[4] Indeed, it is quite clear that "Willingham's choice and expansion of the term 'fable' as opposed to 'fairy tale' is arguably to draw from a larger frame of reference" ([12], p. 97). Like Pinocchio, Willingham also includes materials from other fairy-tale literary fantasies, such as Lewis Carroll's *Alice and Wonderland* and *Through the Looking Glass* as well as Frank Baum's *Oz* books. The vorpal blade of Carroll's "Jabberwocky" is used by Little Boy Blue to dispatch the huge wooden demon that Geppetto has fashioned as the public form of the Adversary ([13], p. 169). Fabletown itself, as Zolkover observes, is "quite literally at the crossroads between a folkloristic and literary genealogy [...] on the corner of Bullfinch and Kipling streets" ([2], p. 48). Reifying literary allusions by spatial representation, Willingham's comic book series revels in the comic book cross-over ethos and materializes meta-storytelling, where nothing is off limits to the creative impulse of synthetic narrative.[5]

Beyond the spatial representation of Fabletown, in his inaugural volume of *Fables*, Willingham's treatment of Pinocchio, explores the literalism of his characters, whether drawn from folklore or print, particularly with regard to the material—and especially carnal—dynamics of magic. During "Remembrance Day" Pinnochio remarks with clear bitterness on his perfectly complected face that "I'm over three centuries old and I still haven't gone through puberty. I want to grow up, I want my balls to drop, and I want to get laid" ([8], p. 87). This blunt confrontation with fleshly sexual identity—and also a parodic jibe at Pinnochio—is a hallmark of the

---

3   See "What Would a Conservative Comic Book Look Like" and "Fables: Just an Analogy?" [10,11].
4   The other well-known perpetual boy—another literary figure with fabulist dimensions, Peter Pan, was not available because of copyright challenges from the Barrie estate [1].
5   Alan Moore's *The League of Extraordinary Gentleman* (1999–2007) is an important precedent to this form of comic book cross-over between genres that enlists a cast of literary characters (especially those drawn from Victorian writers like H.G. Wells, Jules Verne, Robert Louis Stevenson, and H. Rider Haggard): Allan Quartermain, Dr. Jekyll, Captain Nemo, the invisible man, *etc*. Also, Neil Gaiman's *Books of Magic* (1990–1991), which features Baba Yaga, King Arthur, Lucifer, and Thomas the Rhymer is a notable example of a comic book series drawing from legendary characters and working within a comic book universe's franchise characters—John Constantine, Dr. Occult, Dr. Fate—those of the DC property in particular.

rhetorical approach of *Fables*. Aside from the lush fantasy representations and the graphic violence, the direct depiction of sexuality is the reason for the warning on the back of each volume, "suggested for mature readers". Willingham is not sanitizing, idealizing, or infantilizing fairy tales. He is doing his best to materialize them with flesh-and-blood passion and grief for an adult audience that needs something of the earthy amid the fantastic. The sometimes vociferous emphasis of sexuality rhetorically positions the *Fables* series as a vital narrative, pulsing with libido, whether for martial, marital, or metafictional adventure. It's all mapped out on the lurid streets of Fabletown.

3.1. Reclaiming an Adult Genre: Fables' Use of Violence and Sexuality

Fables' emphasis on sexuality, violence, and parody of fairy-tales partly resonates with the larger literary domain of contentious ideological appropriation of the folk tale genre. As Jack Zipes observes in *Fairy Tales and the Art of Subversion*, fairy-tales were revised and repackaged by authors and educators to indoctrinate children; these redesigned fairy-tales inhabited "a type of literary discourse about mores, values, and manners so that children would become civilized according to the social code of that time. The writers of fairy tales for children *acted* ideologically by presenting their notions regarding social conditions and conflicts, and they *interacted* with each other and with past writers and storytellers of folklore in a public sphere" ([14], p. 3). By emphasizing adult features of fairy-tales in *Fables*, Willingham participates in this "literary discourse about mores, values, and manners", though he defies the moralistic and puerile appropriation of earlier treatments of fairy-tale characters.[6] However, *Fables* has its own ideological tendencies: libertarianism, pragmatism, and militaristic heroism emerge as respected principles. However, the *Fables* universe is not defined by moral rigidity or ideological purity so much as by hunger for power and connection. Familial loyalties trump national allegiance; individual acts of ambition and courage are effective if deployed with a sense of strategic practicality rather than dogma or obsession.

Framing these mature themes, depictions of violence and sexuality reinforce the orientation on an adult audience. Like the prose, the artwork pulls no punches: in this opening volume, the full-page illustration of Rose Red's bloody chamber contains puddles of gore from corner-to-corner. Next to the broken mirror in the upper right-hand corner of the panel, the words "No more happily ever after" drips red down the wall, lacerated with numerous bleeding cuts. This

---

[6] Certainly, Willingham is not the most well-known or the first contemporary writer to have emphasized adult material in fairy tales. Many readers will be aware of fairy-tale poetry by Anne Sexton, anthologies edited by Kate Bernheimer, and collections such as Angela Carter's *The Blood Chamber* or Tanith Lee's *Red as Blood: Or Tells from the Sisters Grimmer*.

signature fairy-tale phrase challenges a conventional reader's narrative expectations, subverting complacency because of the bloody script. This morbid slash at the cliché of "happily ever after" is one of many discursive tactics Willingham employs to toy with a reader's assumption about what a fairy tale is, and how *Fables* engages provocation and innovation. Though a reader is led to expect that Rose Red has been murdered, in fact, she has conspired with her boyfriend, Jack, to stage a scam to avoid marrying Bluebeard, from whom Rose had received a generous dowry. Rose's disingenuous engagement with the infamous wife-killer always had money as its object: Jack convinced her that the funds were needed to help finance his dot.com scheme, which did not prosper. After Bluebeard learns that he has been exploited and has no recourse, we can see from his contracted eyes and lips that although he has not yet fully lived up to his villainous reputation yet in the *Fables* series, that he will later express his malignity despite the General Amnesty, and indeed he does so, targeting Snow White and Bigby.[7]

3.2. Mythic Destiny, Fairy-Tale Personalities, Crossovers, and Moral Progression in Fables

Despite such betrayals, the General Amnesty is maintained as a key civilizing institution of Fabletown, and one that continues to interrogate notions of moral rehabilitation and meaningful change. Even after his years of war against the Homelands, Geppetto is offered and accepts the General Amnesty. Mark Buckingham's artwork highlights the significance of this transcendent event by literally extending past the frame into the margins for this double-page spread. Notably, as if to visually remind us of how fairy-tale characters in the *Fables* universe can overcome their traditionally narrow roles, we see major characters in this marginal space, such as Sinbad and Rose Red on the left side and Beauty and Beast (in his dashing human form) on the right ([13], pp. 176–77). Totenkinder, who is a triumph of the General Amnesty's enablement for meaningful rehabilitation further emphasizes the redemptive and transformative potential of the General Amnesty by her remarks about Bluebeard: "Oh, he'll behave. We'll get along famously, Gepetto and I" ([13], p. 177).

The institution of the General Amnesty helps explore a range of personal relationships between social and political power, native desire, spiritual redemption, and absolute evil. By focusing on the process of these characters' changes, Willingham

---

7   Another powerful instance of Bluebeard's inner emotions showing through his facial expressions is when Bigby rebukes him for a coward: "Sure, you're a terror when gutting unarmed brides on their wedding night, or gunning down an unconscious man on a toilet. You're a coward bluebeard, hiding behind a lifetime of wealth and privilege." Bluebeard first appears impassive, but a solitary tear trickles down his face when he stands alone on the street—a close-up panel reveals his lip-curling humiliated rage against Bigby, who has unmanned him by this veracious diatribe ([15], p. 57).

engages diverse perspectives on the meaning of personality. Of course, "personality" is an insufficient term when discussing a literary character—and a fairy-tale character in particular since folktale protagonists' aspects are a nexus of plot functions, patterns, and motifs. There is generally a fixity of traits that define fairy-tale characters, and they aren't often capable of meaningful change. If fairy tale protagonists change, it is often revelation of an underlying essence, not a true transformation. Structurally, change in fairy-tale characters connects to the plot's movement between opposites, as Maria Tatar describes, following Max Lüthi's concept of the folk tale feature of "'extreme contrasts'": "Both character attributes and social conditions can shift from one extreme to the other" ([16], p. 100). In terms of contrasts and character shifts, we tend to see that dichotomy with the consequences of diverse behavior among siblings and other rivals. As for protagonists, usually magical endowments externalize character traits rather than signal meaningful attitude changes: a maiden who by the end of the tale spills golden coins from her mouth had something beautiful and compassionate about her to begin with.[8] An inhospitable son doesn't become hospitable; he winds up with a toad sitting on top of his head.[9] However, in *Fables*, meaningful change is possible, although this very fluidity has disconcerted some critics: "the characters have little connection with their predecessors beyond their names" ([12], p. 101).

On the contrary, *Fables* characters have a strong connection to "their predecessors", and it is in response to their fairy-tale histories, that the *Fables* characters are motivated to change. It is in this regard that the importance of the General Amnesty in *Fables* cannot be overstated. The characters of Bigby (formerly the Big Bad Wolf of folkloric, storybook, and cinematic fame) and Totenkinder (the witch in "Hansel and Gretel") epitomize the possibilities of mythic transformation that Willingham's plot device of the General Amnesty allows for. As such two formidable embodiments of physical and magical power from the fairy-tale tradition, Willingham expands the depth of these characters through epic backstories. We learn that Bigby is the runt son of a she-wolf (Winter) and the North Wind himself. This mythic origin story is a masterstroke of improvisational mythmaking by Willingham; the character's desire to become a legendary monster and the power of gusty wolfish breaths makes perfect sense via this hereditary etiology.[10] Willingham's conception of Bigby's heritage also displays his syncretic

---

[8]   See "Mother Holle." ([17], p. 81).
[9]   See "The Ungrateful Son."([17], p. 461).
[10] The inherited nature of Bigby's potent breath is first introduced in *Fables: Storybook Love* Vol. 3. When he protects himself and Snow White from the intrusion of Goldilocks: "I guess I never mentioned before that I'm the product of a mixed marriage. My father was the north wind—and how he met my mother and took a spark to her—" ([15], p. 139). *Fables: 1001 Nights of Snowfall* provides the details ([18], pp. 72–84).

ethos regarding fairy tales, which derived from his sense of crossovers in comic book culture:

> That was the whole bread and butter of the two big comics' empires, DC and Marvel [...] imagining that characters in one story would show up in another story was already second nature to me when I discovered fairy tales. The big crossover in my mind was that the same Big Bad Wolf appeared to vex poor Little Red Riding Hood and also blow down houses in the Three Little Pigs. There is nothing in those stories that led me to believe that those were different wolves. ([19], p. 40).

Willingham here expands upon the more limited concept of a comic book crossover—featuring different characters from different story worlds owned by the same company—to a larger matrix of narrative where any character in the literary and folkloric tradition can cross over to any narrative world. Drawing from this crossover ethos from comic books allows Willingham to develop a *Fables* universe of significant depth, which merges folkloric, literary, and cinematic sources. The notion of the General Amnesty harnesses the potential for these fairy tale characters crossing over to not only interact in traditional ways but to elicit new connections, relationships, and behaviors.

It is because of the premise of the General Amnesty that so many wicked or destructive characters, such as Bigby, Totenkinder, and Bluebeard, coexist with little Boy Blue, Cinderella, Snow White, *etc.* However, as Martin and Karasek observed, these fairy-tale villains are very different at times from their prior incarnations in fairy-tale lore, and it is instructive to compare their individual development. Bigby struggles with his wolfish identity, and he reverts back to lupine form, such as to threaten Bluebeard when he threatens to torture Jack. In his turn, Bluebeard goads Bigby: "Oh look. After all these years, the wolf has finally shed his sheep's clothing to once more show us the true beast underneath. Most of us knew it was only a matter of time before you reverted to your old ways, Bigby. Nature cannot be denied" ([8], p. 65). However, Bluebeard's essentialist claim is reductive; Bigby does contain himself and rebukes Bluebeard for his brutal intentions with Jack: "That's not the way we do things anymore" ([8], p. 66). Nevertheless, these character interactions reveal the discrepancy between the General Amnesty as a political reality and a personal conviction. Free will is the bridge that Willingham indicates makes a personal transformation convincing, not the political decree itself.

4. Martial Masculinity Meets Community Responsibility: Plotting Subversions of Heroism in Fables

Willingham presents Bigby as an example of a character who is willing to accept the ideal of the General Amnesty and willfully struggle with his destructive passions in contrast to Bluebeard, who conceals his disloyalty and after several betrayals of Fabletown, joins the forces of the Adversary. This is a far cry from Bigby, who not only takes human form as much as he can stand in Fabletown (all the better to perform his role as Sheriff on the down low rather than blowing his cover with big eyes, big nose, or big teeth) but also manifests human emotions. Bigby falls in love with Snow White and develops a sense of responsibility for the Fabletown community. These testaments to virtue in Bigby, do not simply seem to be indications of his capacity for change, but rather to express the nobler potential of his mythic being. In his capacity of Sheriff and commanding advisor regarding the Adversary, Willingham imbues Bigby with a heroic aura befitting the son of a god—the North Wind.

In much of the first-half of the *Fables* series, Bigby manifests his heroism through military conflict, whether in flashbacks during America's participation in World War II or the main war in the Fables universe against the Adversary. In his physical profile, Bigby channels well-known icons of masculinity from the comic-book world of super-heroes and the cinematic genre of noir hard-boiled detectives: Wolverine and Sam Spade. He's impressively muscular, smokes frequently, wears a drab trench-coat, and displays shaggy long hair, a perpetual five-o-clock shadow, and scowl on his hirsute face. Bigby's masculine militarism has alarmed some critics, particularly because of the danger of glorifying war in a simplistic fashion. Mark Hill decries Bigby because of how he epitomizes "the stiflingly rigid masculinity that is privileged within the text" and serves to promote a conservative political perspective on war ([20], p. 182). In particular, Hill is "disquieted" by how Willingham "invokes the cultural memory of the masculine hero-soldier in a war worth fighting" ([20], p. 186). Hill asserts that "if *Fables* is a magic mirror held to American society, then it displays a country that glories war and the soldiers who fight them" ([20], p. 192). There is no denying that Bigby's depiction in *Fables* often glorifies militaristic and nationalistic masculinity. Willingham himself asserts that superhero comic books need to maintain American values. In "Superheroes: Still Plenty of Super but Losing Some of the Hero" Willingham explains how when having the opportunity to write about Batman and Robin he made sure that they performed as "good, steadfast heroes, with unshakable personal codes and a firm grasp of their mission". Yet, Willingham distinguishes between the ambiguous world of *Fables* and nationalistic superhero comic-books: "There's [...] room for [...] moral ambiguity, and the eternal struggle of imperfect people trying to find their way in a bleak and indifferent world. I plan to continue all of that and more in my *Fables* series. But for me at least the superhero genre should be different, better, with higher standards, loftier ideals [...]" [21]. To what degree Willingham succeeded with a more ambiguous nuanced world in *Fables* is debatable, but analyzing the totality of the series, rather than a single moment in the storyline does suggest that the depiction of militarism and masculinity evolved as the plotline transformed from a goal-oriented conflict-based scenario to an exploration of the connections in a community defined by diverse personalities, ideologies, and genders.

Fables representation of military masculinity is not static, nor is the series' engagement with gender roles. Hill identifies how Snow's independence shifts towards subservience in the context of her relationship with Bigby. However, Hill's article was written before significant changes occurred in the storyline that marginalized the male characters and revealed the female fables as the primary movers and shakers of Fabletown and the larger universe. Hill also recognizes Bigby as a "tool of civilization" after his romance with Snow White and her "spell allowing him to shift between wolf and human at will" ([20], p. 184). The truth of the larger trajectory of the Fables story is that Bigby becomes a tool for "civilization" but also vendettas and internecine war because of the manipulations and magic of the more dominant female fables. After his defeat in battle by Brandish, who turns him into a glass statue that he promptly shatters, Bigby returns from the afterlife and is controlled by first Mrs. Spratt and then Rose Red, until she abandons the conflict against her sister, Snow. If one frames the final conflict in gendered terms, this last war in Fables is not won by masculine force but by feminine recognition of the importance of community after the fetish of militarism is discarded. Even in the earlier war against the Adversary, Willingham's story offered indications that masculine militarism was destructive and antithetical towards long-term survival. Although Prince Charming offered one of the Fables series most sexist equations between military force and sexual conquests ("whether it involves a desperate war or a woman's virtue, I always win my battles"), it is through his self-sacrifice first of his looks and then his life that Prince Charming makes his final contribution to the preservation of Fabletown ([13], p. 143). Boy Blue perishes soon afterwards as well. There may be glory in the death of heroes, but by the later volumes of the Fables series, the absence of leading men becomes quite obvious as is the implicit message, whether approved by Willingham's conscious mind or not: a community that bases its ethos on perpetual armed conflict will not endure. While Hill's general remarks on the Fables series' initial exaltation of war and masculinity are incisive and apt, the resolution of the story by Rose and Snow's sororial agreement rather than male conquests dilutes the importance of militaristic and heroic masculinity. The martial prowess that Bigby, Prince Charming, and Boy Blue once represented becomes overshadowed by the enduring connections of the extended Fables family, a community where Rose and Snow reconcile. The recognition of the primacy of civilized communal obligations subverts pretensions of heroic masculinity.

The capacity for civilizing change is perhaps most explicit when Bigby spends some time in heaven after losing his life (temporarily), Boy Blue informs him that his love for Snow White has transformed his destiny: "You fight for Snow and the cubs, and beyond that, for those who matter to you. That's the sole rhyme and reason of the universe. [...] If there is a greater intent, it isn't going to be imposed on you—on us. You get to decide what that will be, all by yourself. Freedom sucks, huh?" ([22], pp. 115–16). Bigby still is capable of violence, but it's meaningful violence because it's focused on preservation of his family and friends, not conquest or even national defense of an abstract ideal. Blue's words emphasize a spiritual existentialism underlying the *Fables* universe. Autonomy and connection supersede other factors. The General Amnesty helps foster an environment for these characters to connect personal autonomy with communal responsibility.

5. Double Double Toil and Trouble? Brewing Feminine Darkness and Occult Redemption in Fables

Similar to Bigby's commitment to Fabletown and his family, Totenkinder demonstrates the tendency to revere pragmatism for survival of a meaningful community. She employs her occult mastery to help divine specific threats and to formulate magical solutions. As the greatest non-divine magic-user in the Fables universe, Totenkinder emerges as an archetype of personal sacrifice in the service of esoteric power. In "The Witch's Tale" of *1001 Nights of Snowfall* not only does Willingham present how Totenkinder is integrated into Fabletown (Snow White and Rose Red discovered her still-living burned body in the oven in her hut), but he depicts the epochal depth of her magical power: "I was born into the fog mountain tribe, seven years after the ice retreated from our current home. I became a woman in my fourteenth summer [...] When my first moon's blood came, I began to have the seeings and premonitions" ([18], p. 98). Gifted by second-sight tied to feminine sexuality, the young Totenkinder is a prodigy, who helps guide the tribe by predicting the migration of game and the outcome of natural disasters. However, she does not foresee the consequence of a battle between her tribe and another, resulting in her husband, the Chief's Son, marrying the daughter of the rival Chief in order to avoid further conflict. She is outcast to the wilderness and sacrifices her baby: "I could never survive on my own, unless I found more power than the moon's blood could provide. [...] Any spirits of sky and moon and stars, behold the gift I give thee. 'And Power Came. In Abundance'" ([18], p. 103). Thus, Totenkinder's desire for the lives of children is elevated to a self-conscious strategy of ritual empowerment that she needs to survive in a patriarchal world. Her powers grow with more sacrifices, and she achieves revenge, as well as virtual immortality: "Sacrificing two a year, I stopped aging" ([18], p. 104). We watch her progress through the ages—her involvement in several well-known tales of magical obstacles and enchantments, such as "The Three Billy Goats Bluff", "The Frog Prince", "Rapunzel", and "Beauty and the Beast". Willingham emphasizes Totenkinder is always the unnamed witch in tales, much like Jack is the ubiquitous young hero.

Hearing Totenkinder's biography, Snow White distrusts her nature, and does not want to take her to Fabletown and recruit her to help against the Adversary, but Rose Red is powerfully moved, as Snow White in her role of frame-narrator emphasizes: "She was always the one who adopted injured animals and broken-winged birds, nursing them back to health" ([18], p. 112). Totenkinder ends up being not only a powerful ally against the Adversary but also against Fabletown's even greater enemy, Mr. Dark—although she is defeated during the confrontation. It is a poignant example of the psychic depth of Totenkinder that when she gathers her magical weapons to use *versus* Mr. Dark that the "oldest shape" she summons is "the altar stone on which I first sacrificed the life of my own child"—she calls this stone "damnation" and lays her withered hand upon it: "and Regret" ([23], p. 67). Willingham does not seek to evade, dismiss, or condemn the moral darkness that Totenkinder navigates; it is right in the open. This direct engagement with the terrible costs of power is one of the underlying themes of the *Fables* series. Rose Red and Snow White themselves are learning about these costs to the psyche and soul, and it is telling that because of Rose's inclination, Totenkinder joins the two sisters. Together this trinity of powerful and conflicted women leaves in search of Fabletown, where the past is allegedly forgiven.

6. "No Friend Like a Sister"? Shadows of Tradition Fall between Snow White and Rose Red

Willingham's use of Snow White and Rose Red reveals his aesthetic regarding innovation and tradition, while also implying possible oversights in distinctions between literary and folkloric sources. Willingham indicates in Volume 2 of *Fables* that Rose Red is a marginal figure in print and popular culture compared to her sister: "They keep making their godawful animated movies and writing their endless children's stories about you. So you can't die! They'll never let you! But who remembers me?" ([24], pp. 108–9). The resentment of Rose Red is a compelling example of the deep and conflicted feelings that Willingham imbues his characters with, and as Zolkover recognizes, the *Fables* characters offer "psychic depth" that is quite a departure from the tenets of Max Lüthi regarding the "depthlessness" of the fairy-tale protagonist ([2], p. 42; [26], p. 11). This psychological depth provides greater resonance for the characters' actions and reknits the web of their connections, combining folkloric and literary precedents with further narrative development.

6.1. Sibling Rivalry vs. Canonical Accuracy: Rose Red's Grievance Against Snow White's Popularity

Rose's complaint against her sister is neither canonical nor accurate. Recent texts do pay homage to the both sisters, and there's a groundswell of interest in Rose Red, including Disney's announcement about an upcoming film [26]. Cristina Bacchilega in "Fairy-tale Adaptations and Economies of Desire" analyzes a range of literary treatments, such as Margo Lanagan's novel, *Tender Morsels* (2008) and Francesca's Lia Block's "short story 'Rose' (2000)" ([27], pp. 87, 90). Willingham's treatment of the Snow White and Rose Red tales to build up sibling rivalries challenges the sororial harmony that Bacchilega observes in those sources: "Their temperamental difference is not the marker of rivalry or a binary opposition, but of their complementarity; and because she is always with Snow White, Rose Red's propensity for wandering and gathering flowers has not the same valence as Little Red Riding Hood's erring off the path" ([27], p. 81).

Bacchilega's emphasis on these two harmonious sisters underscores Willingham's divergent choices. Although Bacchilega invokes "Little Red Riding Hood" as a contrast to Rose Red, in *Fables* we see Rose Red displaying erring behavior throughout the series. Furthermore, although she does not choose an animal consort, she does gravitate towards the Farm, as the wilder alternative to Fabletown. In addition, not only does the wolfish villain of the "Little Red Riding Hood" tale emerge as a mate for Snow White, but these two sisters become rivals who end up commanding armies in their adversarial opposition. Willingham subverts the assumptions of educated readers like Bacchilega about the idyllic sisterhood of Snow White and Rose Red. Much like the *Fables* tendency to undercut the proverbial "happily ever after", the comics reverse and recontextualize conventional impressions about these fairy tale characters.

6.2. Opposites Distract: Adversarial Sisterhood and Gender Diversity with Rose Red and Snow White

Bacchilega only notes *Fables* in passing—paraphrasing the work of Andrew Friedenthal, who analyzes additional adaptations of the Snow White and Rose Red characters, and points out that "More modern figurations of Rose Red demonstrate how contemporary writers interpret her and use this dichotomy [between Rose Red and Snow White] as a kind of shorthand to explore diverse expressions of femininity" ([27], p. 173). *Fables* exemplifies these "diverse expressions", and Friendenthal gives *Fables* special attention in his article's conclusion: "*Fables* offers an extreme exception to a general pattern—Rose Red is silenced by the very fact that she is the symbolic representation of a dangerous, active woman, a femme fatale to Snow White's innocent persecuted heroine" ([27], p. 178). In his footnotes, Friendenthal offers a quotation from *Fables* where Rose explains how she's "grown out of the habit of sleeping with girls" ([28], Note 7, p. 178). Beyond her sexual activity, Rose Red transgresses conventional boundaries throughout the *Fables* series. From her short red hair to her bold fascination with the illicit—faking her murder and stringing along Blue Beard for his money. Rose's incarnations challenge gender norms.

If Snow White's elegant depiction as director of Fabletown continues to some degree the tradition of regal beauty, moral purity, and familial focus, Rose Red presiding over the Farm is very much the heroine of twenty-first-century taboo-breaking heroic femininity. On the level of visual depictions alone, whether Rose wears punk clothes, business wear, no clothes at all[11], or dons traditionally masculine tools of arms and armor, signaling fairy-tale heroism—she maintains one of the strongest personalities among the Fables. Like her appearance, Rose's actions express a diverse array of heroism, morality, and gender roles. She betrays her sister by having sex with Prince Charming, runs a commune of animal fairy-tale characters at the Farm, breaks Blue Boy's heart because he wants more than friendship, raises an army, ascends to the throne of Camelot, defies and devours the Goddess Hope, and ultimately decides to end the family vendetta. Rose spares not only her sister's life but the integrity of the Fables world—all because she comes to feel compassion for the lives of Bigby and Snow's children is more important than her ambition to consolidate matrilineal power in her own person. In a metafictional flourish, the writer of the "History of Fables in the Mundy World" turns out to be one of these children.

Rose Red's speech to her sister about how much she envies Snow White's popularity highlights one of the central metaphysical principles of *Fables*: a fairy-tale character's popularity among the Mundies determines her or his constitution. The most popular fables (like Goldilocks, Jack, Bigby, and Snow White) recover from ghastly injuries, and even death. Despite Rose's outrage about her sister's popularity (so popular is she that she recovers from a gunshot to the head), Willingham nevertheless makes Rose Red one of the primary characters in the *Fables* series. Not only does Rose Red's murder mystery inaugurate the *Fables* series, but her fated epic struggle with her sister, Snow White, becomes the crowning conflict near the close of *Fables*.

As established, Willingham's emphasis on this sisterly feud transforms the dynamics of these sisters' storybook rapport; *Fables* stresses their competitiveness and mutual resentment rather than the idealized unity they manifest in Grimm's tales, and the Grimm's source material, Caroline Stahl's "The Ungrateful Dwarf". Reading Rose Red's words in *Fables*, a reader might get misled about the genesis of the tale of Snow White: "It used to be Snow White and Rose Red. Now it's just Snow White, period. All alone! No sister needed or desired" ([24], p. 109). "Snow White and Rose Red" is categorized as ATU 426, "The Two Girls, the Bear, and the

---

11 Zolkover analyzes Rose Red's "state of undress or half-dress" as well as that of Goldilocks—indicating they are prime examples of how Willingham corporealizes initially abstract fairy-tale characters ([2], pp. 46–48).

Dwarf", and "Little Snow White" is ATU 709—following the classic elements readers are well familiar with [29]. Beyond the tale-type distinctions, there is the matter of chronology: despite Rose's objections to the contrary, "Little Snow White" appears in the first edition of *Kinder-und Hausmärchen* (1812), while "Snow White and Rose Red" did not appear till the third edition in 1837. The story itself, according to Jack Zipes in *The Great Fairy Tale Tradition*, has "no known previous oral versions, but Grimm's text has fostered numerous versions since its publication" ([30], p. 772). This example of the porous borders of folklore and literature is intriguing, but the fact remains that Caroline's Stahl's "The Ungrateful Dwarf" ("Der undankbare Zwerg")—published in 1818—was not folklore, and to equate its status with that of "Little Snow White" is erroneous conflation, though it is not altogether clear if that is Willingham's error, or merely an intensification of Rose Red's self-righteous hyperbole. And, it's certainly not Willingham's purpose or responsibility in *Fables* to separate print and oral sources. Yet, if Willingham had been aware of "The Ungrateful Dwarf" as the genesis for the "Snow White and Rose Red" story in Grimm, one wonders why he didn't integrate that aspect into the sisterly tensions; this further neglect in popular culture would have been fodder for Rose Red's complaints.

Whether or not Willingham knew that "The Ungrateful Dwarf" preceded the Grimm's "Snow White and Rose Red", his portrayal of the two sisters relies on elements of both the Grimm and Stahl narratives. In the Grimm's tale Rose Red is an outdoorsy free spirit while Snow White is dutiful and domestic:

> They were two as pious, good, industrious, and amiable children, as any that were in the world; only Snow-white was more quiet and gentle than Rose-Red. For Rose-Red would run and jump about the meadows, seeking flowers, and catching butterflies, while Snow-White sat at home helping her Mother to keep house, or reading to her, if there were nothing else to do" ([31], p. 656).

Readers are overloaded with images of domestic purity as the two sisters sit "on the hearth" with their Mother: "By their side, too, lay a little lamb, and on a perch behind them a little white dove resposed [sic] with her head under her wing" ([31], p. 659). From Stahl, it appears Willingham may have extrapolated upon the idea that Snow White and Rose Red had other siblings, as the very first line of "The Ungrateful Dwarf" highlights, "A very poor couple had many, many children, and they had great difficulty feeding them all" ([30], p. 772).

Although Willingham presents a flashback retelling the Grimm tale of "Snow White and Rose Red" that focuses on just the two sisters in *Fables Volume 15: Rose Red*, Willingham develops the adversarial dynamics of Snow White and Rose Red by inventing a backstory later in the *Fables* series (*Fables Volume 21: Happily Ever After*) that involves a larger family: specifically how the mother of Rose Red and

Snow White had many sisters, all of whom had magical powers and that each time one sister kills another, she gains the accumulated power [32,33]. Rose and Snow's mother is horrified when she gives birth to twins: "One will surely die and one will bear the sin of fratricide" ([32], p. 186). The Stahl story is a likely candidate for the notion of the larger family drama lurking in the past and the threat of insufficient resources to go around—whether nutritional or magical—for "feeding them all". In *Fables* Rose literally eats the goddess Hope, once Rose has reduced her form to a moth-sized shape. Thus, the classic primal motivation of hunger in fairy-tales appears incarnate in Rose and Snow's competition for supremacy, just as the threat of masculine predation—even so far as it affects one's own family—is manifest in Bigby's wolfish impulses gone amuck, and Snow has to be prepared to kill him to save her children from paternal cannibalism. When Rose spares the children, returns to Bigby the magic ring that was manipulating him, and ends the sisterly rivalry by self-exile, the internecine threat is resolved.

6.3. Dwarfish Aggression and Disconcerting Vengeance: Fables' Uneasy Exploration of Rape and Disability

Fables introduces another innovation into the world of storytelling about Snow White, in the form of sexual masculine predation—as well as female confrontation and individuation. Snow White pursues a vendetta against the seven dwarves. This is another instance of how Willingham may have drawn from Stahl as well as the first edition of Grimm tales or even variants. In Stahl's "the Ungrateful Dwarf" we see dwarfish aggression when the dwarf that the sisters had tried to help attempts to escape from the bear by suggesting the sisters would be a better option: "Oh, dear merciful bear, don't eat me! I'll even give you my sacks of gold, pearls, and jewels. Do you see the girls over there? They are young and juicy and tender. They are much more of a tasty morsel than I am. Take them instead and eat them!" ([30], p. 773). This dwarf's aggression reverses conventional expectations that a supernatural being in a fairy-tale will be grateful to a compassionate protagonist. There is no reward to be had in this case until the dwarf's death. Also, there's an added sense of taboo and transgression against familial safety when the dwarf tells the girls not to involve paternal assistance: "Snow White offered to run quickly to her home, and fetch her father, but the dwarf forbade this" ([30], p. 772). This attempt to separate the sisters from the benign influence of their father implies that the dwarf has ill-intent. Dwarves with malign intent towards Snow White have a precedent in Grimm. The notes to "Little Snow White" reveal a variant of the tale whose synopsis indicates that like the brothers who only spare their sister when she agrees to domestic duties in "The Twelve Brothers" the seven dwarves are intent on killing Snow White before she agrees to tend the house.[12]

Willingham's decision to develop the dwarves as sinister creatures capable of violence may not have relied upon tale variants but cinema. In the Disney film of *Snow White and the Seven Dwarves*, there is the threat of violence against Snow White by the dwarves; we hear the dwarves say "chop it to pieces", "kill it dead", and "let's kill it when it wakes up", when they seek to dispatch the intruder that may be a "monster" and is sleeping in one of their beds. However, their hostility is based on fear, and once Snow White is revealed in her beauty, the dwarves lower their pick-axes. Regardless of any particular prompting from cinema, literature, or folklore, Willingham chose to make the seven dwarves despicable, and in the collection of *Fables* backstories, *1001 Nights of Snowfall*, Willingham reveals how Snow White pursues and kills each of the seven dwarves because they had raped her.[13] While this empowers Snow White as a character capable of administering her own vengeful ambitions, some readers may cringe from the depiction of dwarves as rapists. This macabre rendering of dwarfish sexual assaults contains something of the prejudicial "logic of superstition" that Tobin Siebers identifies as a hallmark of fantastic depictions of the Other, which Siebers argues is implicitly an "act of exclusion" used to validate "false differences among men" ([34], pp. 34, 56). Although Willingham is working with a tradition of literature and folklore that entails dwarves as chthonic and sometimes dangerous beings, Siebers reminds us that traditions carry with them their own dangerous legacy of social prejudices.

The revelation of Snow White's vengeance against the malignant (and perhaps maligned) dwarves is narrated in *1001 Nights of Snowfall*. The frame story imitates the famous *Tales of A Thousand and Ones Nights*, but instead of Scheherazade, it is Snow White who has to make a positive impression on a Sultan and avoid the well-known fate of the previous wives, for though she is divorced from Prince Charming—and not a virgin—this Sultan threatens her with the same gruesome fate. The reason for her audience with the Sultan is that she seeks an alliance with him against the forces of the Adversary that continue to oppress the homelands of the fables. She prefaces her tale about the dwarves with the description that it is "my own small tale

---

[12] "c. In the third version [...] seven dwarfs live in a cave and kill any maiden who comes near them. [...] they want to kill her [Snow], but because she is so beautiful, they let her live, and in exchange for their mercy they say that she should keep house from them" ([17], p. 494).

[13] Zolkover had probably not yet had the chance to read *1001 Nights of Snowfall* (2006) because his article (2008) does not cite the volume, and he suggests the mention of the dwarves in the first volume was an indication of "sexual implications"—not knowing the more disconcerting matter of sexual assault explored elsewhere—"making the taboo" about "sexual implications" with the dwarves a mere "narrative device" whereby "the comic book is explicitly, and quite loudly, mum" ([2], p. 44). In fact, Snow's silence and expression of revulsion was an important foreshadowing of the later revelation of her violent and righteous revenge against those dwarves.

of revenge and its terrible lessons" ([18], p. 21). The tale itself concerns Snow White's request for fencing lessons after her marriage to the prince, who had promised her anything she "desired as a wedding gift" ([18], p. 25). Since Prince Charming himself is reputed to be the deadliest swordsman around, he personally gives Snow the lessons, albeit privately, because he emphasizes that "sword-fighting isn't a fit activity for ladies of the gentry—for any woman in fact" ([18], p. 26). Despite the prince's objections, he trains Snow effectively, and over time her skills significantly improve. Meanwhile, hacked-up bodies accumulate from a particular group of seven dwarves—brothers known to have occupied one of the "diversion cabins" where human women were regularly abused ([18], p. 40). As the prince concludes at the end, although he took steps for a known murderer to take the fall to avoid open war with the king of the dwarves, he recognizes that "by the final murders, the killer needed only a single thrust to do his mortal work—as if he were inexperienced at first, but perfecting his deadly art all along. Much like your progress in our fencing lessons—and remarkably, over the same time" ([18], p. 53). The Sultan, after hearing this tale wonders why this storyteller—Snow White in disguise—had described it as an example of the dangers of revenge, and Snow explains that the woman's "husband never quite trusted her again. One version of the story has it that their marriage ended when he slept with the princess's sister, newly arrived to be a companion to her. But wiser listeners might conclude that the marriage really ended on the day she set out to become a destroyer" ([18], p. 55). Snow's inclusion of her ex-husband's adultery with her sister, reinforces the competitive tensions between Rose Red and Snow White, and the thematic emphasis in *Fables* on emotional consequences of violent power. The narrative closure of achieved vengeance remains fraught with these disconcerting feelings of distrust, destruction, and demonized disability.

6.4. Comic-Book Aesthetics for Snow White and Rose Red: Panel Portrayals of Memory and Personality

The artwork in *Fables* is deployed with both intense emotion and subtle indications of psychic depth for the characters, and the memories shared by Snow White and Rose Red is a compelling example of this dynamic.[14] Near the end of the second *Fables* volume, *Animal Farm*, Rose Red reveals the motive for the affair to Snow when she explains that much of her anger against her sister stems from Snow's lack of attachment to her ([24], p. 108). Forming the middle panel of the page

---

[14] Karin Kukkonen in "Comics as a Test Case for Transmedial Narratology" offers a rewarding analysis of the role of art in the *Fables* series, particularly for *Fables Volume Seven: Arabian Nights (and Days)*. Kukkonen emphasizes how that volume "draws on earlier versions of *Arabian Nights*, particularly the nineteenth-century fairy book and its illustrations, remediating and recontextualizing their storyworld and characters" ([35], p. 35).

there's a picture of Snow White and Rose Red as young girls, and there are no borders whatsoever, evoking a sense of limitless white space, along with the roses and flowers and butterflies flapping beside the girls, whose hands are clasped in fellowship. The text in that white space beside the flashback represent Rose Red's words to Snow at the farm: "When we were young, back in the cabin, we pledged we'd be together forever. You and me against the world. … **remember?**" ([24], p. 109). The smiles on the girls' faces in that telling middle panel are complimentary: Snow has an open-mouthed smile, while Rose sports a closed-mouth grin; Snow has pig-tails and Rose has curls on top of her head; their clothes have some variation with geometric parallels to indicate separate yet compatible personalities that remain in harmony. The idyllic contrast with the rest of the panels where the adult women scowl at each other—Rose with tears in her eyes and Snow with glassy perplexity. Rose alludes then to how "the moment your pretty Prince Charming came along, you rode off with him, without so much as a backward glance" ([24], p. 109). Snow counters with how she soon asked Rose to live with them, but we know from the *1001 Nights of Snowfall* that invitation came from Prince Charming's notion that Snow needed a companion after she had shown herself errant in her act of revenge against the dwarves. Rose also confirms that as Snow suggests, she had "seduced him [Prince Charming] and ruined [Snow's] marriage—all to punish [her]" ([24], p. 109). It is not until volume fifteen, entitled *Rose Red*, that Rose's psychic wound is partly healed by the ghost of Colin—the pig beheaded by Goldlocks—who takes the form of Rose's mother and shares with her Snow White's perspective on the painful legacy of the past. These two sisters only approach healing after many obstacles and battles of personality.

7. Playing the Trickster: Willingham's Metafictional Improvisations of *Jack of Fables*

Healing is not in the final focus, however, in *1001 Nights of Snowfall*, where after having heard Snow White's tale of the dwarves, the Sultan remains ignorant that the tale is so personal. His response underscores the enthusiasm of Willingham (and many folklorists) that "Every good story has a hundred different versions, Snow. That's what makes them endlessly wondrous and delightful" ([18], p. 55). This metafictional gesture towards folklore's diverse variety stresses the many levels of framing, innovation, and syncretic connection in the *Fables* universe, whereby a multiplicity of perspectives—from the medieval to the modern—are engaged through fresh reconsiderations of the role of gender, sex, family, evil, war, and love in the classic tales. The most emphatic of Willingham's improvisational approaches to syncretism and metafiction is with *Jack of Fables*.

One of the many ways Willingham offers both innovation and depth with *Jack of Fables* is by demonstrating wide-ranging familiarity with various tales and traditions. For instance, although the casual reader has no notion of Appalachian, Southern, and

Canadian Jack tales, folklorists are well-aware of the oral tradition concerning Jack in North America. We see allusions to a range of Jack's adventures in the various issues of *Jack of Fables*, and we also see the manifestations of powers that remind us of variety of Jack's folkloric adventures, such as how Jack not only speaks of "visions. Dire omens. They're indistinct and hazy, but they're true. I can sense it", but he has taken the shape of a dragon ([36], p. 75). Both powers are reminiscent of the Canadian Tale, "The First Time Jack Came to America" where he's able to change into a range of shapes and know everything after licking up "all the wisdom of the world" from the pot of a witch ([37], p. 214).

However, Jack's powers in *Fables* are generally much more restricted, and when he witnesses the character Raven turn into animal form, he reflects, "Who knew Raven could turn into a bird? If I could turn into a bird, I'd do it all the time" ([38], p. 79). In the folktale this is a manifestation of the motif of the magicians' duel, and we see Jack in Willingham's *Fables* indeed capable of facing off against magic-wielding opponents at times, though in his dragon-form he is doomed to be killed by his son, Jack Frost, born of the Ice Queen. Patriarchal conflicts are a familiar folkloric scenario, from the usurpation of Uranus and Cronus to the unintentional murder by Cuchulainn of his unknown son. In addition, the entire *Jack of Fables* spin-off occurs after his Fable-town exile, and these meanderings in North America are much in the spirit of the ending sentence of "The First Time Jack Came to America" as well: "And that is the story of how he came to get to America to begin with, and he's been making it on his own ever since" ([37], p. 217). Throughout *Fables*, Jack makes his way through arrogance and serendipity, demonstrating Max Lüthi's notion of "universal interconnectiveness" in the fairy-tale world: "The hero is the lucky one. It is as if invisible ties linked him with the secret powers or mechanisms that shape the world and fate" ([25], p. 57).

There are also power dynamics that Jack engages that don't have a clear folkloric precedence: for instance, when he reveals to his traveling companions that he has a briefcase where he's hidden all the treasure recently retrieved from the lost city of gold, he explains that the briefcase became magical over time: "For years it was just a normal briefcase. But ever since I hit the road, it's just sort of...grown. Must be one of the perks of being at the center of all stories" ([38], p. 102).[15] There are also plenty of folkloric elements for Jack that Willingham does not incorporate, such as the fact that despite folk tale precedents for Jack having brothers, in both British and especially American variants including Richard Chase's versions—usually named Will and Tom—Willingham does not include fraternal characters in Jack's world of

---

[15] There are precedents for magic bags and Jack, but not this precise cause-and-effect: that a bag becomes magical because of being near Jack. One Jack tale with a magic bag is "The Magic Bag" ([39], pp. 84–86.)

Fables. However, one wonders if Willingham read some accounts of Jack's vices, such as alluded to in *Tellable Cracker Tales* where Annette Bruce shares a tale about the three brothers ending with Jack as a mere punch line: "Will is a failure too. But Jack? Jack never did want to be nothin' atall but a lazy, good-for-nothin' Cracker, and he shore is successful" ([40], p. 24).

In terms of sources for Willingham's Jack, besides European collections, it is most likely that Richard Chase's *The Jack Tales* (1943) is the main source, which offers a very arrogant Jack despite Chase's claims that his Jack manifests "easy-going unpretentious rural American manners that make him so different from his English cousin, the cocksure, dashing young hero" ([41], p. x). For one thing, the first panel of *Fables Three: Storybook Love* shows an old human hand holding a book entitled, "The American JACK TALES", which aside from the word "American" appears to exactly duplicate the title of Richard Chase's 1943 collection ([15], p. 7). In addition, on the credits page, which opens a double-page spread of Confederate cannon-fire against advancing Union troops, and offers the title of the original issue, "Bag of Bones", Willingham writes the following: "This story was freely adapted from a couple of the Mountain Jack Tales of American folklore. In true oral tradition, it's been much altered under my care, which is a polite way of saying that I stole everything I thought I could use, changed a bunch of stuff to suit my whims, and made up the rest.—Bill" ([15], p. 9). The ethos that Willingham expresses here is closer to modern creative writing pedagogy that encourages students to not feel guilty about borrowing or endure an undue pressure to be original: "Every artist gets asked the question, 'Where do you get your ideas?' The honest artist answers, 'I steal them.' How does an artist look at the world? First, you figure out what's worth stealing, then you move on to the next thing" ([42], p. 5). While Willingham's flippant directness towards artistic appropriation may reflect this practical vision for creative writers, the attitude may chafe contemporary folklorists, who aim to respectfully represent the oral storyteller as both a person and tradition-bearer, and even nineteenth-century folk collectors, such as the Grimms, in their first edition offered scholarly notes and variants, more intent on assembling a body of tales indicative of their speculated German folk literature rather than stealing anything per se.

Willingham's statement about stealing is a testament to his awareness that folklore is not fixed in stone, and that individual storytellers innovate within a tradition of tales and lore. The phrase "Mountain Jack Tales" might easily be translated "Appalachian Jack Tales", and indeed the subtitle of Chase's *The Jack Tales* is "Folk Tales from the Southern Appalachians". In addition, the honesty of Willingham's admission to theft and revisionism for artistic purposes may resonate with those folklorists familiar with Richard Chase's *The Jack Tales*: significant alterations of material—without such admission—is a charge levied against Richard Chase. As Carl Lindahl asserts, "Not until the appearance of a remarkable study by Charles Perdue, however, was it clear how drastically Chase had altered his oral sources" ([43], p. xxvi).

It also appears that Willingham's use of *The Jack Tales* influenced the depiction of Jack's *Fables* personality. Beyond visual and textual cues in the "Bag of Bones" issue, there are further indications of a Richard Chase model, based on the character of Jack in *Fables*, particularly his arrogance. Charles Perdue himself points out that "art follows life in Chase's tales: Jack is more than twice as likely to be a braggart than he is in the Carter/Adams tales, not inconsistent with Chase's well-known sizeable ego" ([44], p. 120). Willingham's Jack Horner is profoundly arrogant: "I am the coolest. I am the bravest. And I am absolutely the one you most want to have around when the chips are down—provided I like you" ([45], p. 25).

To return to the matter of the expanding briefcase, its powers resemble a magical bag that Jack won (and later lost in his travels) earlier in a game of cards with a bayou devil (Nick Slick) and has the quality of being bottomless ([15], pp. 10–28). However, the comparison with the earlier magical bag is not what is significant but the dynamic of mundane-to-magical transformation and what that represents in the narrative of the *Fables* universe. We've learned from the return of Goldilocks earlier that popular fable characters can return from the dead, but the notion of evolving magical properties rather than innate attributes is a hitherto unidentified feature in the *Fables* comic book series. Generally in folk tales as well, magic is an externalized gift that aids the protagonist rather than an emanation of the protagonist.[16] This enchanted briefcase is a departure from these traditional metaphysics but a continuation of Willingham's endowment of a supernatural aura on his fairy-tale characters. In fact, when Jack beats Nick Slick at cards, it's not a feat that he performs through sleight-of-hand or gambling acumen; Jack beats this bayou devil by producing four jacks because Jack "never did pick up a deck of cards where he couldn't deal himself all four jacks, whenever he liked" ([15], p. 14). Thus, Jack has transformed from his roots as a plucky lad with wit and courage to become in Willingham's *Fables* a supernatural figure with essential powers, not merely aided by magical helpers and objects.

The concept of character-based enchantment and magical expansion of space achieves its logically ultimate conclusion in the last look at Jack's character, which occurs *after* the seemingly final moment when his ghost emerges from his corpse and slips away from the five diabolic figures who are seeking to collect on Jack's various debts ([35], p. 138). The true close for the character of Jack does not occur until the

---

[16] Willingham does not limit this power solely to Jack either: a parallel of how it is the fairy-tale characters themselves that produce enchantment occurs with Rose Red when she learns that the forest she grew up in with Snow White was not magical in its own right but as an emanation of her own being: "You bled magic into the surroundings, rather than the reverse" ([32], p. 138).

penultimate volume of *Fables* where this closing crossover episode of Jack interrupts the showdown between Snow White, Rose Red, and Bigby. We learn that Jack in his phantom form did not escape the five devils, but that they caught him when he was hitchhiking, and then they decided his punishment: "They argued for a while over which of their hells I'd go to and finally decided to get together and make a special hell just for me. To wit: to sit alone on an empty planet with nothing to do but think about everything I'd done wrong" ([33], p. 174). In fact, Jack ends up making a brand new universe along the lines of exactly what he wants. His purgatory becomes pure paradise. Ego unlimited. Heaven equates with narcissistic tall-tale telling.

On the one hand, Jack's besting of the diabolic characters is in keeping with both folkloric and literary tradition. Reading the Brothers Grimm, for example, one finds protagonists in the devil tales evade soul-crushing consequences by trickery or the mere good fortune that the devil has his designs on a longer con game with someone else. As for literary examples, Basil Davenport points out that out of his twenty-five anthologized stories in *Deals with the Devil*, "the mortal gets the better of the Devil in thirteen stories, and loses in twelve" ([46], p. xvi). On the other hand, the precise nature of Jack's solipsistic solution to his diabolic punishment is unparalleled in folkloric tradition, but is a commentary on critical framing by collectors.

To understand Jack's solution to his predicament—and one of the ways that Willingham most profoundly and explicitly engages metafiction—it is important to realize that part of Willingham's engagement with folklore in his *Fables* universe is a critique of bowdlerization. The spirit of censorious revision is personified by the character of Mr. Revise in *Jack of Fables* who is a powerful representative of a class of beings known as Literals—a clear manifestation of Willingham's dislike of hostility towards fantasy storytelling and certain tendencies of fairy-tale editing over the last centuries. When Jack is captured in the first issue of *Jack of Fables* it would bring a smile to many a folklorist's face to see that Jack is at first restricted to *The Golden Bough Retirement Home*, considering the range of scholarly objections to James Frazer "as an armchair anthropologist and folklorist", the place Jack finds himself in is obviously of a highly dubious quality for a folkloric character ([47], p. 109). In this retirement center, Mr. Revise taunts Jack with how fairy-tales have changed: "Do you even remember anymore, Jack? How much more sensual it used to be? How violent? How violent? How concupiscent? My job is to neuter you; to take away all in you that is potent and fearsome. All that is memorable and distinct" ([47], p. 49). The drawings that accompany Mr. Revise's words appear in two panels in the fashion of woodcuts or 18th century broadsides: one panel depicts the Big Bad Wolf devouring a woman's body; the second panel shows fiendish-looking children—evidently Hansel and Gretel—gloating over the burned corpse of the witch. The censorious tyranny of Mr. Revise is only challenged by Jack's rebelliousness, as well as the even greater threat of the mercurial scribbler Kevin Thorn, another Literal, who plans to write the entire Fables universe away. In *Fables: Vol. 13 The Great Fables Crossover* the plot lines of *Fables* and *Jack of Fables* converge with further revelations, such as the arrival of the Literal, Deus Ex Machina and the clever machinations of the Pathetic Fallacy (known as Gary) who helps Mr. Revise expel Kevin Thorn into a new universe where he has to contend with "one great big blank page" ([48], p. 220). The comic book presents a blank page facing this formidable Literal, while Kevin Thorn laments, "I have no idea where to begin!" ([48], p. 220). Unlike in Jack's new universe, there is no companionable Pathetic Fallacy animate the visions in Kevin Thorn's head. Willingham's utilization of these Literals shares with his audience the trials of the creative process and emphasizes his metafictional consciousness of literary criticism, existential philosophy, and most obviously, writer's block. With Jack's triumph against the adversarial limits of the Literals and the punitive constraints of the devils, Willingham harnesses metafiction to construct a story that breaks the fourth wall, repudiates prudish censorship, and builds a network of transcendent storytelling, which navigates through moral, chronological, and metaphysical obstacles in fairy-tale discourse.

Beyond Willingham's engagement with Jack, there is further Americana that he utilizes for metafictional purposes in *Fables*. It is because of Mr. Revise that both Paul Bunyan and Babe the Blue Ox have been reduced in size; however, regardless of the sinister agenda of some of the Literals, Willingham himself takes liberties with Babe in ways that are revisionist as well. Babe becomes a kind of Walter Mitty, who adopts various roles. He serves as a pacing mechanism and comic relief for the more dramatic plots. Also, despite having survived the attempts of the metafictional nemesis—Mr. Revise—Babe himself crosses the border between the comic narrative and the audience when in the penultimate volume he threatens the reader:

> Now I come to find out that when a comic book ends, all of the characters in it cease to exist! [...] So here's what's going to happen. I'm going to sit here and eat these pizzas and drink all this Tab. And you are going to do exactly nothing. See, if you don't turn this page, then you can't finish reading the story. And if you don't finish reading the story, then the story can never end. So you're going to leave the book exactly where it is, and back alway slowly. And then I and all your beloved Fables and Mundys and Literals and Whatchamadoos will live on forever. You didn't want Fables to end, right? Well now it never will." ([33], p. 71).

Accompanying this threatening rhetoric is a sinister man in a dark coat who pulls a revolver out and the final panel of this page is pointed at the reader. In addition, the narrative inset in the right-hand bottom corner proclaims, "Why chance it? Do what the little Ox **says!**" ([33], p. 71). This admonition is about one-third of the way through the volume, and one wonders if even a single *Fables* reader decided to capitulate to Babe's demands after this ominous and comedic breaking of the fourth wall.

8. Superteams and Super Crossovers: Willingham's Genre-Hopping Narrative Dynamics

Significantly, the opening of the penultimate volume of *Fables* highlights allusive metafiction with the title "Bigby Wolf and the Blustery Day: Chapter Four of *Happily Ever After*". One thinks of the children's book *Winnie the Pooh and the Blustery Day* as well as reflecting upon the opening volume of *Fables* where Rose Red and Jack had drawn in blood, "No More Happily After". Willingham is clearly broadcasting his metafictional mode—signaling complicity between reader and writer with regard to the patterns of beginnings and endings, as well as the interpenetrations between folklore and literature. He emphasizes the nexus of genres from comic books to films and literature at every step of the way in the *Fables* universe, but it is especially near the end where we reach the perspective to fully fathom the depth of these allusive crossover storytelling dynamics.

Happily Ever After proceeds with other self-conscious nods to popular culture and narrative innovations as well: Osma of the Oz books joins with Beast (clad in a robotic suit, looking much like a sci-fi mech from Guillermo del Toro's *Pacific Rim*) to fight Bigby, who remains under the control of Leigh Duglas, the erstwhile wife of Jack Spratt and consort of the elementally evil Mr. Dark. Osma sports a red cape and with her hovering in mid-air evokes Supergirl [33]. The visual approximations of superheroes were used in an earlier volume as well: *Superteam*, and as Rebecca-Anne Rozario observes, the depictions of the characters engage "retro superhero-style identities and costumes" that "makes explicit the similitude between fairy tale and superhero" ([49], p. 195). We are also reminded in *Superteam* about Willingham's ethos connecting comic book crossovers and fairy tales.[17]

To return to the struggle between Rose Red and Snow White, we see in *Happily Ever After* this mélange of visual allusions to other comics and books, which renders the scene of conflict akin to the climatic battles between legions of superheroes, such as the X-Men or the Justice League. When the struggle with Mr. Dark has devolved into a struggle with his consort, Mrs. Spratt, Rose Red has yet to realize her hereditary vendetta against Snow White. After Bigby dispatches prior opponents, such as Beast, then Snow White prepares to defend her cubs—for her children are both capable of human and wolfish forms—against the love of her life. She is joined by her sister

---

[17] In terms of the aesthetic of the *Fables* drawings, Rozario also points out that despite some of the series' illustrations' focus on human bodies, such as the "close-fitting" garb of Cinderella in the first volume while fencing "it is no more revealing than Bluebeard's. Her poses stress strength and confidence, not sexual availability" ([49], p. 198).

Rose Red, garbed in her armor of Camelot, and Bellflower (the rejuvenated form of Totenkinder), who has secretly prepared with Rose Red for the clash with Bigby, who is controlled by Mrs. Spratt (and then Rose herself later via the same magical ring). Indeed, Rose and Bellflower leave Snow White behind in the assault against Bigby, although they are not able to defeat him, partly due to the residual power of Mr. Dark that Mrs. Spratt wields. Rose herself then takes the ring and only relents in her use of Bigby as a pawn due to compassion for the children ([33,50]). The defeat of the "superteam" and the betrayal by Rose shows how Willingham subverts comic-book motifs as well as fantasy tropes: he undercuts the superteam expectations with this complicated outcome of shifting loyalties and intrigue. There is no perfect team where chaos cannot intrude and dissolve the bonding magic that crosses genres.

9. There's No Free Lunch—Or Marital Counseling—With *Fables* Libertarianism

It is not just in the domain of fairy-tale, comic-book, and literary criticism that Willingham uses *Fables* to jab at dogmatism or parody storytelling conventions. Although Zolkover insists that Willingham "exposes the rigidness and prescriptive moral didacticism of fairy-tale patriarchs like Perrault and the Brothers Grimm", in fact there are indications of social and political didacticism in the *Fables* world as well ([2], p. 48). Aside from the early prominence of masculine militarism, the most obvious of ideological biases in the *Fables* series, is the emphasis on libertarian attitudes towards government. In the very first issue when Beauty and the Beast ask Snow White for help in their troubled relationship, she dispatches their request based on the libertarian principle of limiting government's role in people's daily lives:

> We can't afford to do marital counseling, and to be perfectly candid, I wouldn't allow it if we could. The mundanes may look to their government to solve their problems, but in the fable community, we expect you to be able to run your own lives. Our only concern is that you're currently in violation of our most vital law: no fable shall, by action or inaction, cause our magical nature to become known to the mundane world ([8], p. 9).

In her plush red chair, Snow coldly delivers this speech. The authority of this utterance is emphasized by the placard indicating "Snow White, Director of Operations". This is no mere opinionated disclosure, but the official position of Fabletown, voiced by perhaps the most famous of all fairy-tale personalities. Beyond the focus on libertarian self-sufficiency, Snow's emphasis about the "most vital law" of Fabletown underscores pragmatism. Snow's disdain for government intervention and belief in pragmatic discretion are pervasive values in the *Fables* series.

Beyond this libertarian ethos and focus on political pragmatism for survival, Willingham makes several political critiques throughout the comic book series. One of his most ferocious characters is Goldilocks, who ruthlessly pursues her ideology of a kind of mixture of animal rights and Marxism; however, her vision is subverted by her bloodthirsty tactics—rationalizing the beheading of one of the three little pigs because it "symbolized that it's time for our revolution to come out of the shadows" ([25], p. 29). Or when she's revealed as having shared the bed in a sexual manner with one of the three bears, it's an indication of "there is no superior species. Bear, human or hedgehog, it can make no difference—even in our most intimate lifestyle choices—or we're all oppressors" ([24], p. 31). It's also Goldilocks who shoots Bigby and later Snow White in the head, so despite the example of an animal and human relationship embodied by Snow and Bigby's union, Goldilocks seeks to destroy them. Clearly, Willingham is implying that despite manifestoes pretending rationalizations and passionate commitments, too many revolutionaries are merely anti-social psychopaths, bent on their own egoistical acts of vengeance.

Beyond anti-revolutionary politics, there are more specifically American matters of partisanship on display in *Fables*, such as when we learn that Pinocchio—considered an ideal candidate because of his inability to tell a lie without his nose growing—has been considering running for president of the United States, it is the republicans who successfully draft him ([51], "The Last Pinocchio Story"). Although we don't get to see Pinocchio enthroned in the White House, our current commander-in-chief (implicitly President Obama) is advised to take decisive action to deal with the imminent threat to New York due to magical warfare: "Hold off even an hour longer and it's Benghazi all over again, multiplied by hundreds—thousands probably. You can't take another hit like that. It's a guaranteed legacy-killer" ([51], "In a Castle Dark").

This stab against American foreign policy also recalls King Cole's Remembrance Day speech from the first *Fables* volume, with its echoes of Martin Niemöller's famous quote regarding passivity in the face of Hitler's nationalism: "First they came for the Socialists, and I did not speak out—Because I was not a Socialist" [52]. In King Cole's speech he refers to the Adversary's initial attacks against the lands of Oz and Narnia: "When the Emerald kingdom fell, we tisk-tisked and tut-tutted in our homes [...] but we weren't tempted to intervene. [...] Then the kingdom of the great lion fell, and again we did nothing, because we always found the old lion to be a bit too pompous and holier-than-thou for our tastes" ([8], pp. 82–83). The similarity is unmistakable, and the critique against political dithering is also clear. Beyond this inveighing against passivity, further equivalency is implied between the ideals of Fabletown and the West, particularly America: King Cole conferring with Snow White—also in the very first volume—refers to Fabletown as a "noble experiment" ([8], p. 58). Americans may recognize that phrase from Herbert Hoover's description of Prohibition, but it is a phrase sometimes used by pundits about America and democracy itself. In her discussions with Bluebeard about his grievance against Jack and Rose, Snow White reminds him that "This is America, where we all have freedom of choice" ([8], p. 115).

10. Freedom in *Fables*: What's it Good For? Defying Fairy-Tale Motifs for Identity's Sake

Freedom of choice is validated as the chief value of the *Fables* plot because it is what saves the Fable characters when Rose Red decides to end her vendetta against her sister. Despite the Lady in the Lake's warning to Rose Red that when she finds herself in the role of King Arthur that the Fates "are likely to step in and force everything to happen this time just like it did last time" we see that Rose navigates past the destiny of Arthurian epic as well as the matrilineal legacy of fratricide ([22], p. 151). For all its representations of battles and bloodshed, *Fables* offers closure through the development of personal autonomy in the face of ideological and magical pressures and rejects martial power in favor of reconsideration of familial and communal ties of identity.

Willingham reminds us in these numerous volumes of the tension between mythological, metafictional, and folkloric tendencies of characters following plot functions as opposed to claiming personal autonomy. While Osma laments that she "was never destined" to help defeat Mr. Dark, Pinnochio challenges her philosophic assumptions: "What's Destiny got to do with it? You don't really think everything's preordained, do you?" ([50], p. 123). Preordained or not, Bigby's father, the North Wind, navigates past his oath "to kill my grandson" because of his duel-to-the-death against Mr. Dark: "Death cancels all obligations" ([50], p. 114). Like Bigby, who had once sworn to destroy his father because of his abandonment of his mother, the North Wind finds an option beyond formal vendetta. The North Wind's example suggests that even one of the mightiest of mythic characters can elude the power implied by oaths by enlisting the greatest of existential limits: death. Or, to be more precise, he decides upon endless imprisonment in a casket with Mr. Dark, the most powerful evil in the Fables universe. North Wind decides upon imprisonment and stasis—yes—but a prison of the North Wind's own volition—a paradox that dynamically reinforces the indelible power of a single choice to accomplish a meaningful sacrifice to protect infinite worlds whose vivid narratives entail growth, life, movement, and connection. The storybooks remain forever open.

Like so many of the best known fairy-tale protagonists—Snow White, Cinderella, Little Red Riding Hood, Rapunzel, and Briar Rose—the *Fables* characters who most determine the final outcomes of the struggles of Fabletown are female. As Do Rozario concludes in her analysis of Cinderella, in "a comic series like *Fables*" Willingham's Cinderella appears as "more than simply an object of male desire"; the series offers "a grown up, independent Cinderella [which] is required for the twenty-first century" ([49], p. 201). Beyond Cinderella, Rose Red and—of course—Snow White assert themselves throughout the *Fables* series: as Snow explains to her grown-up daughter, Therese Wolf, her focus on survival is what sustained her against the evil of the seven dwarves, and she extends her fierce resolve to her family: "I dug in deep, hardened my heart, and vowed to endure every single day, no matter what they did to me, and survive. [...] Monsters of the woods couldn't kill me. The armies of kings, sorcerers and empires couldn't. I'm Snow goddamn White. I look after myself. I look after my own. And I never lose" ([22], pp. 88–90). In fact, all of the major female characters display independence, competitiveness, and resolve, as do most of the males—despite Bigby's protracted manipulation by the magical ring wielded by Mrs. Spratt and then Rose Red. Bigby contains his bestial impulses and achieves familial contentment; Snow White protects her family and successfully directs the community of Fabletown; Rose Red finds her autonomous identity separate from her sister and evades bloodshed; Jack, although banished from the very universe of other fables due to his arrogance, reconfigures the dogmatism of Satanic punishment into a paradise of his own imaginative conception. Willingham ultimately allows most of his primary fable characters to be emancipated from their fairy-tale functions, and it is that narrative liberation which permits them to attempt to live—if not happily—relatively freely based upon the passionate autonomy of their own principles ever after.

Conflicts of Interest: The author declares no conflict of interest.

References

1. Willingham, Bill. "Bill Willingham on *Fables vs. Once Upon a Time*." 4 December 2011. Available online: http://www.comicbookresources.com/?page=article&id=35737 (accessed on 21 February 2016).
2. Zolkover, Adam. "Corporealizing Fairy Tales: The Body, the Bawdy, and the Carnivalesque in the Comic Book *Fables*." *Marvel & Tales: Journal of Fairy-Tale Studies* 22 (2008): 38–51.
3. De Voss, Gail. "Storytelling, Folktales, and the Comic Book Format." In *Fairy Tales in Popular Culture*. Edited by Martin Hallett and Barbara Karasek. Tonawanda: Broadview, 2014, pp. 151–60.
4. Jameson, Fredric. "Reification and Utopia in Mass Culture." In *Signatures of the Visible*. New York: Routledge, 1990, pp. 9–34.
5. Hutchinson, Linda. *The Politics of Postmodernism*, 2nd ed. London: Routledge, 2002. E-book.
6. Zipes, Jack. *Why Fairy Tales Stick: The Evolution and Relevance of a Genre*. New York: Routledge, 2006.
7. Kelly, Stuart. "Bill Willingham's Fables Heads to a Fairy-Tale Ending." 5 May 2015. Available online: http://www.theguardian.com/books/booksblog/2015/may/05/bill-willinghams-fables-heads-for-a-fairytale-ending (accessed on 21 February 2016).

8.   Willingham, Bill. *Fables: Legends in Exile*. New York: Vertigo (DC Comics), 2003, vol. 1.

9.   Miller, Andrea Nicole. "Review of Coloring America: Multi-Ethnic Engagements with Graphic Narrative." *MELUS (Multi-ethnic Literature of the United States)* 32 (2007): 253–55.

10. Wagner, Darin. "What Might a Conservative Comic Book Look Like? We Already Know." 12 January 2012. Available online: http://www.bleedingcool.com/2012/01/12/might-conservative-comic-book-look-like-by-darin-wagner/ (accessed on 17 May 2016).

11. Wong, Devon. "Fables: Just an Analogy? " 15 May 2010. Available online: www.steelbananas.com/2010/05/fables-just-an-analogy (accessed on 3 April 2016).

12. Hallett, Martin, and Barbara Karasek, eds. "The Comic Book and the Graphic Novel." In *Fairy Tales and Popular Culture*. Tonawanda: Broadview, 2014, pp. 95–101.

13. Willingham, Bill. *Fables: War and Pieces*. New York: Vertigo (DC Comics), 2008, vol. 11.

14. Zipes, Jack. *Fairy Tales and the Art of Subversion: The Classical Genre for Children and the Process of Civilization*. New York: Wildman, 1983.

15. Willingham, Bill. *Fables: Storybook Love*. New York: Vertigo (DC Comics), 2004, vol. 3.

16. Tatar, Maria. *The Hard Facts of the Grimm Fairy Tales*. Princeton: Princeton University Press, 1987.

17. Grimm, Jacob, and Wilhelm Grimm. *The Complete First Edition: The Original Folk & Fairy Tales of the Brothers Grimm*. Translated and edited by Jack Zipes. Princeton: Princeton University Press, 2014. Volume 1 appeared in 1812 and Volume 2, dated 1815, was printed in 1814.

18. Willingham, Bill. *Fables: 1001 Nights of Snowfall*. New York: Vertigo (DC Comics), 2006.

19. Alverson, Brigid. "Not Your Grandmother's Fairy Tales." *Publishers Weekly*, 30 September 2013, pp. 40–41.

20. Hill, Mark C. "Negotiating Wartime Masculinity in Bill Willingham's *Fables*." In *Fairy Tales Reimagined: Essays on New Retellings*. Edited by Susan Redington Bobby. Jefferson: McFarland, 2009, pp. 181–95.

21. Willingham, Bill. "Superheroes: Still Plenty of Super but Losing Some of the Hero." 9 January 2009. Available online: http://www.breitbart.com/big-hollywood/2009/01/09/superheroes-still-plenty-of-super-but-losing-some-of-the-hero/ (accessed on 3 April 2016).

22. Willingham, Bill. *Fables: Camelot*. New York: Vertigo (DC Comics), 2014, vol. 20.

23. Willingham, Bill. *Fables: Witches*. New York: Vertigo (DC Comics), 2010, vol. 14.

24. Willingham, Bill. *Fables: Animal Farm*. New York: Vertigo (DC Comics), 2003, vol. 2.

25. Lüthi, Max. *The European Folktale: Form and Nature*. Translated by John D. Niles. Bloomington: Indiana University Press, 1982.

26. Kit, Borys. "Disney Plans Live-Action Film about Snow White's Sister." 31 March 2016. Available online: http://www.hollywoodreporter.com/heat-vision/disney-plans-live-action-film-879528 (accessed on 3 April 2016).

27. Bacchilega, Cristina. "Fairy-tale adaptations and economies of desire." In *The Cambridge Companion to Fairy Tales*. Edited by Maria Tatar. Cambridge: Cambridge University Press, 2015, pp. 79–96.

28. Friedenthal, Andrew J. "The Lost Sister: Lesbian Eroticism and Female Empowerment in Snow White and Rose Red." In *Transgressive Tales: Queering the Grimms*. Edited by Kay Turner and Pauline Greenhill. Detroit: Wayne State University Press, 2012, pp. 161–78.
29. Uther, Hans-Jörg. *The Types of International Folktales: A Classification and Bibliography*. Helsinki: Suomalainen Tiedeakatemia, 2004, vol. 3.
30. Zipes, Jack. *The Great Fairy Tale Tradition: From Straparola and Basile to the Brothers Grimm*. New York: Norton, 2001.
31. Grimm, Jacob, and Wilhelm Grimm. *The Complete Illustrated Stories of the Brothers Grimm*. London: Chancellor Press, 1984.
32. Willingham, Bill. *Fables: Rose Red*. New York: Vertigo (DC Comics), 2011, vol. 15.
33. Willingham, Bill. *Fables: Happily Ever After*. New York: Vertigo (DC Comics), 2015, vol. 21.
34. Siebers, Tobin. *The Romantic Fantastic*. Ithaca: Cornell University Press, 1984.
35. Kukkonen, Karin. "Comics as a Test Case for Transmedial Narratology." *Substance* 40 (2011): 34–52.
36. Willingham, Bill. *Jack of Fables: Vol. 9 The End*. New York: Vertigo (DC Comics), 2008.
37. Davis, Donald. *Southern Jack Tales*. Atlanta: August House, 1997.
38. Willingham, Bill. *Jack of Fables: Vol. 4 Americana*. New York: Vertigo (DC Comics), 2008.
39. Roberts, Leonard W. *South from Hell-fer-Sartin—Kentucky Mountain Folk Tales*. Lexington: The University Press of Kentucky, 1988.
40. Bruce, Annette J. "Successful Cracker Jack." In *Tellable Cracker Tales*. Sarasota: Pineapple, 1996.
41. Chase, Richard. *The Jack Tales: Folk Tales from the Southern Appalachians*. New York: Houghton Mifflin, 1971.
42. Kleon, Austin. *Steal Like an Artist: 10 Things Nobody Told You about Being Creative*. New York: Workman, 2012.
43. Lindahl, Carl. "Jacks: The Name, the Tale, The American Traditions." In *Jack in Two Worlds: Contemporary North American Tales and Their Tellers*. Edited by William Bernard McCarthy. Chapel Hill: The University of North Carolina Press, 1994, pp. xiii–xxxiv.
44. Perdue, Charles L. J. "Is Old Jack Really Richard Chase? " In *Perspectives on the Jack Tales and Other North American Märchen*. Bloomington: Indiana University Press, 2001, pp. 111–38.
45. Willingham, Bill. *Jack of Fables: Vol. 3 The Bad Prince*. New York: Vertigo (DC Comics), 2008.
46. Davenport, Basil. *Deals with the Devil: An Anthology*. New York: Dodd, 1958.
47. Willingham, Bill. *Jack of Fables: Vol. 1 The (Nearly) Great Escape*. New York: Vertigo (DC Comics), 2007.
48. Willingham, Bill. *Fables: The Great Fables Crossover*. New York: Vertigo (DC Comics), 2010, vol. 13.
49. Do Rozario, Rebecca-Anne C. "Comic Book Princesses for Grown-Ups: Cinderella Meets the Pages of the Superhero." *Colloquy: Text Theory Critique* 24 (2012): 191–206.

50. Willingham, Bill. *Fables: Superteam*. New York: Vertigo (DC Comics), 2011, vol. 16.
51. Willingham, Bill. *Fables: Farewell*. New York: Vertigo (DC Comics), 2015, vol. 22.
52. "Holocaust Encyclopedia." Available online: http://www.ushmm.org/wlc/en/article. php?ModuleId=10007392 (accessed on 10 May 2016).

MDPI AG

St. Alban-Anlage 66

4052 Basel, Switzerland

Tel. +41 61 683 77 34

Fax +41 61 302 89 18

http://www.mdpi.com

Humanities Editorial Office

E-mail: humanities@mdpi.com

http://www.mdpi.com/journal/humanities

www.ingramcontent.com/pod-product-compliance
Lightning Source LLC
Chambersburg PA
CBHW051314020426
42333CB00028B/3328